MINNESOTA STATE FAIR

Minnesota State Fair

AN ILLUSTRATED HISTORY

Kathryn Strand Koutsky
and Linda Koutsky

IN COLLABORATION WITH

MINNESOTA STATE FAIR

COFFEE HOUSE PRESS
MINNEAPOLIS

We owe profound gratitude to many individuals who helped us compile this remarkable history of the Minnesota State Fair. Our admiration for State Fair staff runs deep and their assistance was immeasurable. From executives, archivists, superintendents, volunteers, employees, and all the countless friends of the State Fair, the knowledge and enthusiasm was simply awe-inspiring. Thanks to the State Fair Museum who provided a wealth of artifacts and guidance, and to museum founder Gale Frost for his spellbinding tales of fairs-gone-by. State Fair Foundation staff gave us our start on this exciting ride and will benefit with preservation funds from this publication for State Fair buildings and grounds.

The staff at Coffee House Press, Allan, Chris, Molly, Lauren, and Esther, lent unparalleled support and guidance in an unusually complex project. Mercifully, their keen observations and patience never waned.

We owe lasting gratitude to those who gave us valuable time and talents by sharing favorite fair memories. Garrison Keillor and *A Prairie Home Companion* staff delighted us with observations that capture the very heart of Minnesotans at fair-time. Songwriter Charlie Maguire put whimsical words to lilting music that will sing on forever in the minds of fairgoers. Special thanks to David Steinlicht and cropart.com for preserving an unusual State Fair art form for the whole world to enjoy.

Friends who follow fair history diligently reviewed our words and photos. Our thanks go to Susan Larson-Fleming and the Hennepin History Museum, creative food editor Ann Burckhardt, our steadfast detail organizer Madeline Betsch, and Judge Harriet Lansing for the u.s. Supreme Court decision story. Over the decades, known and unknown photographers who worked for the fair documented many fair-time activities—we thank them for a vibrant visual record. But most of all, we give our appreciation to husband and father Dean Koutsky who dubbed himself assistant art director and spent tireless hours on preliminary page layouts, hunting for missing photos, and indulging in experimental bake-offs.

That doesn't begin to cover all the friends and acquaintances who brought us artifacts, photos, postcards, stories of fair escapades— along with moral support when we felt as tired working on the manuscript as we did after a long day at the fair. To all who made this an exhilarating year-long Minnesota State Fair adventure for us—thank you so much!

Copyright ©2007 by Kathryn Strand Koutsky and Linda Koutsky
Cover and book design by Linda Koutsky
Author photograph by Kent Flemmer

"The Great Minnesota State Fair" words and music by Charlie Maguire,
©2007 Mello-Jamin Music, All Rights Reserved, used by permission.

Manufactured in China by Pettit Network, Inc., Afton, Minnesota
First edition | First printing
10 9 8 7 6 5 4 3 2 1

Library of Congress Cataloging-in-Publication Data
Koutsky, Kathryn Strand
Minnesota State fair : an illustrated history /
Kathryn Strand Koutsky and Linda Koutsky.
p. cm.
ISBN-13: 978-1-56689-207-0 (alk. paper)
ISBN-10: 1-56689-207-4
1. Minnesota State Fair—History.
2. Minnesota State Fair—Pictorial works.
I. Koutsky, Linda. II. Title.
S555.M666K68 2007
630.776'58—dc22

COFFEE HOUSE PRESS books are available to the trade through our primary distributor, Consortium Book Sales & Distribution, 1045 Westgate Drive, Saint Paul, MN 55114. For personal orders, catalogs, or other information, write to: Coffee House Press, 27 North Fourth Street, Suite 400, Minneapolis, MN 55401 or visit our web site: www.coffeehousepress.org.

Coffee House Press is a nonprofit literary publishing house. Support from private foundations, corporate giving programs, government programs, and generous individuals helps make the publication of our books possible. We gratefully acknowledge their support in detail in the back of this book.

To you and our many readers around the world,
we send our thanks for your continuing support.

Good books are brewing at coffeehousepress.org

Photo credits: Half title, looking toward the Midway, 1950s; title page, fairgrounds, late 1800s; contents, 1914 Minnesota State Fair & Exposition brochure

CONTENTS

Foreword by Garrison Keillor   vi
Introduction from the Authors   viii

1   The First Fairs   2

2   The Bountiful Harvest   38

3   All About Animals   56

4   Grandstands & Bandstands   70

5   The Midway   94

6   Creative Competitions   114

7   Exhibits & Concessions   136

8   News, Politics, & Education   156

9   Food & Dining   170

10   Recipes   186

Recipe Index   210
Index   211
Photo Credits   213

Foreword

by Garrison Keillor

This is a joyful book for us fair lovers—it brings to mind the joys of the fair itself and those Twelve Thrilling Days and Fun-Filled Nights in late August up to Labor Day when we troop over to Como Avenue at Snelling

1) to experience centrifugal force
2) to resist the pitches of barkers and hawkers
3) to make contact with animals farther down the food chain
4) to eat food we've been warned against and build up fat for the winter
5) to be in a crowd.

No. 5 is the crucial motive. We live insular lives, working in cubicles, riding around in cars, hanging out with people a lot like ourselves, and the fair is where you can see, at long last, who else lives in Minnesota other than you and your family. You get to walk down Commonwealth Avenue past the spun-sugar booths and Tom Thumb donuts and Corn on the Cob stands in a river of humanity jostling and milling and brush against them and be brushed, smell each other, hear other parents haranguing their children, see teenagers in love and geezers holding hands, and where else can you do this in Minnesota? We're shy and instrospective people, wary of strangers and skittish about body contact, and the State Fair is where you go to try to get over that.

Of course the fair is not what it was in my youth. The fair of my childhood was more parklike, with expanses of grass where our family spread a blanket on the grass and ate a picnic brought from home. My parents distrusted food bought from vendors: how could you know it wasn't teeming with bacteria? Machinery Hill was bigger then and there were girlie shows like the Harlem Revue. The World's Largest Piece of Toast is gone—1.3 acres, beyond the old Dairy Building, whole wheat one year and pumpernickel the next, it took half a ton of butter to cover it—they needed the space for parking lots. And the Salad Spinner is no more—a cylinder full of silage and you went around so fast you were pinned to the wall. The Maggot Man is gone: you paid $1 to watch him eat worms and maggots with a little Miracle Whip on them. And his children ate dirt.

Some people say they don't care for the State Fair because of its sameness, which is what the rest of us love it for. It's a religious experience. The Horticulture Building smells of apples and grain and the livestock barns are the same as when you were six years old, and the fish drift around in their tanks at the Conservation Building.

I took my daughter to the fair for her first visit when she was nineteen months, to make her officially a Minnesotan. She ate part of a Pronto Pup, pre-chewed for her by her father, and part of a soft bean taco, and a honey sundae. She was taken through the Poultry, Sheep, Swine, Cattle, and Horse barns and touched a newly-shorn sheep, and a pig: she was stunned. She went on the carousel, and the Giant Slide: she laughed all the way down. We've gone every year since and now we've advanced to the double Ferris wheel on the Midway. I am afraid of heights and my daughter, who is nine now, is not. We rise into the air and I get that heart-clutching feeling when you stop a hundred feet above the ground and try not to look down. It is terrifying for me with my beloved daughter along—DAD AND DAUGHTER PERISH IN MIDWAY MISHAP—and it is hilarious for her to see me scared. The wheel goes through its convolutions, revolving at the end of an arm that is revolving, so that once every three revolutions you make the big death-defying stomach-churning drop to the ground, and I grabbed onto her hand, and back up we went, the sun setting over St. Anthony Park, the music and rumble and greasy smells exactly the same as they were in 1952 when I was her age. What a joy.

Thank you for these pictures and all the sounds and tastes and sensations they bring back.

Introduction

from the Authors

Our family immigrated to Minnesota about the time the State Fair opened its permanent grounds in 1885. Ole Olson ran the Oxlip store near Isanti and brought his family by horse and wagon to see what was new at the fair and to pick up store supplies. Since then, Ole's daughter, granddaughter, and great-granddaughters have attended the fair as visitors, exhibitors, and volunteers. These days, the sixth generation is enjoying Kidway and the animal barns, and the fair has become our longstanding family tradition.

After writing a book on restaurant history, *Minnesota Eats Out*, then *Minnesota Vacation Days*, we decided our third book had to be about the State Fair. We thought we knew all the nooks and crannies of the fairgrounds. But even with a crop-art winner and exhibiting fine artist in our family, we were in for a lot of surprises.

We began our search at the State Fair archives and museum, looking for photos, premium books, programs, and artifacts—the towering piles of records went back more than 150 years. Logs were kept, day-by-day, year-by-year, in books beginning in 1854. Along with fabulous photos and fragile glass negatives from the early 1900s, the vast resources were spellbinding. But how to decide which pictures to use—and what did other fairgoers like about the Minnesota State Fair?

No one escaped our inquiries: "Do you go to the State Fair?" Almost always a yes. "What do you do first?" Check out the animals, try out the food, and pick up a bag for giveaways, usually in that order. "What do you like best?" Food was number one, then animals, people-watching, music, creative competitions, and the Midway. Of course, looking at merchandise and machinery, giant vegetables, corndogs, cotton candy, talent and Grandstand shows did get plenty of mentions. Everyone had a favorite. Many also told us that 4-H and other youth programs had been huge influences on their lives. After all the impromptu surveys, we found that what everyone liked best is what everyone has liked since the very first fairs.

We found State Fair staff to be a perseveringly dedicated group. From executives to maintenance staff, everyone was knowledgeable, insightful, helpful, and encouraging. They don't just work at the fair, they *love* the fair and focus all year on ways to make next year's fair better. Concessionaires and exhibitors are a diverse bunch bringing fairgoers an ever more unusual sampling of products. Many booths are staffed by several generations of hard-working family members who have said: We pitch in every year, loving every exhausting minute.

Our recipe chapter is filled with flavors that have been served at fair stands and dining halls or came from booklets distributed at company booths over the years. Dozens of tasters and testers prepared old-fashioned recipes—some with obsolete ingredients or inadequate instructions—and made them more suitable for today's cooks. Competition winners willingly shared their prize recipes with us.

Many collectors brought us their State Fair photos, postcards, souvenirs, and family memorabilia as rare reminders of what fairgoers took home throughout the ages. Donors to the State Fair Museum also helped preserve history, both in this book and for visitors in Heritage Square. Of the thousands of photos, artifacts, and recipes we looked at, only a small percentage could fit in this book. The sheer volume of information left us wanting more pages.

Surprisingly, early fairs were similar to those of today. Minnesota agricultural exhibits continue to impress and livestock are shown off for urban admirers. Aromas of frying onions and roasting corn waft over hay bales and road apples while lilting sounds of music blend with noisy tractors.

The great Minnesota State Fair remains a grand and glorious finale to our summer season. There's one last look at raucous roosters, prancing horses, colorful art, fine needlework, and award-winning pies. It's a celebration of the abundance of our land, the talents of our community, and everyone is invited to the last great picnic of the year. Lifelong fairgoer and State Fair Executive Vice President Jerry Hammer sums it up with his favorite saying: "Every time I walk through the gates, I feel like I'm ten years old again."

Let's go to the fair!

In the 1920s, Hart-Kaiser provided colorful poster art to State Fairs across the country and fairs printed their local dates at the bottom. The stunning art called attention to dates of the fair and the next Minnesota State Fair became quite irresistible.

Agricultural fairs have been held throughout the world for thousands of years. Ancient markets were important connections for buying and selling food and providing everyday necessities, but early festivals were also respected places for education—and they nearly always included some form of entertainment.

American fairs honored their ancestral roots in similar marketplaces. In our young country, growing the nation's food was serious business and agriculture was a major contributor to the national economy. But cultural quests and educational advances were also deemed important to the growth of the nation, and fairs and expositions gave significant time and space to nurturing those pursuits as well.

In Minnesota, State Fair time became the celebration of our own agricultural history. As our population grew, county and state fairs became windows for the progress and culture of our state, a mirror on what we value and find motivating. Fair activities grew to encompass the entire family and developed into a very real sense of community pride. Agriculture, along with creativity, education, amusement, and festival food became the way we enthusiastically celebrated our increasingly urban marketplace.

Minnesota fairgoers have witnessed amazing technological advances since the first fairs in 1850. Plows, pulled by oxen for centuries, were replaced by highly technical farm machinery, horse and buggy became powerful shiny automobiles, and space travel brought new materials to every aspect of our lives. In the future, whole new generations of agricultural innovations are certain to have important impacts on our lives in Minnesota. Exciting advances await us and the State Fair may be where we first experience these amazing discoveries.

Who owns and operates the Minnesota State Fair?

The Minnesota State Fair is defined by law as a public corporation and a quasi-state agency. The fair receives no government support, depending financially on gate receipts, space rental, Grandstand and Coliseum tickets, Midway attractions, seasonal rental of fair buildings, and contributions to the nonprofit State Fair Foundation.

The State Fair is governed by the Minnesota State Agricultural Society, which was formed in 1860 by an act of the State Legislature. The Society is charged exclusively with governance of the State Fair and serves no other purpose. Delegates represent 95 fairs in 89 Minnesota counties, along with a few dozen statewide agricultural groups. An elected ten-member board of managers sets policy and provides oversight for the State Fair and the 320-acre fairgrounds.

History of State Fair Buildings

Administration Building	1870–1951
Main Building	1885–1944
First Grandstand	1885–1908
Art Building	1887–1920
Racetrack Club House	1890–1903
Aircraft Building	1890–1951
Livestock Amphitheater	1906–1942
First Agriculture Building	1887–1940s
Machinery Hall	1902–1938
Drivers Club	1890–1903
Manufacturers/Women's	1904–1950s
Rest Cottage	1904–1960s
State Exhibits/Progress Bldg.	1907
Dairy/Fine Arts Building	1907
Officer's Cottage	1907
Current Grandstand	1909
Ye Old Mill	1913
Greenhouse	1916
Cattle Barn	1921
Conservation Building	1934
Swine Barn	1936
Horse Barn	1937
Poultry & Sheep Barn	1938
Territorial Pioneers Cabin	1938
Arcade/Commissary	1938
4-H Building	1939
Agriculture Horticulture	1947
Cafeteria, Food Building	1948
Hippodrome/Coliseum	1951
Children's Barnyard	1956
Empire Commons	1967
Creative Activities	1971
CHS Miracle of Birth and FFA Center	2006

Premium Books

Premium Books contain the rules for entering State Fair competitions. They include lists of categories for each class and the prizes awarded in each category.

Prize Ribbons

First Premium is the same as First Prize, Second Premium is Second Prize, etc. Blue Ribbons are awarded to first place, Red to second, White to third, and Pink is fourth place. Sweepstakes and Grand Champion Best-of-Show are awarded a special Purple ribbon.

Employees

The fair in 2007 has about 71 year-round full-time staff. During the summer, about 150 seasonal staff are added to complete opening preparations. Fair time staff is in excess of 3,000 people.

Years Without A Fair

Since 1854, only five fairs have been canceled: in 1861 and 1862 due to the Civil War and Dakota Indian conflict, 1893 to participate in the World's Columbian Exposition in Chicago, 1945 to conserve fuel for World War II, and in 1946 because of the polio epidemic.

Hamline

Hamline was the Minnesota State Fair postal address until 1927 when the U.S. Post Office repositioned the area into the St. Paul Post Office.

One Million Fairgoers

1955 was the first year over one million people attended the fair. The one-millionth person entering the gate was given a wristwatch and silver trophy.

Street Names

One fast horse and several early board members were rewarded for their tireless efforts—they could walk on State Fair streets and avenues named after them.

Fairchild

Board member H. S. Fairchild served the fair for many years at the turn of the century and shared his name with a future State Fair mascot.

Fair Dates

The first Minnesota fairs were held for three days in late September. Later, fair dates were moved to early September and more days were added. Finally, the fair moved into late August and early September. In 1939 a ten-day fair ending on Labor Day was initiated, and in 1975 the first 12-day fair began.

The first Minnesota Territorial Fair was to be held in 1853, but officials decided that it was important to promote the territory at the New York World's Fair instead. As a special attraction, a young Minnesota buffalo bull was trusted to the watchful eye of Minnesota Fair Commissioner Wm. G. Le Duc. But on the long trip east, the buffalo chased several boatmen into the water, cleared an entire street of pedestrians, and escaped its guards, and a platoon of policemen that were sent to take it into custody. The Minnesota handlers finally settled the cantankerous young bison into the New York Exposition Building, but the determined little bull butted down the gates and ran amok throughout the grand stables. Fair authorities scolded Le Duc for bringing the buffalo to the show, and threatened him with arrest if he did not remove the unmanageable brute immediately. Minnesota's buffalo became the talk of the New York World's Fair and the nation became aware of the state's agricultural richness and industrial potential. The very next year, Minnesota's first Territorial Fair opened in Minneapolis.

CHAPTER ONE

The First Fairs

Minnesota Territorial Fairs were established to convince skeptical newcomers that the state's soil was productive and the weather wasn't so bad. The territorial boundary was huge; it included the present state of Minnesota and most of North and South Dakota. Settlers had plenty of choices for land. They came because the earth was fertile, the soil produced profitable crops, and the fields offered good grazing to produce sturdy livestock.

Fairs presented early settlers with agricultural information and a rare chance to enjoy a little culture and entertainment. Rural and urban families soon embarked on the great tradition of annual journeys to the fair—and for pioneering families it was often their only vacation. The first Territorial Fair held in Minnesota opened in 1854. When Minnesota became a state in 1858, the new fair wandered to southern Minnesota towns and the Twin Cities—until a permanent location was found in 1885. Fifty years later, the fairs were so popular, the President of the Minnesota State Agricultural Society observed that the fair had become the largest on the continent. It had grown to be an accurate reflection of the agricultural prosperity and cultural progress of the state.

As the success of the growing region was celebrated, flags and streamers flew and bands played. Specimens of livestock and horticulture, along with the latest machinery, were the finest west of the Mississippi. Exhibits were described as brilliant bazaars of merchandise, while dining halls and baking contests offered food to tease the appetite. Racetrack events ranged from gracefully trotting horses to grand battles between imaginary armies. The Minnesota State Fair became an irresistible event.

PREMIUM LIST
MINNESOTA STATE FAIR
SEPT. 2 TO 7, 1912

NEW ENGLAND FURNITURE & CARPET CO.

NEVER FORGET THAT
YOUR CREDIT IS
GOOD AT THE
NEW ENGLAND

THE NEW ENGLAND
BUILDING IS DIRECTLY
OPPOSITE THE HORTI-
CULTURAL BUILDING.

State fair machinery displays, 1885.

The First Fairs, 1854–1860 ▰

Although the Minnesota Territory was a rich and promising land, it was Territorial Fairs that became the center of information and education for the success of pioneer farmers. Fairs featured new seed and livestock developments as well as recently invented labor-saving farm equipment. As settlers began to arrive in large numbers, early real estate offices were the first stop for information on newly available farmland in the state.

Second Avenue South and Washington Avenue looking at St. Anthony Falls, Minneapolis, 1850s

From 1854 to 1856, Territorial Fairs were held near Bridge Square in Minneapolis. Farmers exhibited selections from their fields, flocks, and herds. Displays of huge cabbages, pumpkins, squash, turnips, and beets from the fertile land were said to have "astonished even the natives." Cultural growth was equally important: the few ladies present in the territory at the time brought examples of their domestic work, including baked goods, needlework, hand-woven rugs, and flowers. Dairy competition arrived in 1858 when Mrs. Joel B. Bassett of Minneapolis exhibited the best display of cheese.

The first real estate office in Minneapolis, 1855

Mechanical innovations, such as the Esterly reaper promised easier harvests, St. Paul, 1860

The 1857 fair in St. Paul hosted the first balloon ascension in Minnesota, and it was dubbed the "Balloon Fair." Inflated at a St. Paul gas plant and hauled to the fairgrounds, it launched with five young men aboard and flew off to a landing at White Bear Lake. As the balloon car touched the ground, one man sprang out to fasten the tether rope and the balloon, relieved of 160 pounds of weight, shot skyward. It sailed away to a final landing at Forest Lake. The unlucky riders were returned to the fair in a settler's wagon.

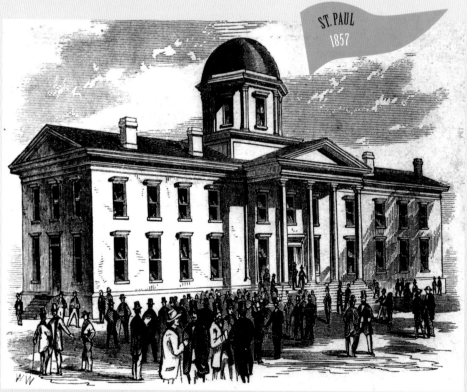

Territorial Capitol Building, St. Paul, 1857

In 1857, the Territorial Fair moved to Capitol Square in St Paul. Fine arts and the latest in merchandise, including the first sewing machine, were shown inside the Capitol building. A huge racetrack shared grounds with livestock and horse barns; fairgoers gathered around lush harvest displays that overflowed in spacious horticulture buildings.

STATE FAIR AT FORT SNELLING

held on the 26th, 27th and 28th days of September.

When the Territory of Minnesota became the State of Minnesota on May 11, 1858, the country was in deep financial hardship. The first official State Fair was held the following year in Minneapolis, but funding was scarce and attendance was sparse. The admission price was 25 cents, but cold rains kept the meager 3,000 fairgoers shivering in small frame buildings.

In 1860, as the country recovered financially, an expansive State Fair opened at Fort Snelling, sponsored by the newly formed Minnesota State Agricultural Society. The vacant fort had become a sheep farm. Parade grounds were converted into a racetrack, buildings turned into halls for various departments, military bunkrooms became pleasant hotel rooms, and equipment displays rambled throughout the grounds. River steamboats and wagon trails brought fairgoers from all directions—it was the largest number of people assembled in Minnesota in any one place up to that time.

The old fort never looked so attractive. Men arrived in top hats and Prince Albert coats; the ladies in pretty bonnets and billowing crinolines. Attendees viewed new farm equipment, including the first combined reaper and mower. A record 650-pound hog was entered by Wyman Elliot of Minneapolis. Onions 17 inches in circumference, radishes 28 inches long, and foot-long Irish potatoes were examples of what the fertile soil of Minnesota could produce.

The principal address was delivered by Hon. Cassius M. Clay of Kentucky, but his language was so complicated that people hurried away to watch the fire engine water-throwing contests.

Politics was on everyone's mind as the Republicans had nominated Lincoln for president, although few fairgoers thought about the prospect of Lincoln's election and civil war.

No fairs were held for the following two years as Union Soldiers occupied the fort and the Civil War and Indian uprisings exhausted the energy of state residents. In 1863 the State Fair was held outside the walls of the fort. Agricultural displays and creative activities were plentiful and it was reported that the ladies—who were described as the sterner sex and complimented on the fruits of their labor—added to the success of the exhibition.

FORT SNELLING
1860, 1863

STATE & COUNTY FAIR!

1864!

The State and County Fair will be held in Red Wing, on the 6th, 7th, and 8th of October. A general interest is being displayed in the matter, and it is earnestly hoped that all friends of Agricultural and Mechanical pursuits will do all they can to promote this object.

SENATOR RAMSEY

WILL DELIVER THE ADDRESS.

The FAIR GROUNDS have been fitted up in splendid style, and every preparation has been made to make it a

COMPLETE SUCCESS.

FARMERS

Are requested to exhibit their STOCK and PRODUCE, with a view to encourage the improvement of stock, and the developement of the highest order of Agriculture that it is possible to attain to.

MECHANICS

Are invited to exhibit the best specimens of their labor, for this is not only an Agricultural Society, but a MECHANIC'S INSTITUTE.

LADIES

Are cordially invited to compete for PREMIUMS. Exhibitions of their handiwork, of whatever kind, whether Needle work, Embroidery, Painting or the more needful art of Culinary, will greatly add to the attraction of the Fair.

☞ The citizens of Red Wing will make every possible arrangement to accommodate such of our visitors from the country as cannot be accommodated at the Hotels.

☞ Citizens of Goodhue County : it is a special honor that the STATE FAIR has been appointed at our county this year, and if we properly appreciate it, we shall be ready to take right hold and make it a perfect success—It only needs that every FARMER and MECHANIC in the county take an interest in it to make it such.

Newspaper notice for Red Wing's combined state and county fair, 1864

Early farms were located in southern Minnesota and civic leaders frequently convinced the Minnesota State Agricultural Society to hold the State Fair in their town. For several years the fair moved around the state and varying locations sometimes made the fair hard to attend for exhibitors and fairgoers alike.

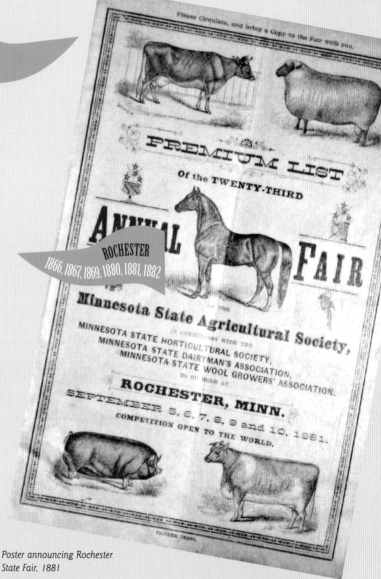

RED WING 1864

ROCHESTER
1866, 1867, 1869, 1880, 1881, 1882

Poster announcing Rochester State Fair, 1881

Red Wing hosted the fair on a Mississippi River landing near Barn Bluff. A half-mile racetrack held various events including popular ladies riding competitions. The lady who rode most gracefully in the best looking outfit won—but subjective judging of winners became mired in controversy. Politics also held people's attention and State Fair speaker Senator Ramsey noted that while agriculture in the state was flourishing, the old Union must be restored, and slavery must be abolished.

Rochester citizens produced noteworthy events for thousands of fairgoers arriving by the first trains. Railroads served rapidly growing Minnesota cities, thousands of new farms had opened, and farmers were prospering. Wheat and grain yields were abundant, and cattle, hogs, and sheep were thriving. Large crowds viewed Minnesota-made plows, mowers, reapers, and binders along with displays of Vermillion Range ores including lead, iron, gold, and silver. The fairgrounds state baseball championship between the Gophers of Rochester and the Saxons of St. Paul resulted in a whopping 54 to 54 tie. President Cleveland's future Secretary of Interior, Col. Wm. F. Vilas, spoke so eloquently on the "American Farmer" that his address was printed in pamphlets for distribution around the state.

Giant produce on display

Winona erected an amphitheater with a thousand seats for races and musical entertainment. Bountiful exhibits confirmed that area fruit orchards were flourishing and local gardens produced a profusion of giant vegetables and grains. The plowing match was as popular as the trotting races and the fair awarded T. M. Busbee of Winona first prize as the champion plowboy of the state.

Mrs. Elliott received a souvenir card of her weight courtesy of Fairbanks Standard Scales, 1867.

Jobbers Union complimentary lunch menu at the Owatonna State Fair, 1884

Carriage and farm equipment store, Rochester, 1882

Citizens of Owatonna went to work enthusiastically on their fairgrounds. Then a tornado struck that completely wrecked the exposition buildings. Described as "plucky" and "public-spirited," Owatonna workers reconstructed and repaired all damage in time for opening day. Unfortunately, hotel accommodations were few, and the grounds were small. Local ministers decried the arrival of thieves and pickpockets and other bad characters that demoralized and corrupted youth and maidens. But exhibits and displays were excellent and the fair was deemed a success,

St. Paul and Minneapolis Vie for the Fair ▰

Over the years competition became passionate between Minneapolis and St. Paul as to who would host the State Fair. City governments planned popular and profitable events—and no expense was spared in attracting and entertaining fairgoers.

ST. PAUL
1871–1876, 1878, 1879

WHEAT
OATS
RYE
GRAPES
APPLES
TOBACCO
LUMBER
SHINGLES
STAVES
BROOMS

Harper's Weekly *poster of the 1878 fair in St. Paul*

St. Paul rallied to put on fairs with expansive exhibits and lively entertainment. The Kittsondale fairground was located midway between the Twin Cities. Northern Pacific, Lake Superior & Mississippi, and St. Paul & Pacific railroads erected a 100-foot exhibition building. Inside were displays of North Shore magnetic ores, Beaver Bay arsenical ore, and Northeastern iron deposits—all having come to the fair by rail. Attendees viewed a squash weighing 120 pounds, 17-pound beets, 30-pound cabbages, giant turnips and potatoes. Mankato sent bricks, Rochester showed fine carriages, and Red Wing displayed strong, steel safes. St. Paul won the fire engine water-throwing tournament and the fairs were pronounced huge successes. President Hayes spoke at length in 1878 reminding listeners that St. Paul and the neighboring city of Minneapolis are "one great city."

*Northern Pacific State Fair trophy
awarded for the best bushel of apples.*

Agricultural Hall, Minnesota State Fair

In Minneapolis, the 1877 fair was held under the direction of Colonel William S. King, president of the Minnesota State Agricultural Society. It was going to be a "Big Fair." New buildings were erected, including an enormous Agricultural Hall, an Art Hall, and a fine racetrack. Marino sheep and Cashmere goats were featured favorites and the Minneapolis Woolen Mills received ribbons for the best and greatest display of woolen goods made in the state. Crowds were the largest ever assembled on a single occasion in the state and the fair was a financial success.

▼ *Grandstand at King's Agricultural Exposition, 1878*

In 1878, Colonel King, who had resigned from the Minnesota State Agricultural Society, opened his own agricultural exposition in Minneapolis and it competed with the traditional Minnesota State Fair that was held in St. Paul that year. Although the two cities were constantly expanding toward each other, these rivalries between them began to seem insurmountable and everyone agreed that a permanent location must be found for the Minnesota State Fair.

From 1878 until 1882, King's competing expositions were extravagant and popular attractions. One year, the main event was an ambitious hot-air balloon voyage to Boston or New York—depending on wind directions. Representatives of national newspapers were passengers, and on the day appointed, the balloon successfully sailed away, but in just a few hours, and only seven miles later, it descended into a Ramsey County cow pasture and remained there while the gas— and the newsmen—escaped.

General view of the fairgrounds

In 1884, after months of discussion, a permanent home for the Minnesota State Fair was chosen in the little town of Hamline. Located equally between Minneapolis and St. Paul, Hamline won over the second-place option at Minnehaha Falls. The Minnesota State Agricultural Society took possession of 200 acres at the Ramsey County Poor Farm that were donated outright to the new Minnesota State Fair.

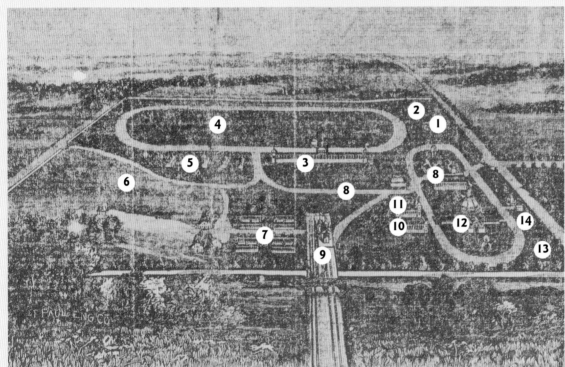

1 Machinery Hill
2 Campgrounds
3 Grandstand
4 Racetrack
5 Horse barns
6 Lagoon
7 Animal barns
8 Exhibits, dining, amusements
9 Entrance
10 Horticulture building
11 Institute Hall
12 Main Building
13 Adminstration building
14 Officer's Cottage

Minneapolis Daily Tribune front page plan of the fair, 1885

The Minnesota State Fair opened in 1885 on its new fairgrounds. Site plans changed very little through the years. The Grandstand, animal barns, livestock and agriculture buildings, and Machinery Hill have remained in virtually the same locations for over 100 years.

Rural folks found the new fairgrounds to their liking. They came to the Cities for business or to shop, now they could also attend the fair. Railroads from their hometowns offered reduced-rate transportation and trains steamed right up to a fanciful depot at the fairground gates. Now everyone—from cities and rural towns—united to make the Minnesota State Fair an everlasting success.

THE STATE FAIR.

A Fairly Successful Inaugural Day—The New Grounds a Bonanza.

The Exhibits in Place and the Work Substantially Completed.

A Remarkable Showing of the State's Varied Resources—The Stock Exhibit.

The Races Closely Contested—To-day's Programme—Notes on the Fair.

Arriving at the fair, 1900

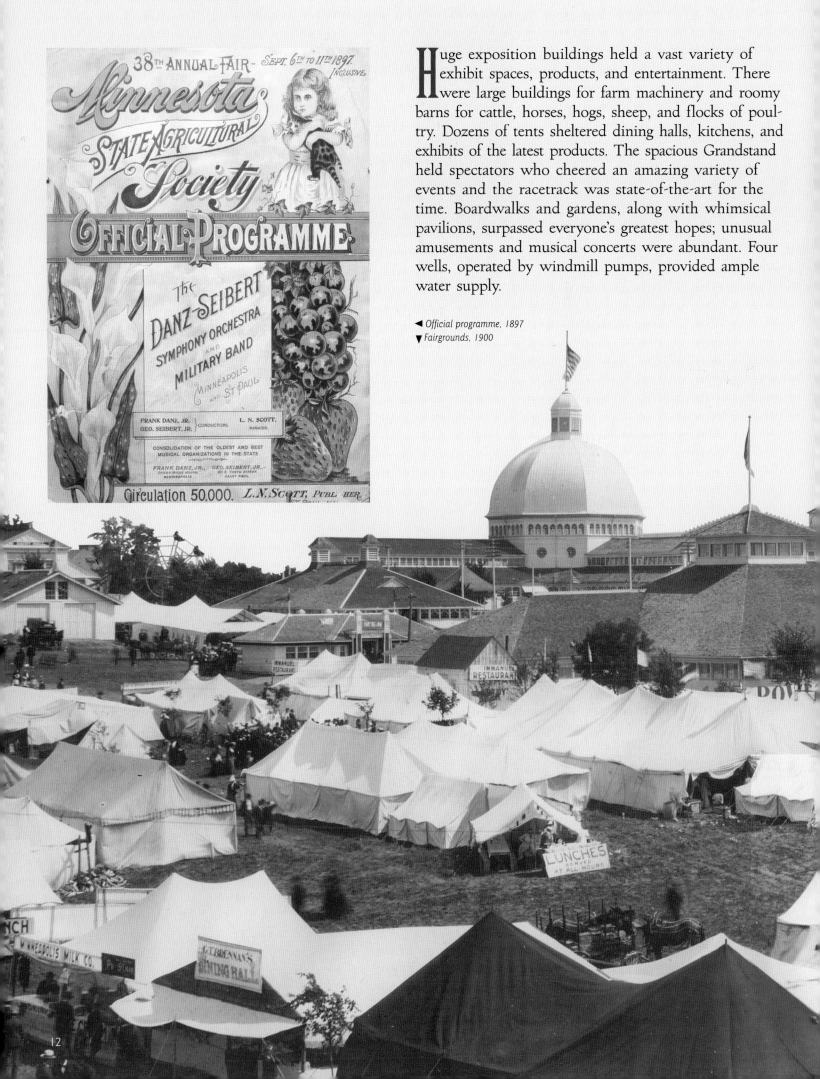

Huge exposition buildings held a vast variety of exhibit spaces, products, and entertainment. There were large buildings for farm machinery and roomy barns for cattle, horses, hogs, sheep, and flocks of poultry. Dozens of tents sheltered dining halls, kitchens, and exhibits of the latest products. The spacious Grandstand held spectators who cheered an amazing variety of events and the racetrack was state-of-the-art for the time. Boardwalks and gardens, along with whimsical pavilions, surpassed everyone's greatest hopes; unusual amusements and musical concerts were abundant. Four wells, operated by windmill pumps, provided ample water supply.

◀ *Official programme, 1897*
▼ *Fairgrounds, 1900*

Entrance, 1905

27th ANNUAL State Fair
J. H. Mahler Co. Carriages, Sleighs, Harness, &c.
SAINT PAUL
Saint Paul 1885

EXIT ONLY

Crowd scene, 1900

RHINE'S CAFE
ZIEVE
DELICIOUS GOLF CLUB COFFEE

13

S t. Paul architect James Brodi created an imposing main building topped by a 150-foot dome that could be seen for miles. It was a stirring adaptation of the world's first great exposition building, London's 1851 Crystal Palace. The building was monumental in scale, impressive in design, and attracted crowds from every corner of the fairgrounds to become the architectural icon of the fair.

The Main Building, later called the Exposition or Agricultural Building, was the center of activity from 1885 to 1944.

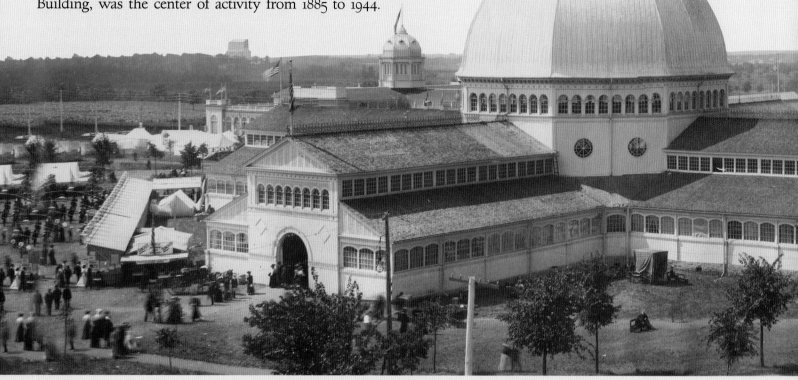

Inside the Main Building

Four cavernous exposition wings could take a day or more to explore, 476 windows provided light to all the exhibit spaces, and hardly a product existed that wasn't among the Main Building's offerings. Calling for a woman's attention were exhibits that included new cooking products from Pillsbury, Red Wing Syrup, Snowflake Baking Powder, and Minnesota Coffee. Instructions that made life easier came in giveaways like *The Housekeeper on Domestic Economy*.

Nathan Ford's piano exhibit in the Main Building, 1886

Kimball pianos and organs, Mason & Hamlin organs, Steinway pianos, and Domestic and White sewing machines appealed to fairgoers looking to furnish a home. Quinby & Abbott's assortment of rich furniture, mahogany sideboards, mantels, and mirrors sat by samples from the carpet dealers of St. Paul. Fancy millinery and the latest fashions in clothing, fur goods, embroidery, silk, and quilts occupied a booth near the Florida display of seashells made into pretty table ornaments.

Men visiting the Main Building inspected an assortment of fine hand-sewn hats and shoes, leather, and saddlery. Handsomely made baggage shared space with office, church, and home equipment along with rubber stamps, baggage checks, and trunks. The Northwestern Paint Works offered color samples and Archibald's Business College gave out exacting specimens of penmanship.

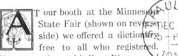

St. Paul shoemakers Foot, Schulze & Co. offered free dictionaries to visitors who registered at their booth in the Main Building. The dictionaries were late in arriving and required a postcard apology.

The First Livestock Amphitheater and Agricultural Building ▶

In impressive Mission Style architecture, the 1906 Livestock Amphitheater held 6,000 spectators beneath rows of airy windows and intricate ironwork. Livestock judging occupied the big arena during fair time, other shows used the cheerful space throughout summer and winter months.

MINNESOTA STATE FAIR.

STALLION, 2 Years old and under 3—Third.

1896

▲ *Livestock Amphitheater, 1910*
◀ *Interior of Livestock Amphitheater, 1910*

State Fair postcard mailing, 1910

First-prize herd of herefords, 1906

16

The Agriculture Building—
later called the Horticulture
Building—offered vast spaces
for impressive displays of horticulture and bee products.
Packed with well-stocked fruit
and vegetable arrangements, the
classically styled building held
a celebration of Minnesota's
agricultural richness. Counties
from around the state, as well
as companies in agricultural
businesses, constructed exhibits
to capture prizes for the most,
the best, or the biggest in horticulture excellence.

The 1901 Agriculture Building provided shelter for exhibits until 1952.

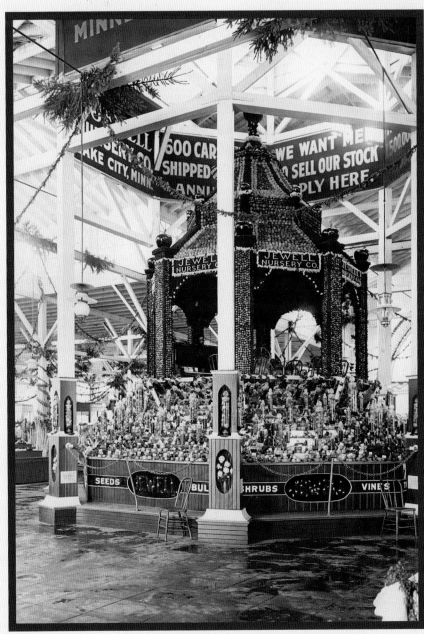

Jewell Nursery display under the center dome, 1900

Interior view of Agriculture Building, 1905

Produce exhibitors, 1910

The First Grandstand ▶

The huge wooden Grandstand was ready for the first fair in 1885.

In classic racetrack architecture of the day, the tiered wooden Grandstand sported viewing towers, box seats, and seating for 15,000 shaded spectators who gazed upon an amazing diversity of events.

Grandstand after viewing towers were removed from the roof, 1905

Horse races, 1905

Balloon ascension, 1905

The field and surrounding track adapted easily for horse races, cattle parades, balloon ascensions, stagecoach robberies, band concerts, baseball matches, orchestra concerts, bicycle feats, aeronautics, stage shows, elaborate thrill shows, and finales of thunderous fireworks.

Cattle parade, 1905

Grandstand, racetrack, and bicycle loop, 1905

19

Machinery exhibit, 1906

By 1905, machines that planted, harvested, fed stock, and milked cows covered several acres on Machinery Hill. Thousands of family farms required thousands of tractors, reapers, mowers, binders, manure spreaders, and milking machines—and the Minnesota State Fair was the best place to see them all.

Tractors, 1905

Outside the Women's Building, 1910

Champion canning team, Boys & Girls Club

After the crops had been harvested, along came a few great cooks! Minnesota grains went into hearty breads, sweet cakes, and flaky pies; canning competitions transformed plump fruits into gem-colored jams, jellies, and preserves; fresh vegetables morphed into spicy relishes and savory sauces. Competitions for a variety of talents grew in both size and artistic creativity—and the Women's Buildings held them all. If viewing delectable food brought thoughts of lunch or supper, dining halls provided convenient dining experiences. Cooks obligingly fried up sweet onions, grilled fat hotdogs, browned hearty potatoes, buttered ears of corn—then served up big wedges of apple pie topped with slices of farm-fresh cheese.

Amusements by the racetrack, 1905

Talkers tempted fairgoers with irresistible amusement and leisurely rides. Fair-time fun for all ages was provided with games like Guess Your Weight, Test Your Skill, and an occasional peek at life inside a curiosity show tent. Prizes and souvenirs went home along with memories of the good times.

Roller coaster and train by the Grandstand, 1912

Getting Ready for the Fair ▶

At the turn of the 20th century, a botanical showplace was planned for the fairgrounds. Eighty thousand bulbs poked their heads up in springtime gardens and thousands of flowers were planted in artistically designed floral plots. Insightful caretakers maintain many historic gardens in trample-proof locations throughout the grounds.

Flower gardens at entrance gates, 1900

Liberty Bell, 1920s

Liberty Bell and Gates Ajar topiary from the early 1920s are painstakingly replanted each year for fairgoers to enjoy nearly a century later.

Greenhouse interior

Built in 1916, greenhouse caretakers stoked the coal furnace day and night all winter long to protect the sprouting seedlings and sleeping cannas for next year's fair.

Officer's Cottage, 1916

Greenhouse caretakers lived next door in the former Officer's Cottage. Renamed the J. V. Bailey House, the building houses the State Fair Foundation, whose mission is to preserve and improve State Fair buildings and grounds, and to provide educational programs.

Floral sculpture Gates Ajar

Tens of thousands of cannas were planted during Victorian times and their plentiful off-spring capture admiring glances from fairgoers today.

As early as 1900, a farmer's tent city was available for rural campers. When autos entered the fairgrounds in 1931, tent city was replaced with a tent and trailer camp. Prices in 1910 to rent family tents for the week were $7–$12.50, concessionaires rented pavilion-size tents from $3–$60.

Bird Eye View. Minnesota State Fair.

Tent City, 1920s

C. J. Hoigaard premium book ad, 1920

Farm Boy's Camp and campground operated by Minnesota Tent and Awning, 1925.

Tents, awnings, and flags from St. Paul, premium book ad, 1922

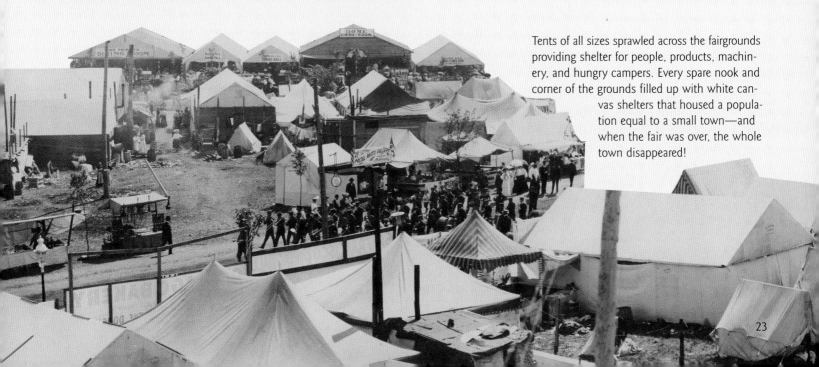

Tents of all sizes sprawled across the fairgrounds providing shelter for people, products, machinery, and hungry campers. Every spare nook and corner of the grounds filled up with white canvas shelters that housed a population equal to a small town—and when the fair was over, the whole town disappeared!

Great Northern and Northern Pacific ran rail spurs to the fairgrounds and passengers arrived at a fanciful depot right in the heart of the fair. Other Minnesota railroads offered special rates, observation-café cars, and "velvet roadbeds" to the cities during fair time.

Minneapolis & St. Louis Railroad poster, 1920s

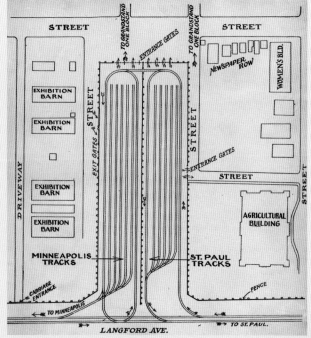

Streetcar track plan from Minneapolis and St. Paul, 1905

Separate loops existed for streetcars from St. Paul and Minneapolis with space for over a hundred cars. Passengers got off at the entrance gates and when the day was done, the streetcars were nearby, with a wicker seat awaiting tired fairgoers.

State Fair special train, Northern Pacific Railway, 1915

The popcorn cart came by with an afternoon treat for streetcar conductors, 1910.

Streetcar terminal, 1905

24

Ticket taker readies for a coming rush, 1920

Fair visitors arrived at the main entrance, 1924

The main gate, 1947

Minnesota STATE FAIR

It was easy to hop on an open-air bus for a rest and a ride to the other side of the fair.

Although roads were dusty—and muddy when it rained—automobile drivers had their pick of parking spaces in 1912.

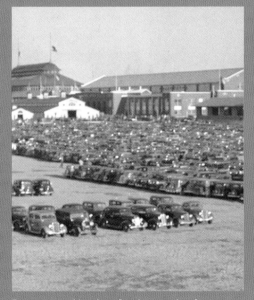

By 1941, parking lots for thousands of automobiles relieved growing street congestion. Boy scouts manned nine big parking lots and parking was free!

When all rows looked the same, finding a car at the end of a tiring day tested a fairgoer's memory in 1969.

Postcards were the most common pictorial remembrances of fun-filled days, since hardly anyone carried heavy cameras around in the early 1900s. Postcards of buildings and crowds were shown to families or mailed off to friends as teasers of the fun they missed.

The Minnesota State Fair sent yearly photo reminder cards of coming fair dates. Postcards mailed at the fairground's special post office were stamped with a State Fair postmark.

Since personal messages were not allowed on the address side, senders squished their notes on the front. "Martha got here safe and sound. This is one of the postals that the Minn. State Fair send around. Papa got four."

Case Engines invited customers to see their latest tractor display amidst a field of attention-getting flags in 1910.

SCENE AT MINNESOTA STATE FAIR GROUNDS

V. O. Hammond was a prolific postcard publisher at the turn of the century. His Minnesota State Fair cards captured the spirit and excitement of the day and have become highly collectible even a century later. Hammond fair cards were available in a numbered set of 12—buy a set and mail them all for two cents.

AGRICULTURAL BUILDING.
MINNESOTA STATE FAIR GROUNDS.

Paul and Minneapolis
O 7, 1907
IUMS AND PURSES

"SOME CROWD" at the GREAT MINNESOTA STATE FAIR, midway between MINNEAPOLIS and ST. PAUL, 1908 FAIR, AUG. 31—SEPT. 5.

Early morn', waltzing through the dawn
Toward the sights and the sounds
Summer is leaving, the fair is appearing
Autumn's pulled closer with each turn
Of the Merry-go-round, the grounds
With a walking cane
Tapping out which way to go where
Down streets that are found in no other city or town
But the Great Minnesota State Fair!

"THE GREAT MINNESOTA STATE FAIR" BY CHARLIE MAGUIRE

27

Architecture of the Fair—Farm Style ⚑

Architecture at the fairgrounds followed fashion and design trends as the fair grew in size. Early architecture imitated farm and homestead buildings that went up in rural style. They were quickly joined by buildings in fanciful exposition architecture, and later with structures in elegant and ornate Beaux Arts designs. By the 1930s, sleek Art Deco and Moderne was the preferred style, and in the 1960s, simple Modern buildings arrived.

Poultry Building, 1905

Cattle Barn, 1903

Poultry Building interior

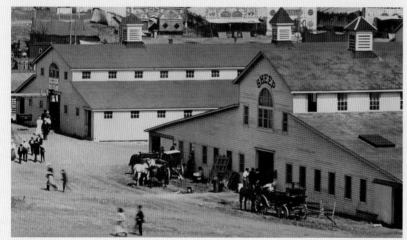

Sheep Barn, 1925

Whitewashed barns and wooden stables filled up fast with ever-popular four-footed animals awaiting competition.

▲ *Windmill exhibit*
▼ *Animal barns, 1900*

Animal buildings in 1900s had monitor roofs along the ridge to let in light and air. It was healthier for animals and more comfortable for fairgoers to admire the sturdy stock inside.

The few houses on the fairgrounds were of popular American Foursquare Style. Practical and economical, their simple roofs and painted clapboard siding held honest appeal. While they lacked adornment, a cool and restful porch wrapped around the front. The adaptable style was built on country farms as well as city streets and whole houses in Foursquare designs could be mail-ordered from Sears Roebuck & Co.

Visitors at the Administration Building, 1911

Originally the Ramsey County Poor House, the Administration Building was believed to have been erected about 1870 and was razed after the 1951 fair. It had been used as offices, residences, and dormitories. Many celebrities were entertained in the house, including Theodore Roosevelt, Horace Greeley, Calvin Coolidge, Warren G. Harding, the King and Queen of Sweden, and Dwight Eisenhower.

State Fair Police Headquarters occupied a painted clapboard house in 1906

Architecture of the Fair—Exposition Style ▶

In the late 1800s, American fair buildings were erected in Exposition Style architecture that radiated playfulness and optimism. Domes with flags-a-flying and fanciful ornamentation suggested high-spirited entertainment in one irresistible place. Inside, building structures provided nearly endless room for huge displays of the latest merchandise and machinery. But throngs of visitors and natural disasters took their toll on fragile glass and wood buildings and most of these genial structures did not survive more than a few decades.

Entrance, 1890

Dairy Hall, 1903

Institute Hall held programs for the Farmers Institute, 1900

Clubhouse for the Minnesota Driving Club on the racetrack, 1890

Machinery Hall, 1903

Machinery Hall exhibits overflowed the grand spaces inside

Fish and Game Building, 1903

Architecture of the Fair—Beaux Arts ➤

Beaux Arts Style came into vogue for fairs and expositions in the early 1900s. Inspired by the 1893 World's
Columbian Exposition in Chicago, the famous Neoclassical
panorama of the "Great White City" became the design to
emulate. Visitors were enticed through a profusion of ornate
columns, pilasters, cornices, and balustrades into bright and
airy interiors, and despite the elaborate facades, the style
was friendly and flexible inside.

Grandstand, 1909

The 1904 Manufacturers' Building was assigned to the Women's
Department in 1907, and later became the Home Activities Building.

Agriculture Horticulture Building under construction in 1901

Agriculture Horticulture Building

POULTRY BUILDING.
MINNESOTA STATE FAIR GROUNDS.

COMPLIMENTARY Not Transferable 1907
MINNESOTA STATE FAIR
48th Annual Exhibition.
Good for One Admission of Person named on Cover, and Lady
On Monday, Sept. 2, 1907, only.
NOT GOOD IF DETACHED.
1
No. 2890
Cosgrove SECRETARY B. F. Nelson PRESIDENT

The 1907 Poultry Building later became the State Exhibits Building, then the Progress Center ▲

The 1907 Dairy Building later became the Fine Arts Building ▶

Two of the oldest fairgrounds buildings have lived through many names and uses. Modern engineering techniques and durable materials provided stability, and the remarkable buildings are still in use after one hundred years.

Interior of Cattle Barn, 1947

Classically designed in red brick, the Cattle Barn held comfortable quarters for herdsmen, 1,000 animals, and several washing rooms.

Animal ornaments on the Cattle Barn

Architectural rendering of the Cattle Barn, erected in 1921. Fanciful bovine motifs animate the exterior.

Architecture of the Fair—WPA-style ▶

State fairs embraced Art Deco and Moderne Style architecture during the 1930s. The vertical emphasis and solid towers reflected enthusiasm for a new era. The greater advantage was the use of inexpensive materials and efficient construction for Works Progress Administration (WPA) workers who built many structures on fairgrounds and public sites throughout the country.

WPA worker with Horse Building relief sculpture

Many artists were employed by the WPA: they spent their years sculpting, painting, and creating fine works of art that survive on buildings across the country today. Their fanciful embossed designs celebrated the show inside.

WPA buildings were the result of a nationwide depression-era employment project initiated by President Franklin D. Roosevelt in 1935. Congress appropriated five billion dollars for programs with 85% going directly into wages. Nearly 300 men worked at the Minnesota State Fairgrounds from 1935 to 1946. The fair became the recipient of more than a dozen buildings, sidewalks, paved roads, hundreds of trees, and various ramp, camp, parks, and Grandstand improvements.

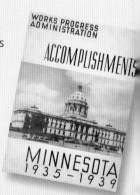

Horse Building

4-H Building, 1941

Sheep and Poultry Barn

WPA workers cutting stone for a Grandstand wall

Arcade Building, 1940

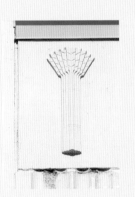

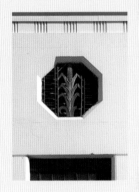

Crop motifs and sculptural ornamentation pay homage to Minnesota's agricultural heritage.

The Agriculture Horticulture Building

The Agriculture Horticulture Building replaced the Main Building and it honored the original central tower and exhibition arm design.

The Agriculture Horticulture Building, built in 1947

Although built just after the WPA period, the building reflected a similar architectural style.

35

Architecture of the Fair—Modern ⬤

Modern architecture was driven by new developments in technology and engineering that resulted in simpler buildings of steel and concrete. Like the changing styles of art and fashion, the architectural style evolved with the times. Since State Fair structures needed to be festive, bright colors and attention-getting flags livened up many of the buildings.

Coliseum, built in 1951

The Coliseum was designed like a military armory: strong, sturdy, and mostly utilitarian. When it was built, it was one of the largest arenas in the country, with a seating capacity of 5,200. Large WPA-style reliefs depicting the state motto, *l'Etoile du Nord,* added architectural interest to the massive, minimal building. The building was named in honor of Lee and Rose Warner in 2006.

Education Building architectural rendering

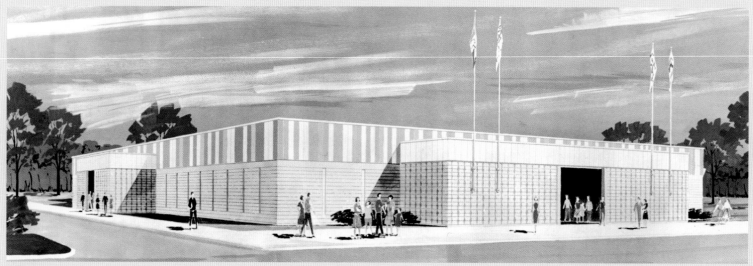

Architectural rendering of Dairy Animal Products Building, later called Empire Commons.

Fair Administration Building architectural rendering

Creative Activities Building

Decorative concrete block with patterned metal panels called attention to creative work inside the Creative Activities Building.

The Food Building attracted cheese curd connoisseurs and walleye gourmands from the first day it opened.

▼ *Electri City became the Modern Living Building, 1963*

Merchandise Mart

State Fair Souvenir Shop

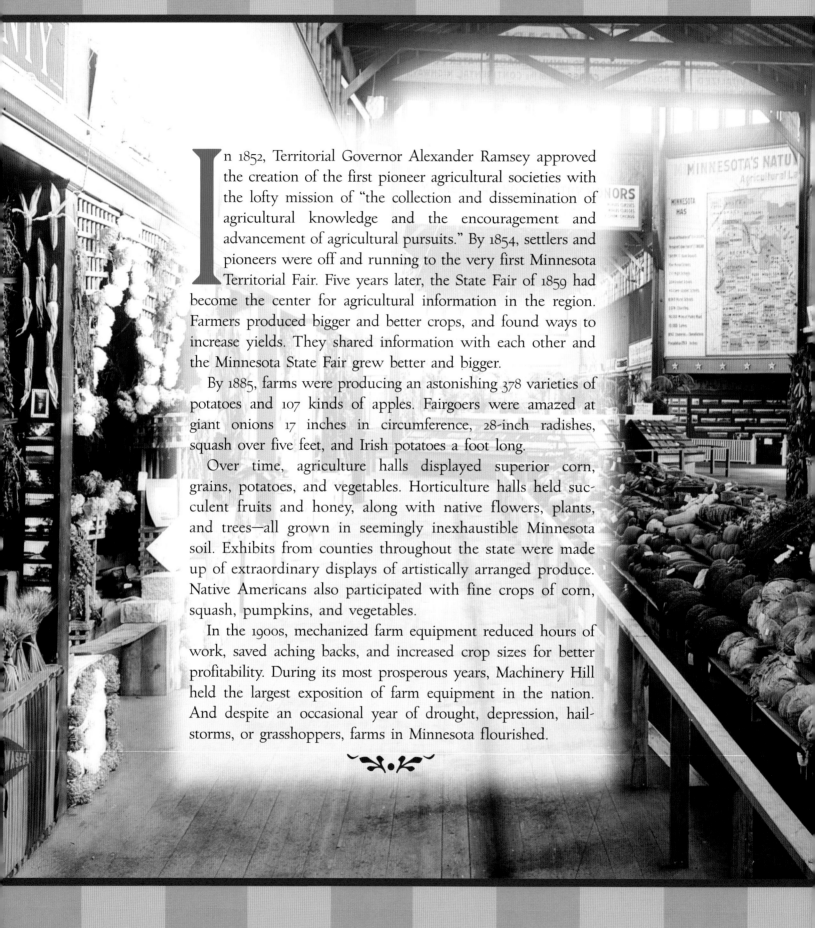

The Bountiful Harvest

In 1852, Territorial Governor Alexander Ramsey approved the creation of the first pioneer agricultural societies with the lofty mission of "the collection and dissemination of agricultural knowledge and the encouragement and advancement of agricultural pursuits." By 1854, settlers and pioneers were off and running to the very first Minnesota Territorial Fair. Five years later, the State Fair of 1859 had become the center for agricultural information in the region. Farmers produced bigger and better crops, and found ways to increase yields. They shared information with each other and the Minnesota State Fair grew better and bigger.

By 1885, farms were producing an astonishing 378 varieties of potatoes and 107 kinds of apples. Fairgoers were amazed at giant onions 17 inches in circumference, 28-inch radishes, squash over five feet, and Irish potatoes a foot long.

Over time, agriculture halls displayed superior corn, grains, potatoes, and vegetables. Horticulture halls held succulent fruits and honey, along with native flowers, plants, and trees—all grown in seemingly inexhaustible Minnesota soil. Exhibits from counties throughout the state were made up of extraordinary displays of artistically arranged produce. Native Americans also participated with fine crops of corn, squash, pumpkins, and vegetables.

In the 1900s, mechanized farm equipment reduced hours of work, saved aching backs, and increased crop sizes for better profitability. During its most prosperous years, Machinery Hill held the largest exposition of farm equipment in the nation. And despite an occasional year of drought, depression, hailstorms, or grasshoppers, farms in Minnesota flourished.

MᶜLEOD COUNTY

NOBLES COUNTY.

NICOLLET COUNTY.

Premium List
MINNESOTA
STATE FAIR
and
NORTHWEST DAIRY
EXPOSITION
September 4th to 11th
1926

Main Building produce exhibit, early 1900s

Business on Machinery Hill

Machinery Hill and Machinery Hall showcased the future of farming for coming years. Thousands of people came to see firsthand the latest agricultural equipment and innovations that would simplify, improve, and add comfort to all facets of farm life.

Machinery Hall, 1905

"The Great Minneapolis Line"

With its reputation of nearly thirty years behind it, has something of the greatest interest to show you. Look at this Farm Motor. The highest grade Four Cylinder Farm Motor on the American Market. Absolutely the most for the money in any gas motor built.

Don't fail to look us up while at the fair.

THE MINNEAPOLIS THRESHING MACHINE CO.

HOPKINS, MINNESOTA

▲ *The Great Minneapolis Line, premium book ad, 1912*
▼ *Machinery Hill in 1905*

Twin City Gas Tractors, premium book ad, 1912

Early farm implements had big steel wheels, and while they offered new efficiency, they were bone-rattling rough riders. In the early 1900s, tractors were a rare sight on farms, but fifty years later, millions were working on nearly every farm in the country.

Wege Concrete Machinery, premium book ad, 1916

The 1916 premium list ad stated: "Drive it like an automobile—or shift a lever and have a concrete mixer, or run the engine power-plant for corn shredding, feed grinding, water pumping, and hay bailing." How could a farmer resist?

Independent Silo Co., premium book ad, 1938

Independent Silo Company offered functional and attractively designed models such as Triple Wall, Redwood Stave, Tapestry Tile, Korok Tile Stave, and Utility.

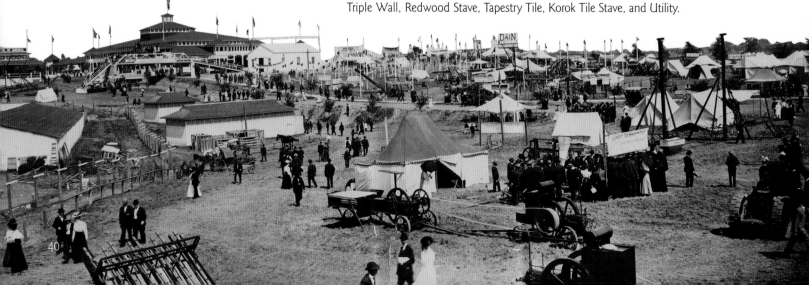

achinery Hill, at its largest, covered nearly 80 acres that held over 100 manufacturers of agricultural implements and farm vehicles. Dealers invited farmers into imaginative tents that offered refreshments and places to rest. Demonstrations followed of more efficient, safer, and softer riding rubber-tired farm machinery. The State Fair was the best place to compare the latest in agricultural equipment in nuts-and-bolts detail.

John Deere building, 1940

International Harvester, 1950

Ferguson Tractors, 1951

Farmall tent, 1954

Allis-Chalmers tent, 1950

Oliver display, 1950

Fairbanks Morse & Co., 1947

Minneapolis-Moline, 1950

Fun on Machinery Hill

Innovation in equipment wasn't the only draw for crowds on Machinery Hill—lively displays and interesting events were entertainment for whole families.

Fairgoers heading for the famous hill in 1947

The giant Lee overall became a legend on Machinery Hill, perhaps because it was sized to fit another Minnesota legend—Paul Bunyan. Miniature jeans were sewn right at the fairgrounds and given out as souvenirs.

Farmland Shows provided amusements for toddler farmers along with their patient parents, 1950s.

Little boy at a big steering wheel in 1956

Urban and rural visitors found it exciting just to sit on oversized masters of the soil.

Testing the latest tractor with encouragement from an interested friend, 1944.

P roving tractor power and agility were creative challenges for equipment dealers. They quickly invented interesting spectator tricks to show their worth, while serious plowing demonstrations left no soil unturned on Machinery Hill exhibition fields.

Case Engine doing stunts, early 1900s

Famous race car drivers raced with tractors in 1933

Practicing for a popular tractor square dance program

Power parade of State Fair maintenance vehicles on the race track

Kids checked out what was new on Machinery Hill—some would go on to ride a tractor at a farm of their own.

Buildings for Agriculture and Horticulture

Grand spaces in architecturally stunning buildings were full to capacity with bountiful crops and perfect produce. Artistically arranged displays impressed fairgoers from near and far—and overflowing exhibits left no doubt that Minnesota was an agriculturally prosperous place to live and work.

Vegetables ready for judging in the early 1900s

Highly decorated displays of fruit and vegetables under the central dome, 1905

The Agriculture Horticulture Building opened in 1887

The Art Deco Agriculture Horticulture Building replaced the old Main Building in 1947.

Concert under the dome in the new building, 1950

Agricultural shows included more than traditional produce displays in the 1950s. Fairgoers also came to see food demonstrations, apiary shows, and entertainment.

University of Minnesota apple varieties on display, 1947

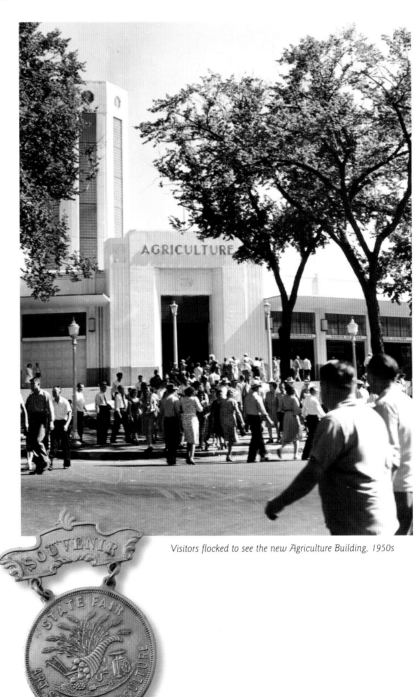
Visitors flocked to see the new Agriculture Building, 1950s

Alluring County Exhibits

In the early 1900s, fair officials observed that the fairgoing public was primarily interested in seeing what is produced agriculturally in each county. State Fair management increased the scope of county exhibits and designers outdid each other with glorious displays.

Olmsted County, 1907 ▲
Judges evaluating grain in the Main Building, 1911 ▼

Beautiful stained glass windows were featured in Minnesota's exhibit building at the 1904 St. Louis World's Fair. Later, the building and windows were moved to the Minnesota State Fair. Stylistic leaves surrounded center glass panels that included the names of every county in the state.

Isanti County, 1912

Washington County, 1912

The fair of 1912 was called the "Bumper Crop Fair." With 50 county exhibits, the first Horticulture Building was rated the largest agricultural exposition structure in the world.

Exhibits were judged on agricultural importance and profitability to the county. Coveted awards were given for arrangements that showed off produce in a new and novel manner in a neat, well-balanced, artistic display.

Wilkin County, 1912

Otter Tail County, 1911

Meeker County, 1911

Prize Winning Corn and Grain

Original Native American Indian corn was small and multicolored, but true golden corn evolved over the years. Corn did not change much in appearance over the next decades, although yields increased dramatically. Colored corn was later used for products like blue corn chips and decorative accents.

Selecting corn and canned goods for the fair, 1957

Award-winning corn in 1943

Pioneer hybrid cornfield planted for a State Fair exhibit, 1941

Only field corn was exhibited at the fair, sweet corn was sold at food stands. There are always an even number of rows on an ear of corn, 14 rows was standard in early days, now corn cobs have 16 or 18, but never have an odd number of rows.

Corn exhibit, 1947

Corn is the largest crop in the United States, both in terms of acres planted and value of crops produced. In Minnesota, corn is also the largest crop and new product developments may make it a larger crop yet.

Milling companies like Pillsbury, Washburn Crosby, General Mills, Robin Hood, Ceresota—and hundreds more—made Minnesota famous worldwide. The fast-growing companies enthusiastically participated in exhibits and events at the Minnesota State Fair. Over the years, the famous spring and winter hard red wheat used for bread and baking remained a Minnesota standard, but crops of durham wheat, used to make pasta, declined in production.

Display of grains, 1956

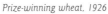

Prize-winning wheat, 1926

Prize-winning sack of Minnesota milled flour, 1935

Trophies for wheat, 1911

Trophies were presented in the early 1900s for the best grains and corn. Winners took the expensive trophy home, but it had to be returned before the next fair began—and the winner was required to give a two-hundred dollar surety bond guaranteeing that the trophy would be carefully cared for. A trophy became the property of the exhibitor only if it had been won three times in five successive years.

Plentiful Produce

Varieties of fruit and vegetables have always played important roles at markets and fairs. At the 1885 Minnesota State Fair, people viewed an amazing 376 varieties of potatoes and 107 kinds of apples. But displays also indicated years of good or bad weather, or if pests and other disasters had damaged the crops. Over many decades, produce became more robust, more flavorful, and gained favor for its undeniably healthy attributes.

A lighted candle topped St. Paul Growers Association's fall harvest in 1937

Duluth Harbor promotion at the State Fair, 1912

Duluth promoted its international seaport as the best way to ship Minnesota grain and produce to the rest of the world. The proud claim was convincing and displays were artfully arranged to prove the point.

Small produce rested in bushel baskets, 1947

Pride for area farmers was apparent in St. Paul Growers Association exhibits.

Exhibitor in the largest produce competition, 1926

The largest radish, heaviest pumpkin, fattest carrot, longest bean, and tallest corn stalk stood for fertile soil and successful farming. It was so in 1850, and remains true over 150 years later.

Potatoes were one of the largest crops in Minnesota, but many other vegetables in colorful baskets and paper trays also vied for a judge's ribbon.

During World War II, amateur gardeners won awards for outstanding wartime Victory Gardens. Vegetables recommended by the government were given preference in judging and prizes ranged up to $25. It was a tidy sum in war years.

Vegetables, looking good enough to eat in 1960

4-H Vegetable Queen, 1950

A closer look at bags of potatoes, 1941

A winner is selected in 1941

Sweet Halls of Fruit and Honey

Dozens of varieties of native Minnesota apples were on display in the late 1800s. But over the years, new apple varieties arrived from local growers and the University of Minnesota that really put the state on the map. Along with those big juicy apples, aisles of succulent pears, plums, peaches, cherries, raspberries, and strawberries were admired by fairgoers as well.

Acres of apples, 1912

Deciding on the best for their State Fair entry, 1956

Perfectly displayed, 1957

As early as 1916, over 30 varieties of table grapes appeared on State Fair competition tables. But, in the 1980s, Minnesota vintners began cultivating winemaking grapes and a new competition category was established. Wine was first served at concession stands in 2003, but it had to be Minnesota wine to encourage development of more vineyards for northern climates.

Winemaker Robert Mondavi grew up in Virginia, Minnesota, and attended Hibbing High School. The family later traveled to California where they established a wine-making business. Mondavi reflected that he was greatly influenced by old world traditions from his family in Minnesota.

Judge checking the "nose" on a Minnesota wine

Minnesota blazed a path in beekeeping at an early date when it officially recognized bees and honey as important state resources. The University of Minnesota division of beekeeping, the first of its kind in the nation, served as a model for other American universities. Minnesota consistently ranked in the top six honey-producing states and was the largest in the country in the 1960s.

▲ *Bee and Honey Exhibit Building, 1930*
◄ *Clover display inside the Honey Building, 1912*

Bee and Honey exhibit space, 1958

Introduced in the 1970s, Kemps began making the popular State Fair honey/sunflower ice cream—and the scrumptious combination is only found at the State Fair!

A beekeeper gets ready for a trip to the fair. Live bee shows and bee beards fascinated— and sometimes frightened—fairgoers.

Crowds gathered to hear the benefits of using pure, golden honey, 1971

53

Glorious Flowers

State Fair flower shows were more than a passing fancy as new generations of growers followed in the footsteps of flora-loving ancestors. Flower displays looked their best for only two days; a new variety was staged in exhibit halls every other day. Flowers, plants, and trees have been grown to be hardier, with more colors, in bigger or miniature sizes, and over the years, heritage plants, like roses that lost their scent, have been resurrected.

Cutting flowers in a flowered dress for a State Fair flower arrangement, 1946

Minnesota flower and table arrangements, 1951

Dahlia winners after the judging, 1960

Dahlia fancier Harold Nelson claimed that growing dahlias was habit-forming, 1969

Perfect flowers came in by wagonloads, wheelbarrows, even by pickup truck, and growers often stayed all night to make their display perfect. The most popular flowers with fairgoers were dahlias, orchids, gladioli, bonsai, and African violets.

Mrs. Dougherty won more than a thousand prizes for flowers and arrangements by 1946

Gourds with gladioli challenged the imagination in 1957

Competitions for artistic arrangements included thought-provoking themes like "dangerous curves" or "just desserts." Flowers with vegetables and greens provided lots of creative choices.

Extravagant Sculptures in Produce

Produce suppliers created vegetable and fruit displays with inspired imaginations. Onion man was one of a series of palatable sculptures, but over the years fairgoers also viewed Minnehaha Falls made of vegetables, or the State Capitol reproduced in onions, even Fort Snelling fashioned from Minnesota red apples.

Big onion man, 1953

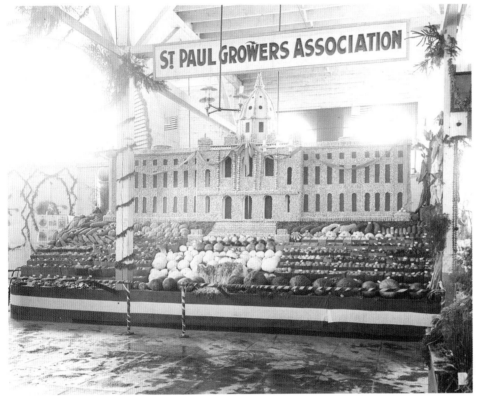

Minnesota State Capital in onions, 1906

Northrup King house of corn with a potato chimney

Jewell Nursery plant display and postcard mailer

Professional growers and university gardens were important fair exhibitors as they were often the first to show new varieties of flower, vegetable, plant, and tree hybrids. Inside the 1920 Jewell Nursery State Fair handout were planting recommendations for the hardiest Minnesota apples, plums, grapes, raspberries, blackberries, currants, and strawberries.

Corn palace from Houston County, 1912

CHAPTER THREE

All About Animals

Farmers in the state concentrated on raising fine livestock and horses—and the place to show and admire Minnesota's best was at the fair. Selective breeding generated first-class stock and prize-winning animals brought recognition to their owners along with added value to their herds.

During the late 1800s, pioneers like James J. Hill and Col. John H. Stevens became promoters of raising hardier cattle and crops by encouraging and supporting farmers throughout the state. According to reports in 1916, the livestock show had become one of the largest in the world and breeders from all parts of America sought the privilege of exhibiting their stock at the Minnesota State Fair.

A farmer's institute on the fairgrounds provided information and lectures on new techniques in agriculture as well as modern methods of stockbreeding. Over the decades, brawny workhorses were no longer needed to pull plows, graceful riding horses gained in popularity, fat hogs became lean hogs, dairy cows gave more milk, and stocky cattle grew to be fine beef cattle.

Country smells mixed with raucous noises from the barns were as entertaining as the animals themselves. In the swine barn, a snort and a huff brought attention from owners who kept watch on their prize Chester Whites. Squawking chickens scolded neighboring turkeys and geese; around the corner, sheep and goats bleated for a scratch from passing would-be farmers.

Animal lovers cruised the barns from dawn to dusk in unhampered admiration of beauty and beast. Beribboned manes, braided tails, polished horns, fluffy sheep, noisy swine, and fancy feathered poultry fascinated country and city dwellers alike.

The Livestock Amphitheater and animal barns, early 1900s

PREMIUM LIST
MINNESOTA STATE FAIR

HAMLINE, MINN.
1910
SEPT 5 TO 10

Livestock Shows and Parades

Spacious amphitheaters and hippodromes were among the largest buildings at the fair. Audiences marveled at handsome animals that paraded around arenas to show off their fine physiques. Cattle and horses shared the large spaces with sheep, goats, and other four-footed creatures in spirited competitions. A busy schedule of events occurred throughout summer months; in wintertime, ice shows, circus performers, hockey, and figure skaters made the Hippodrome their home too.

In 1946, livestock buildings were turned into World War II propeller factories, requiring all livestock and horse shows to be canceled for the following two years. The Livestock Amphitheater building was structurally damaged after four years of hard patriotic duty and the building was replaced in 1951.

Judging tent, 1900

Tent judges, 1900

Early livestock competitions took place in big tents with bleacher seats. No two- or four-legged creature snuck past the discerning eyes of the judges.

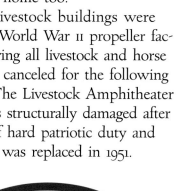

James J. Hill dedicated the Livestock Amphitheater in 1905.

Contemplating winners, 1900

MAMMOTH LIVESTOCK AMPHITHEATER---MINNESOTA STATE FAIR GROUNDS.
Building, 350x250 ft; Arena, 270x120 ft. Seats 7,500. Fair of 1906-Sept. 3 to 8.

Horse show, 1928

Cattle judging, 1919

Work-oxen, 1906

Teams of prize-winning work-oxen were exhibited at early Minnesota fairs; they were reported to have been the best in the country well into the twentieth century.

Beef shorthorn parade at the Grandstand, 1930

Cattle and horse parades were long-standing traditions at the fair and the Grandstand track was the best place to promenade for appreciative audiences.

Draft horses in front of the Grandstand, 1908

Beef and Dairy Cattle ◢

Doors opened in the cattle barn in 1922 to welcome Minnesota's best breeds of cattle. Plank-lined stalls and fresh hay awaited stout beef cattle, angular dairy cattle, and their proud owners.

The Northwest Livestock Show in the Cattle Barn, 1928

Cattle show, 1958

Balcony around the Cattle Barn, 1926

A balcony around the Cattle Barn held dairy-related exhibits providing observers with panoramic views of the cattle below. A balcony exhibit, "The Cows' Contribution to Civilization," drew 98,000 people in 1927. The well-used balcony was removed in the 1940s.

Judging Arena, 1960s

Cattle and their young owners relax in a stall, 1960s

Livestock competitions required long hours from both cattle and caretakers at State Fair competitions. Farmers, future farmers, and 4-H'ers moved into barn stalls during the day and dorms at night to be near their animals.

Campbell Aberdeen Angus "Highland Mary," 1950s

Generations of Campbell brothers exhibited their famed Aberdeen Angus herd at the Minnesota State Fair as early as 1884.

Man and his affectionate friend, 1938

Pine tar bath for a Mayowood Farm Holstein, 1950s

Pampered cattle were "fitted" in preparation for a show. They enjoyed morning washes, an invigorating brush and clipping on coats, ears, and tails, topped off by shiny polish for horns and hoofs.

A stiff brushing for a shorthorn bull in 1957

Vacuum cleaner time, 1953

Smoothing the horns, oilcloth polish to follow, 1950s

State Fair horses showed their talents in a variety of ways. Hefty draft horses pulled plows and wagons, show horses pranced with their elegant English riders, and Western horses could square dance. Milk wagon competitions emphasized the neatness of horse, wagon, and driver: agility tests with crates of empty milk bottles tested the quickness of the horse for starting and stopping—and not spilling the milk.

Draft horses provided farm power in the early 1900s

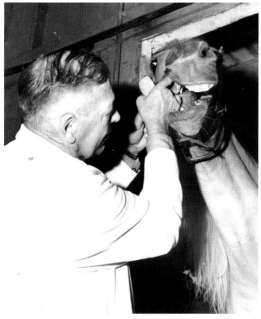

Vet check, 1953

Dr. Elmer Berg was the Minnesota State Fair veterinarian for over thirty years. In 1953, Dr. Berg took care of more than ten thousand animals and birds at the fair. New births, accidents, illness, sickness, and contagious disease could be risky with so many animals together.

Horses and ponies pulled a variety of wheeled vehicles in State Fair competitions.

Percherons, Belgians, Clydesdales, Shires, and Farmer's Teams were the sturdy workhorses of their day. Later they were bred to be taller and not as heavily muscled, but they retained their stately character hitched to colorful wagons.

Ribbons and trophies for a proud horse and Western rider in 1955

Ample ribbons in 1955

Western horses and their riders participated in barrel racing, rescue races, barrel jumps, paint pole bending, pole weaving, square dancing, tandem bareback, prairie stump races, precision drill teams, and pleasure riding. There was something for everyone to watch.

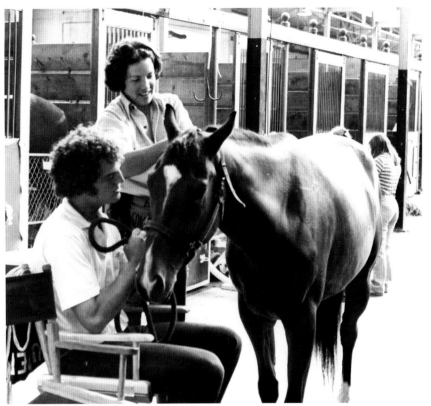

English horses were a talented group: they walked, loped, trotted, cantered, galloped, jumped fences—and they must stand quietly and back up readily. After that, they are judged on attitude, manners, presence, obedience, alertness, responsiveness, performance, and suitability as a pleasure mount. Their riders are judged on horsemanship, elegance, and style. It was a big job for the judges!

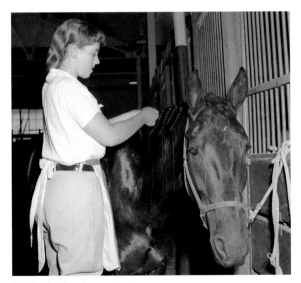

Braiding her horse's mane in 1959

Practicing on the Grandstand infield, 1953

English horse and rider heading for the show, 1979

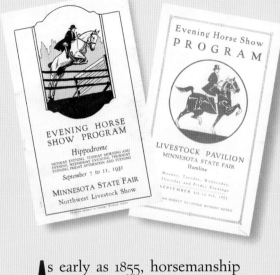

As early as 1855, horsemanship contests between ladies drew huge crowds. All were superb riders and their horses were the best in the country, but disagreements arose constantly over the judges' selection of winners. Through the years, contentious arguments caused ladies horsemanship to be discontinued and reinstated several times, but eventually riding contests between lady riders became very popular fair attractions.

In 1855, Committee chairman Ex-Governor Ramsey wrote on the difficulty of judging:

"Your committee on ladies' horsemanship beg leave to report that they have been most highly gratified with the equestrian exhibitions of the day; and while they find it exceedingly difficult to determine as to the superiority of any one lady equestrienne, yet they feel it to be their duty to determine that the first prize for the best exhibition of ladies' horsemanship must be awarded to the lady in the black bodice and blue habit, Mrs. Alvaren Allen. For the second best we have given the premium to the lady in the drab hat and habit, Mrs. John G. Lennon..."

Swine, Sheep, and Goats

Massive swine drew curious crowds at livestock exhibits as they were often judged on the theory that "bigger is better." As early as 1892, an owner from Pipestone exhibited his Poland-China hog weighing 900 pounds; in later years a huge 1200-pound entry astounded fairgoers.

Through the years, the raising of champion swine became more scientific as nutritionists monitored their diets almost as closely as infant formulas—and pigs became longer and leaner.

Swine Barn, 1952

WPA workers completed the big red-brick Swine Barn in 1936. It also held sheep and a few lucky animal owners who bunked on the second floor near a breezy balcony.

A pair getting ready for the fair

Champion swine by the early animal barns, 1925

Hogs, who are independent and not very obedient, amused audiences in show rings—perhaps because studies have confirmed that they are more intelligent than other farm animals.

First and second place Chester Whites chowing down, 1955

On parade for judges, 1973

Many types of soft, elegant wool came from sheep raised on Minnesota farms—including fine merino wool. Shears and combs made fleece shapely and smooth. Rabbits came in fanciful colors and patterns. Homer pigeons competed with pouters, archangels, tumblers, or trumpeters, and some geese breeds were named Toulouse, Canada, Chinese, Egyptian, and African.

Goats have served mankind earlier and longer than even cattle and sheep. Dairy goats are judged for milk and cheese production; others are exhibited for their luxurious cashmere and angora mohair.

Sheep show, 1957

White-face sheep produced the best wool, some wore covers to protect their fleece from dirt, plus it grew faster under the covers. Black-face sheep were raised for milk, cheese, and meat.

Haircut for his shaggy sheep, 1967

Two curly friends, 1967

A sheep in sheep's clothing, 1960s

Bins of prize-winning fleece, 1940s

A huggable wooly sheep, 1920

Poultry have populated barnyards throughout the world for centuries, and State Fair breeds read like an around-the-world fashion map. Asiatic, Mediterranean, English, American, and Continentals nested along with well-attired Bantams who sported feather legs, clean legs, single comb, or rose comb; Hamburgs come golden spangled or silver spangled.

Poultry Building workers, 1939

A handsome trio in the Poultry Barn

Duane Urch exhibited prize-winning chickens for nearly 50 years

Famous Minnesota turkeys were known by their colors: bronze, white, red, black, and slate.

Fine feathered friends

Rooster Crowing Contests became popular events at the fair. Handlers couldn't touch the birds but could talk, clap, whistle, throw food, or use other tricks to make them crow.

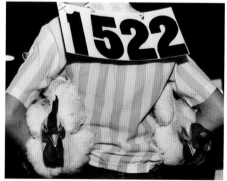

Chickens heading for judgment

Pekin Duck, 1934

Preparing for the Fair

Entering an animal in the State Fair took a lot of planning. Where to eat and sleep was a big priority. Bunks were provided in animal barns, the 4-H Building, and various on-site campgrounds—but great fair food was an added attraction that could be found just about everywhere.

Campground dinner for four, 1954

Heading for the fair, 1954

The Green family of Kasson prepared to leave for the fair with a truck full of Chester Whites, and a few hay bales for snug beds in the swine barn.

Well-rested exhibitors ready to start the day, 1954

Hay was distributed to animal barns one bale at a time, 1958

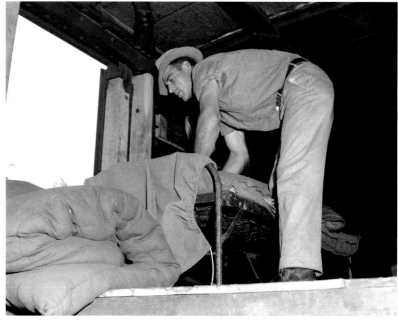
Bunks in the cattle barn near a door of fresh air

Entertaining Animals

Animals did more than show off for judges, they also provided fairgoers with some great entertainment. Clip-clopping of huge hoofs turned heads as awe-inspiring Clydesdales approached the crowds. It was grace and power all wrapped up in one well-coordinated team, and Clydesdales became the darlings of State Fair parades.

Swift & Company Six-Horse Team, 1922

Grandstand parade of draft horses, 1940s

Getting a soapy wash before the parade

A smooth ride on top of eight well-coordinated hoofs

A rare trained buffalo leads the rodeo parade

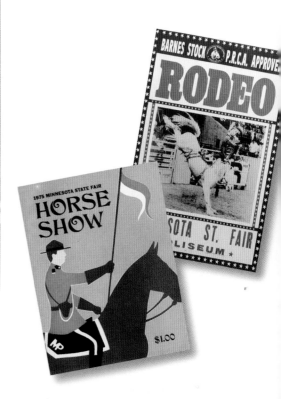

Rodeos came to the Coliseum with no shortage of lively shows, along with balancing acts that provided a little tension for arena crowds. Audiences were no less amazed by precision perform-ances from Austrian Lipizzaners and exacting musical routines by the Canadian Mounties.

Barnyard visitors, 1940s

Future Farmers of America, now FFA, built the Children's Barnyard in 1956. Adorable baby animals were the center of the bustling exhibit—both kids and their parents found it hard to leave. An animal birthing center became part of the Barnyard; it later moved into a bigger barn with FFA headquarters and an even more popular CHS Miracle of Birth Center.

Poster for 1912 dog show

In the early 1900s, the State Fair opened a building exclusively for showing all breeds of dogs and cats. Competitions also included puppies and kittens—little furry creatures endeared themselves to children and adults alike. For decades it was the only dog and cat show held at an American state fair.

Three little lambs with their friends, 1971

One-year-old baby with one-day-old pig

Downey ducklings on display, 1958

The chickens are hatching, 1954

Goats like the attention at the Barnyard

Bedding down, with the sheep and the cows,
More brushing can't do any harm.
Win, place, or show, keep her head up and go
Around the ring circle, long practiced at home on the farm.
Equipment turned out in rows, on Machinery Hill everywhere
Smallest to biggest, to brightest to best
At the Great Minnesota State Fair!

"THE GREAT MINNESOTA STATE FAIR" BY CHARLIE MAGUIRE

Napping with a Holstein, 1971

CHAPTER FOUR

Grandstands & Bandstands

In the 1850s, plowing contests were popular events at rural fairs as powerful horses and their exacting drivers competed on untilled fields in front of State Fair onlookers.

But eventually fairgoers wanted more exciting entertainment, and after the Civil War, horse racing emerged as the biggest crowd pleaser at state fairs. When the first permanent wooden Grandstand opened in 1885, crowds filled the stands to overflowing. They cheered and yelled at harness racers, trotters, and pacers as they thundered to finish lines with hoofs pounding and manes flying.

A sturdy new brick Grandstand was built in 1909 for popular horse racing and a few early automobiles—to the distress of racehorse owners who were told they had to share their racetrack with Locomobiles and Duesenbergs. In a few years, speed races, auto polo, demolition derbies, earsplitting collisions, and the possibility of breathtaking accidents put wound-up spectators on the edge of their seats—and horse racing began a slow decline in popularity.

Grandstand infields were the first launching sites for balloon ascensions and parachute drops, and later, for aeronauts who appeared in dirigibles that could be steered around the grounds. Flying machines came to the fair in 1910. Wing-walkers and loop-the-loop stunts kept hearts pounding in the bleachers until they were finally banned in the 1950s.

That wasn't all there was to see at the busy Grandstand. Thrill shows, human cannonballs, diving animals, movie stars, all-star revues, aerial high divers, famous singers, sham battles, and colossal pyrotechnic spectacles filled seats day and night. And if that wasn't enough, those extravaganzas were topped by a grand finale of exploding fireworks and rockets bursting in midair!

The latest automobiles parked on the infield at the first wooden Grandstand amid dusty views of horse racing in 1900.

MINNESOTA
STATE FAIR

N.W. LIVESTOCK SHOW
25¢ ADMISSION
SEPT. 2 to 9

The Grandstand Building

GRAND STAND, MINNESOTA STATE FAIR GROUNDS

A new concrete and steel Grandstand opened in 1909. The old wooden structure had taken a pounding from enthusiastic spectators, and the tired building was razed in 1908. The new solid, brick Grandstand held seating for 12,000 plus 10,000 bleacher seats. It sprawled along two complete racetracks—a half-mile track and a one-mile track that provided flexible racing distances for all types of competitions.

The new 1909 Grandstand held spectators on solidly constructed tiers with good visibility for everyone.

Opening day, 1909

Grandstand box seats allowed close viewing for Minnesota Governor John A. Johnson and friends.

Grandstand, 1909

Seating on upper tiers was provided with thousands of wooden chairs. A hole in the seat let the rain water drain out.

An elegant turn-of-the-century crowd in casual dress filled the stands in 1909.

The Grandstand and Music Gazebo, 1912

An earthen ramp and wooden trestle bridge led fairgoers straight to their seats in the highest tiers. The famous Art Exhibition Halls with local and national displays were located on the upper floors, while main floor spaces accommodated large auto and merchandise shows.

The Auto Show, 1912

Auto shows were readied for huge crowds coming to marvel at the newest designs. On the spacious main floor, Reo, Hupmobile, Maxwell, Auburn, and Paige parked with dozens of eye-catching models as well as ambulances and hearses. And for those frequent repairs on early automobiles, drivers found exhibits for batteries, rims, tires, seals, and tire patches.

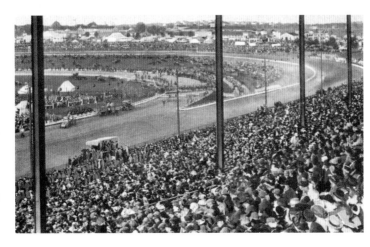

Growing automobile populations created congestion at the fair and the long one-mile track was removed in 1939 to make room for additional parking spaces.

1900

1910

1920s

1930

Judging stands evolved over the years from fanciful parasol-covered stages into high tiers of unobstructed viewing platforms. The newest "apparatus capable of transmitting the human voice five miles" was installed by Northwestern Bell Telephone Company in 1922.

Horse Racing

Harness racing enjoyed the highest attendance of any amusement at the fair for decades, but racing created conflict, as prizes were often higher than those awarded in other competitions. Betting was legal during some years and contributed an irresistible element of suspense, but betting also had its critics. Race crowds ignored all the controversy by the tens of thousands. As early as 1900, fervent fans cheered a variety of unusual and spirited races such as steeplechases, polo matches, eight-horse Roman chariot races, stagecoach robberies, and plug horse derbies. But after many prize-winning decades horseracing began to lose favor with fairgoers and the last race took place in 1949.

Harness racing, 1915

Harness race at finish line, 1915

Rounding the bend, 1925

Lines were long to get a good seat, 1935

The Plug Horse Derby was sponsored by the St. Paul Dispatch and Pioneer Press.

Ladies relay race, 1896

Ladies races drew crowds at the first fairs as riders combined high speed with high style. In 1891, a serious collision between four racers prompted a local newspaper to observe that the sidesaddle was not a good racing seat. Ladies usually raced each other, but a twenty-mile race between a lady and a man energized audiences at the turn of the century—to the crowd's delight, the woman won.

Rows of stables next to the Grandstand were built exclusively for racehorses.
Spacious stalls allowed fans to view the best breeds in American horse racing.

Everything necessary for the health of a racehorse, including new shoes, took place in tents near the Grandstand. For fifty years, Frank Bundy ran the training stable and George Loomis trained pacers that went on to earn fame and money nationally for their Minnesota owners.

Cooling down after the race, 1905

DAN PATCH
1896–1916

Dan Patch, a pace horse who pulled his driver in a sulky, became the most famous racehorse in America in the early 1900s. With a crooked back left leg and an endearing disposition, he flew to finish lines in harness competitions—the most popular form of racing at the time. He never lost a race, and repeatedly set, then broke, his own world records. In 1906, in front of 90,000 feverish fans at the Minnesota State Fair, the seven-year-old Dan Patch set his world-famous record of one minute, 55 seconds for the mile. He was soon regarded as unbeatable, and owners of other horses refused to race against him. Fans loved Dan Patch, and he loved the crowds. His record has been tied—but never broken.

Owner Marion Savage built an idyllic Eden of stables and racetracks for Dan Patch, his stable-mates, and an army of attendants in Hamilton, Minnesota. Consumer goods distributed by Savage's companies featured a Dan Patch likeness on quirky collections of products—coffee and tobacco tins, washing machines, songs, beer, and cars were but a few. Dan Patch traveled in celebrity-style luxury throughout America, then ended his days in Hamilton in 1916. Marion Savage died 24 hours later—some say of a broken heart. The town was renamed Savage in his honor.

Entrance to see the "Fastest Harness Horse in the World"

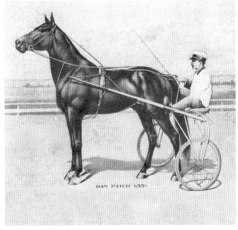

Dan Patch after his famous run

Automobile Racing

Fascination with automobiles swept the country at the turn of the century. As drivers revved their engines, auto racing took off. At first, horse racing and auto racing took turns using the track—and horses were a lot faster. But over a few decades, automobile racing steadily increased in popularity. Speed and a constant threat of crashes attracted huge audiences who saw breathtaking accidents at almost every race—and automania eventually took over all the days of the fair. Regular passenger cars raced first, then dirt racers on a dirt track, and later, sprint and stock cars on a scientifically banked, paved surface.

The first autos to appear at the Grandstand simply paraded around the track. Waverley automobiles driven by Swan Turnblad with his wife Christina, and car dealer George Duncan led the first track parade in 1900. The first actual race between automobiles was held in 1907 and won by 93-year-old Dr. C. E. Dutton, a retired physician who drove a Locomobile Steamer.

Passenger cars lined up for races, 1907

Eddie Rickenbacker survived spectacular crashes at the fair. He went on to become the most famous American flying ace in World War I, and later became president of Eastern Airlines.

Speed on four wheels came in 1905 when Earl Kiser clocked a record time of five miles in 4.75 minutes.

Gus Schrader beat Emory Collins by less than three feet in a ten-mile U.S. championship in front of 78,000 fans in 1936. It was the largest crowd in the history of State Fair racing.

Norwegian-born Albert Lea native Sig Haugdahl reached speeds of 180 mph in 1922 and drove one of the first rocket-powered cars at the fair, 1930.

In 1918, in his Lightning Benz car, Barney Oldfield set a track record of a mile in 49 seconds flat.

Wild Bill Endicott's Blitzen Benz is said to have cost $27,000 in 1916.

Stock car races were first held in 1949. By 1966, the half-mile dirt racetrack was paved to become one of the fastest and safest in the country—to the dismay of old dirt track fans.

Start of a race before a full house

A midget sprint car zoomed on the paved banked track

Auto fans soon clamored for more heart-stopping crashes and frightening midair collisions. Thrill Day ads declared: "Daredevil autoists will flirt with death on the race track, spinning, rolling, broad jumping, and crashing automobiles, amazing the crowd with their skill, daring, and miraculous escapes."

Auto polo was the perfect excuse for smashing old cars to pieces and became the forerunner to demolition derbies. Stripped-down cars drove around the infield bumping big leather balls toward goalposts, ramming and sideswiping each other along the way. The last car still moving was declared the winner.

Demolition derbies were the noisiest of all events, the object being to destroy all other cars. Throwing cars into reverse and using trunks to ram into other vehicles' engines provided the best offense. The last car still running limped through the wrecking yard to claim the prize.

Crews from local body shops rushed to clear the track

Demolition derby gridlock, 1970s

Flash Williams clears the hoods, 1938

Joie Chitwood, 1949

Gilmore Daredevils crash through a flaming fence, 1937

Thrillcade auto daredevils, 1950s

Swenson Thrillcade attendants stood ready to help troubled drivers or clear the track of wrecks.

Elephants were daredevils of their own, 1960

Clearing a row of vehicles, 1963

Daredevils jumped over cars and walked away from midair crashes leaving audiences cheering for more.

THE GREAT TRAIN WRECKS

Train crash, 1921

Head-on railroad collisions attracted huge audiences who fancied thunderous crashes. In 1920 and 1921, locomotives collided at speeds of 15 miles per hour, but in 1933 and 1934 the tracks were inclined and faster engines raced toward each other at combined speeds of 100 miles per hour. Clouds of hissing steam spewed over the grounds as engineers leaped for safety seconds before the deafening impact. The crashing locomotives were engulfed in billowing masses of sooty smoke while shooting flames poured from the mangled hulks. It was the scrapyard for some lovely old locomotives.

Special Added Attraction

Saturday, Sept. 4th
Opening Day.

A DUEL TO THE DEATH

between

TWO RAILROAD LOCOMOTIVES

in a

Thrilling Head-on Collision

Bicycles and Motorcycles

When bicycles were an important mode of transportation, cyclists showed off their talent in competitive races or difficult loop-the-loop feats. Valiant two-wheel entertainers took to the air riding on whirling contraptions or traversing high wires with specially built bicycles and cars.

Bicycle rider in the loop, 1932

Amazing car somersaults were described as "the hazardous terrific automobile double forward somersault that out-thrills all other thrillers." Fairs around the country booked the unusual show and audiences watched in anticipation as the little cars completed their somersaults successfully.

Auto thrill attendants watch the trick car, 1950s

Open cars were custom fitted to race down slides and whiz around loops. Most of the time they completed their tricks, but cars occasionally went off the track. Drivers were rarely injured, but audiences were excited to see a small mishap or two.

Bicycle rider shoots down the ramp ending with a dive in the pond, 1902

MOTOR MADNESS
The Newest 20th Century Thriller

A Whirling Maze of Death

Billed as "the best sensational novelty before the public," 1915

At the starting line, 1953

Raising dust on a speedy dirt track

M otorcycle races were huge crowd pleasers, as powerful machines and fearsome drivers roared around the track in a haze of dust occasionally colliding with fences—or each other.

Number one comes in number one

Hot motorcycles on a paved track

Champion motorcycle racer Bill Truman, 1954

Motorcycle thrill show, 1951

Hot Air Balloons and Aerial Thrill Shows

Flight became a passion for fairgoers the instant the first hot air balloon left the ground. Free-floating balloon ascensions and dirigible airships fascinated would-be-flyers as early as 1857. That lasted until the turn of the century when the first airplane swooped near the Grandstand and took off with people's dreams of flight.

The start of a race, 1907

Over time, balloon ascensions became everyday events to fair crowds, but two or more balloons in a heated race offered spectators the wonder of flight along with the exhilaration of a lofty competition.

Parachutist jumping from his platform, 1905

To keep audiences looking up, aeronauts jumped out of their balloons in parachutes; in later years they performed a basketful of dangerous airborne stunts while anxious spectators held their breath below.

Filling the balloons at the State Fairgrounds in 1907 for a long-distance flight record. "The America" on the left won the race, British entry "King Edward" is at the back.

Dirigibles appeared over the grounds in 1907 and were thought to be the future of flight, since early airships could be maneuvered.

An airship pilot walked along scaffolding between the propeller and tail to control flight direction—or to perform a trick or two for apprehensive audiences watching on land.

In 1928, Army Observation Balloon Captain Walters gave hourly passenger rides to fairgoers. Parachute jumps from the balloon provided additional excitement.

For pure entertainment in 1936, after giving rides all day, Walter's gigantic gas-filled observation balloon was shot down in flames before Grandstand audiences.

A Few of THE MANY ATTRACTIONS TO BE SEEN AT THIS YEAR'S

MINNESOTA STATE FAIR

360 Acres Crowded with Wonderful exhibits

Premiums Increased $15,000 Total Amount Now Offered $60,000

1ST NORTHWESTERN CORN SHOW AND LIBERAL ARTS EXHIBITS
ADDED SPACE IN AGRICULTURAL AND HORTICULTURAL DEPARTMENTS

The Largest Spectacle Ever Produced ~ "THE PAGEANT OF NATIONS

WONDERFUL AMUSEMENT PROGRAM
DAILY FLIGHTS OF WRIGHT BROS. AND CURTISS
~ AEROPLANES ~
$30,000 Racing Program - Automobile Races
MILLER BROS. 101 WILD WEST RANCH

Navassar Ladies Band

30 High Class American and European Vaudeville Acts

Gorgeous Display of Fireworks each evening

EXCURSIONS ON ALL RAILROADS

State Fair postcard mailing, 1910

The first airplane exhibition at the Minnesota State Fair Grandstand was staged by the Wright Company in 1910. The first year they were required to fly at least 40 feet off the ground, but the very next year, after amazing progress in aviation, the contract specified that planes must fly 200 feet or more, staying in the air for ten minutes.

Ten years later, wing walking, roll-overs, loop-the-loops, dive bombing, flame plunges, parachute drops, catapult crashes, auto-to-plane and plane-to-plane transfers became commonplace.

Women aeronauts made headlines for their brave and often dangerous aerial performances.

LADY WING WALKERS

Gladys Roy performed midair acrobatics, 1926

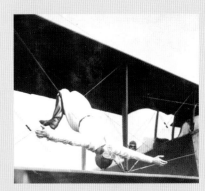

Gladys Roy hangs from the wing strut, 1926

Lillian Boyer, called "the thrill queen of the roaring twenties," in a car-to-plane transfer, 1922

Stunt pilot Captain Frank Frakes crashed into fairground houses for 20 years. His fine aircraft were destroyed along with the flimsy houses, but audiences loved every minute and he walked away every time, unhurt.

THRILL DAY FRIDAY AUG. 29

Some feats were so dangerous that federal authorities in the late 1920s prohibited aircraft from flying within 300 feet of each other.

Flying in formation and aerial drills by the U.S. Government Flying Air Circus thrilled grandstanders in 1922.

In 1950, stunt pilot Carl Ferris and wing-walker Kitty Middleton were killed as their plane crashed north of the Grandstand in full view of the crowd of 18,000. Stunt flying was banned at the fair after their tragic accident.

High-wire Thrill Shows

High-wire aerialists had one thing in mind—to make audiences gasp while they performed death-defying tricks overhead. Contraptions to fling human bodies through the air came with tall ladders, swaying poles, and sky-high diving platforms. But it wasn't all fun and games: serious accidents took place. German aerialist Frederico lost his life in a fall on the last night of the fair in the 1950s.

"Stratosphere Man" thrilled Grandstand audiences in the 40s

The Great Wallenda Family performed their famous pyramid of seven at the Grandstand, 1947

Death-defying cyclist rides with acrobats, 1961

Defying gravity, trapeze artists were among the most graceful show-stoppers at the fair in the 1940s

Two in an elephant suit walk a tight line, 1945

Fair shows always featured a diving horse and rider who dove head first from an 80-foot platform into a five-foot tank of water, 1923.

A daring diver in flames heads for a water tank; audiences always let out a sigh of relief upon his safe landing, 1937.

For three fairs during the 1980s, internationally famous wirewalker Jay Cochrane walked a very long wire stretched from the 4-H Building to the top of the Space Tower. Crowds formed throughout the fairgrounds and on nearby streets as he performed the breathtaking feat with no security harness or net.

Back dive from a U.S. High Diving team member

◄ *Egle Zacchini about to be shot 175 feet into the air*

The famous double cannon shot utilized compressed air to launch both Zacchini sisters from the cannon at nearly 30 miles per hour. In classic carnival romance, Egle Zacchini later married Carl J. Sedlmayr Jr., owner of Royal American Shows.

Sham Battles and Spectacular Firework Shows

In 1899, gaslights allowed the fair to stay open evening hours and elaborate nighttime shows were staged with panoramic spectacles that ended with mammoth fireworks. The first show in 1899 was an elaborate affair called "The Battle of Manila," which represented Dewey's Fleet in the heat of conflict against the exploding Manila skyline. For the next thirty years, new sets were built and then demolished in blazing flames. Famous cities received the most conflagrations: "The Last Days of Pompeii," "The Burning of Rome," "Tokyo Through Quake and Fire," "The Fall of Troy" "Siege of the Dardanelles," "Battle of the North Sea," were only a few.

Preparing for battle, 1887

"The Fall of Port Arthur," 1905

Rudimentary sets were wired with massive amounts of explosives and substantial quantities of fireworks that demolished hundreds of feet of panoramic stage sets and elaborate scenery.

Daytime Grandstand shows in the late 1800s consisted of battles between imaginary armies that brought in capacity crowds. The greatest spectacle was a Grand Army Day Battle in 1887 that included 2,000 veterans of the Civil War and more than 75,000 spectators.

By noon the Grandstand was packed. People continued to arrive until they filled the grounds around the track, crowded onto the track itself, and overflowed onto roofs of buildings nearby. The 15,000 people jammed into the old wooden Grandstand were warned for their own safety not to stamp their feet for fear the structure would collapse.

The epic "sham battle" was between "Union" and "Confederate" forces. They battled for the possession of "Camp Ramsey," over which flew a large Confederate flag. The shouts and cheers of the multitudes could hardly be heard over the tumultuous charging of troops, roaring musket shots, and ear-splitting cannon retorts. By the end of the fierce fighting, "Union" troops were victorious.

Thearle-Duffield
FIREWORKS
and
Thearle-Duffield's Fantastic Oriental
Fireworks Spectacle
"A NIGHT IN
BAGDAD"
Are the Feature Night Attraction at
Minnesota State Fair
Write for Free Illustrated Fireworks Catalog
Thearle-Duffield Fireworks Co.
Largest Producers of Fireworks Displays and
Spectacles in the World
624 S. MICHIGAN AVE.   CHICAGO, ILL.

In 1928, the last great epic "A Night in Bagdad" was staged complete with sheiks, caliphs, Nubian guards, and a replica of the city that burned to the ground in a colorful inferno of explosions and fireworks.

Crowds demanded more spectacular effects each year. Pain Fireworks and Thearle-Duffield Fireworks Companies pioneered new technology in the art of pyrotechnics. Considered the bellwether of all firework displays, the Minnesota State Fair was the first in the nation to stage firework extravaganzas designed as fair amusement. The shows were rated the finest in the country and the stunning epics were always shown first at the Minnesota State Fair.

Wiring for fireworks

THEARLE-DUFFIELD'S FIREWORKS PRESENTATION.
"Last Days of Pompeii,"
at MINNESOTA STATE FAIR.—1929.

"The Last Days of Pompeii," with Mt. Vesuvius erupting to destroy the city, 1929

In 1910, 500 participants in the "Pageant of Nations" took part in costumed parades and native dances representing the United States, France, Japan, Germany, China, Sweden, Italy, and a replica of the Paris Exposition building. Moments after the players departed the show, the elaborate 628 feet of scenic splendor was reduced to ashes resulting from blazing explosions and dazzling fireworks.

"Pageant of Nations," 1910 ▼▲

State Fair Revues

Beginning in 1930, State Fair revues and vaudeville shows replaced the pyrotechnic spectacles of the past. Audiences were entertained by popular music and lively dance routines performed on elaborate stages. Some shows featured bands, dancers, and large orchestras all on stage together in one spectacular musical program. The grand finale always included stunning firework displays that rocketed skyward over the infield.

Stage show ending with fireworks, 1920s

▲ *Grandstand revue, 1950*
▼ *London Palace Girls*

Barnes-Carruthers Theatrical Enterprises produced the State Fair revues. Staging was promoted as offering "showmanly-selected casts, hilarious cavalcades of fun, long lines of dancing girls, and unforgettable scenic and lighting splendor." The enormous productions entertained Grandstand audiences for decades.

MINNESOTA STATE FAIR

STATE FAIR REVUE OF 1941

WORLD'S GREATEST OUTDOOR PRODUCTION SEE IT SUNDAY NIGHT

NEW! DAZZLING! DIFFERENT!

Famous Celebrities

By the 1940s and 1950s, Hollywood celebrities became the darlings of the Grandstand stage. Personalities like Jane Russell, Dennis Day, Art Linkletter, Edgar Bergen and Charlie McCarthy, Roy Rogers and Dale Evans, were all huge drawing cards for fans of stage, radio, and T.V.

In the 1960s, audiences found their all-time favorite entertainment as star-powered celebrities and Grammy-winning musicians packed Grandstand seats night after night.

State fair audiences swayed to the rhythm of hundreds of famous voices. Loretta Lynn, Linda Ronstadt, Hank Williams Jr., Tammy Wynette, Olivia Newton-John, Barbara Mandrell, Barry Manilow, Reba McEntire, Peter, Paul, and Mary, Tom Jones, Merle Haggard, Jimmie Dean, Garth Brooks, Captain and Tennille, and The Carpenters were but a few.

Christina Aguilera holds the all-time record for ticket sales to a Grandstand show—she performed for over 22,000 fans in 2000.

In 1972, when John Denver suddenly wanted to juggle three balls during his performance, a stagehand brought him three oranges from Steichen's fairground grocery store.

Bob Hope

Miss Land O'Lakes and Art Linkletter, 1951

Johnny Cash with fair princesses and a supply of wild rice, honey, and milk

Garrison Keillor

Stars with Minnesota connections played to crowds of hometown audiences. Garrison Keillor combined sage commentary with satirical comedy many times to a cheering Grandstand, Bob Dylan performed in 1990, John Denver, Jonny Lang, and Bonnie Raitt also performed for cheering fans.

The Old Bandstands

All types of musical tempos rated high on the list of fairgoer "must see" activities. Bands, orchestras, and vocalists performed from well-appointed bandstands—and the music was diverse. As stage lighting and voice amplification improved, larger orchestral shows also performed at the Grandstand.

Lindquist Ladies' Symphony Orchestra of Minneapolis, 1909

Signor Cervone's Band was featured at the Grandstand, 1928

The Sousa concert in the plaza bandstand, 1927

SOUSA'S BAND

The greatest band in the world is to play afternoon and evening at the coming State Fair, Saturday, September 3, to Friday, September 9, inclusive. Directed by Lieut. Commander Sousa himself, it is certain to be one of the outstanding features of the Fair

Lt. Col. John Philip Sousa and his 74-piece band was the musical attraction at the 1927 fair, and he played to large appreciative audiences. The Minnesota March, his original composition for the University of Minnesota, was unfortunately not heard by the University president and was performed instead at the fair. Between concerts, Sousa visited the barns and was photographed with a cow, looked over the new model automobiles, ordered hamburgers by the dozen, and was made an honorary Blackfoot Indian Chief. Then he visited the Midway where he met with the leader of the Midget Band and was reported to have established himself as an "all-around good fellow."

An early tented bandstand, 1911

In addition to a musical place to rest during a tiring fair, bandstand concerts offered listeners a whimsical variety of architectural styles.

The popular old tented bandstand received a colorful makeover in the 1920s.

Helen Butler's ladies military band at the turn of the century

Plaza Park Bandstand, 1928

Pillsbury band members posed on the company's exhibit, a miniature of the Stone Arch Bridge, 1920

Bandstands and Marching Bands ⬩

Musical groups found appreciative audiences everywhere on the fairgrounds. Local musicians looked for fame and fortune during successful performances at bandstands, and amateurs had their chance in highly visible talent contests.

Harmonica players in Dixie vests and straw hats

Riders in the Sky played to Heritage Square crowds who hoped for return appearances—and were granted the favor many times.

Fair Tyme Singers at the Bandshell, 1971

Western music played by Picident's Cowboys was appreciated by man and beast alike, 1961

Modern musical group, Baldwin Park, 1980s

Aztec Indian trio, 1937

Duet with guitar accompaniment

Amateur talent contests brought forth musical skills in pop-rock, barbershop quartets, violin solos, fiddle players, guitar, vocal, gospel, piano, and cello. But that wasn't all, Ukrainian dancers, comedy groups, comedy dancers, duets, ballet dancers, baton twirlers, story-tellers, and clog dancers had their chance to shine for fair audiences, too.

Life is a cabaret my friend

Steele Family Singers, winners of the vocal contest, 1980

A needed energy boost and curbside rest

Bands have marched at State Fairs since 1864 when the Great Western Band of St. Paul played at the Red Wing State Fair. In later years, a bicycle band played while riding in formation around the fairgrounds; a 1930 high school band competition was so popular that 15,000 people sat in Grandstand rain to hear them perform.

Talent contest parade float, 1950s

Drum Majorettes from the Albert Lea High School Band, 1946

Any Grandstand seat, welcomes the beat
To music of shiny guitars.
Brass trumpets were made, for the outdoors to be played
Under spun candy clouds and the passionate evening.
Stars on the track, Dan Patch came back
To make history in the open air.
From Wright Brothers, to cars loudly racing on tar
At the Great Minnesota State Fair!

"THE GREAT MINNESOTA STATE FAIR" BY CHARLIE MAGUIRE

CHAPTER FIVE
The Midway

Fairgoers just couldn't resist the alluring temptation of the Midway. For adults, the long, glitzy stretch held childhood memories of whirling lights and penny arcades, easy laughter and uninhibited screams. Youngsters came along bent on creating memories of their own with an adrenaline rush on every ride and a determined attempt to win every skill game.

Historically, fair amusements in the 1800s were limited. They consisted only of sideshows, with talkers out front who convinced onlookers to take a peek into fortune-telling tents and bawdy distractions.

New recreational experiences came to the Minnesota fair when rides arrived in the late 1800s. Carousels featured magnificent carved horses, Ferris wheels took the bravest fairgoers to un-dreamed-of heights, and when the roller coaster arrived, breathtaking thrills were added to the growing list of fairgoing adventures.

Water excursions on a shallow lake provided fairgoers with immensely popular boat rides, but the water continually escaped. When the lakebed was filled, a grand area was created for acres of Midway rides and exotic sideshows. Skill game players found it hard to resist a ring toss or cat on the rail. Winning a prize looked easy, and nearly everyone wanted to take home a souvenir.

The value of the Midway was controversial: should the fair provide amusements for fairgoers who went to the fair for more important interests? But rides and games added a popular dimension to an already entertaining State Fair and the Midway grew larger each year.

Midway attractions, 1890s

Minnesota
STATE FAIR
PREMIUM LIST
Aug. 31–Sept. 7
1935
Admission 25¢

The Early Midway

During the 1800s, amusement shows were scattered throughout the fairgrounds, a sideshow here, a palm reader there, all mixed in with dining halls and exhibits. At the Chicago World's Fair in 1893, a central midway-style amusement concept had proved enormously successful and State Fair officials began to merge all the shows and rides into one location.

Willie Christine show, 1900

Sideshow, 1917

Girls and Fortune-tellers, 1900

Luna entrance, 1905

Amusement areas were called Pike, Luna, Wonderway, or Mid-way, and the alluring zones grew more popular each year.

Gaskill's Big Show, the Mighty Pike, 1904

In 1904, Gaskill Carnival Company put together the first combined traveling midway show at the fair. Admission was charged for entry into the secured area and sideshows lined up all around, but rides were not yet part of the spectacle offered inside.

Roberta and the Great Train Robbery show, 1904

Palmist's tent, 1900

In 1904, workers created a wide canal in a shallow pond heading west from the Grandstand. Boats carried passengers on scenic excursions and the shore was lined with pleasant picnic and camping sites. But the water constantly escaped and it became increasingly difficult to run the boats. Reluctantly, in 1916, the lagoon was filled in and amusement tents expanded into the old lakebed area.

Lagoon boat launch by the Grandstand, 1910

The Cannon Ball Coaster in 1920

Rides became important attractions at expositions after LaMarcus Thompson opened his Coney Island Switchback Railway in 1884. The State Fair's 1914 Cannon Ball Coaster provided apprehensive fairgoers with Minnesota's first truly terrifying ride. When it was dismantled in 1934, fans of wooden roller coasters found thrills on even more exciting rides coming to the fair.

Sideshows

Early sideshows intrigued fair-goers with banners that promised exotic attractions inside—and they had strong appeal to human nature's inquisitive side. Persuasive talkers projected their "bally-hoo" from "bally stages" in front of tents and coaxed nickels and dimes from fairgoer pockets for palaces of wonder and freak shows. "Ripley's Believe It or Not" offered oddities that pulled in large and curious crowds.

▲ *Ripley's, 1937*
▼ *Talker, 1937*

▲ *Fat man and lady, 1935*
◄ *Siamese twins, 1920s*

People marveled at so-called freaks: the smallest boy, fattest girl, tallest man. Siamese twins sang duets, midget companies formed orchestras, and the rubber man danced to popular tunes.

Community leaders became increasingly compassionate about freak shows and eventually a more humane attitude came about. By the 1960s, extraordinary physical feats took their place as sword swallowers, fire-eaters, contortionists, and tattooed bodies took over carnival sideshows.

Bonnie and Clyde Death Car, 1950s

An assortment of infamous characters promised a dime well spent for a little gangster adventure inside the tent.

The All American Cowboy Show, 1950s

Western star Johnny Mack Brown entertained audiences with his tricks and scenes from rodeo shows and stage productions.

Arabian Giantess, 1960s

Doctors and nurses were admitted free to this "archeological exhibit." All others paid 35 cents.

Monkey-Town, 1938

Bozo the Chimp and other animals who were dressed in fancy human clothing entertained their two-legged counterparts.

Royal American Show personnel train cars, 1959

Royal American Shows traveled on the largest privately owned train in the world—90 cars in length.

When the State Fair began its relationship with Royal American Shows in 1933, the popularity of the carnival was already huge. Now called the Mighty Midway, the area attracted large crowds and Minnesota's was billed as the most successful twelve-day carnival on any fairgrounds in the world. To honor the association that lasted more than sixty years, Royal American Shows donated one of their historic train cars to the State Fair Museum.

Starting up the Double Space Wheel

Setting up a funhouse banner

It took crews many days to set up sideshows, games of skill, and hair-raising rides on the long Midway.

Colorful tents for the performers, 1960

Back of the Midway, 1960 ▲
Midway ad, 1941 ▶

Entrance to the Midway, 1937

Crowds entered another world in the 1930s when they passed through the Royal American arches to lilting calliope music, hand-painted wagons, colorful merry-go-round horses—and rides that didn't yet turn the stomach or take the breath away. Flashing neon lights and electrifying paints were still on the horizon and ride calculations did not include the effects of gravitational forces.

Ride developers designed endless spinning contraptions that made fair visitors dizzy, 1970s

World's Smallest Midget Actors, 1948

The famous four-wheel Ferris wheel and popular airplane ride, 1937

Sideshow Girls

As early as 1894, saucy sideshows and gambling tents came under scrutiny by public officials. The following year, the fair was declared a "clean" fair: no liquor was allowed, all gambling devices were banned, and racy "hoochie-coochie" shows were not permitted on the grounds. As expected, they all sauntered back within a few years—only to be expelled again, then reinstated, many times over.

Sideshow poster, 1930s

Harlem in Havana, on the Midway, 1950

Fan dancer, 1934

Fan dancers were popular in the 1930s and '40s, and many became famous stars with Royal American Shows. Dancers like Sally Rand, Gypsy Rose Lee, and Bonnie Baker were appreciated for their creative dance routines and beautiful costumes. Really!

Sally Rand, 1948

The infamous Sally Rand made fan dancing an alluring hit at Chicago's 1933 Century of Progress World's Fair. She also performed at the Minnesota State Fair. A sulky rider not only won his race, a flower-bedecked Sally Rand presented his trophy.

A shimmering beauty in 1940

Club Lido showgirls, 1955

Showstopper, 1959

Standing 6'–8" tall, Ricki Covette, billed as "The World's Tallest Exotic," drew crowds anxious to see her dance performances and high kicks with her legendary long legs.

Midway talkers coaxed audiences to pay the ticket seller for a peek at belly dancers in "culturally educational" foreign dances. But once inside the tent, burlesque-style revues featured dancing girls in flowing costumes performing sensuous dances that beguiled spellbound audiences.

All ages checked out the dancing girls, 1969

Minnesota governors were asked if the "naughty shows" contributed to the delinquency of youngsters from 4-H, FFA, and Boy's and Girl's Clubs. But the full "educational experiences" encountered at the fair won out and the shows continued.

Most of the elaborate carnival revues disappeared in the 1980s when now-famous dancers moved their shows to Las Vegas and points west.

The Early Rides

ranquil merry-go-rounds began to turn in the late 1880s, and within a surprisingly short time, truly spectacular Ferris wheels and hair-raising roller coasters appeared—and they revolutionized amusement at fairs throughout the country.

Ye Old Mill, 1950s

One of the country's only tunnels of love opened in 1913. Four generations of Keenan family members have kept it a beloved fixture at the fair ever since. Famous faces like Hubert Humphrey and Sonny and Cher, along with countless flirtations and wedding parties, floated through the darkness to sounds of splashing water and stolen kisses.

Minnesota's first Ferris wheel, 1896

George Washington Gale Ferris Jr. presented his magnificent Ferris wheel at the 1893 World's Fair in Chicago. The Pittsburgh bridge-builder's gigantic wheel towered 265 feet over the fairgrounds, its 125-foot diameter carried streetcar-sized glass-enclosed gondolas on leisurely ten-minute revolutions.

In 1896, Minnesota fairgoers rode their first Ferris wheel, a modest sixty feet tall. They rode on the nation's first combination of four integrated Ferris wheels in 1932—and from then on, Ferris wheels kept getting higher, more elaborate, and more exciting.

Four-wheel Ferris wheel, 1958

Double Space Wheel, 1980

GOOD FOR ONE RIDE ON
YE OLD MILL 1969
ANY TIME
Not Good on Saturday, Sunday,
Childrens Day or Holidays

Kiddieland, 1963

Pint-size amusements relocated around the fairgrounds every few years as they grew larger and more popular. It was an added attraction for youngsters—a game of hide-and-seek—to find the rides.

MINNESOTA
STATE FAIR
1969
OUTSIDE GATE
ADMIT ONE   Est. Price .97   State Tax .03 $1.00

State Fair Carousel, 1969

The first rides at fairs were merry-go-rounds and Minnesota's first appeared at the fair in 1892, but the most beautiful horses pranced on a memorable carousel that was built in 1914 by the Philadelphia Toboggan Company. By 1988, having been used only a dozen days a year, the privately owned and increasingly valuable 68 hand-carved wooden horses were scheduled to be sent to an auction house. The public strongly objected. Eventually, the carousel moved intact to continue its musical rounds at Como Park.

Tot-sized Empire Builder, 1954

Sellner
TILT-A-WHIRL

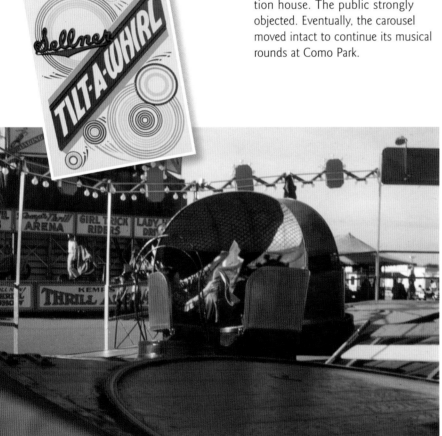

Tilt-A-Whirl car ready for a spin in 1959

The Tilt-A-Whirl has stood the test of time. Seven cars, each fixed to a central pivot, rolled around a circular track of hills and valleys putting centrifugal and gravitational forces on the cars. Invented by Herbert Sellner of Faribault in 1926, the Tilt-A-Whirl's crack-the-whip motion provided a source of fun that brought people back again and again—even all around the world!

Giant slide, 1972

GIANT SLIDE
GOOD FOR
ONE RIDE

Fun House and Carnival Attractions

In his 1947 "I Like It Here" column, George Grimm observed: "You say, 'Isn't it time for the Fair to grow up?' No, it never will be. The Fair must have its roots in better farming, 4-H'ers, the farm boys and girls, the livestock, the quilts, the jams and the breads. But it must keep young and remain a little foolish at heart. It must have tinsel and silly exhibits and a Penny Arcade . . . pink floss sugar candy concoctions . . . and the Fun House."

Inside the funhouse, floors heaved up and down, piles of barrels looked like they were headed for a big fall, air jets blew up skirts, and bent mirrors made everyone look goofy. It was fun!

Hofbrau House, 1980s

Glass House, an a-mazing walk, 1980s

Bug House offered bite-free adventure, 1980s

A visit to foggy London town, 1980s

Welt Bummler whisked riders on little cars through animal scenes, 1963

Dancing Waters, 1960

A record 55,000 fairgoers packed around awe-inspiring displays of misty clouds, splashing fountains, and leaping streams of water.

Ice Palace Revue, 1962

Costumed skaters on cool ice were pleasures on a warm summer day.

The Circus set up on the Midway or at the Grandstand: elephants, lions, and high-wire artists could be seen up close. But the Hippodrome Coliseum provided a more perfect place for animal and acrobatic feats and the menagerie moved to the big arena to perform at other times of the year.

Lux Memory Doll House, 1947

Tiny rooms were full of tiny furnishings, including some that depicted prairie life one hundred years earlier. All were handmade from fine woods and fabrics, or with real pewter and silver: even miniature oil paintings on the walls were hand-painted.

Motordrome, 1937

Marjorie Kemp rode the circular walls of the Motordrome with a lion as a passenger. Shaped like a gigantic bowl, the Motordrome track rose vertically to the top of the walls. Drivers revved up their speed, climbed up the wall, and tried to keep running fast enough to not fall down—the faster they went, the higher they went. Exhilarated spectators watched from platforms around the top.

Riding High and Fast ⚑

As the 1960s approached, carnival fans looked for bigger thrills on taller contraptions in faster cars. Royal American Shows peppered the Midway with improved hair-raising excitement each year, while the State Fair installed lofty sightseeing rides of their own.

The 330-foot Space Tower was billed as the first of its kind at any state fair in the country. Built in Germany, it was shipped by freighter from Holland to Duluth, then loaded on 20 trucks headed for the Minnesota State Fair. When it opened in 1964, the revolving double-decker car offered a view of the entire fairgrounds as well as peeks at both downtowns' skyscrapers.

Sky Ride, 1970s

The Seattle and New York World Fairs had Sky Rides and so did Minnesota in 1964. Made by a Swiss company known for its peak-to-peak gondola rides in the Alps, the Sky Ride offered fairgoers a welcome seat for weary feet and the very best view for long-distance people watching.

MINNESOTA
STATE FAIR
1969
SKY RIDE
ADMIT ONE
Est. Pr. .50 52¢ 0011
St. Tax .02

MINNESOTA
STATE FAIR
1966
SPACE TOWER
ADMIT ONE
50¢
Globe Ticket Co.   TAX EXEMPT

Man in Space, 1970s

Astro-Liner, 1980s

Carnivals indulged space age enthusiasts after the walk on the moon in 1969. Riders were hard to convince that the Astro-Liner didn't go anywhere—inside it felt like a real spaceship.

Thunder Bolt, 1980s

Mad Mouse, 1958

Super-Loop's, 1970s

Fairgoers hung on tighter as carnival ride inventors employed the first space-age gravity tricks. Gleeful riders were sent flying down slippery slopes like those in the Alps or the Himalayas.

Matterhorn with chilled breezes on hot days, 1980s

The Midway became a magical place at night. Rides seemed more mysterious in the dark as brightly colored lights whirled and twisted against the evening sky.

Space Wheels, 1975

Carnival rides through the end of the 1900s were relatively tame compared to the undreamed-of amusements of the future. Huge increases in velocity and altitude would fling bodies through the air in unimaginable ways in the 21st century.

Skill Games and Souvenirs

In the early 1900s, tent games such as Mice in the Hole and Pitch a Penny were considered gambling because winning players received cash instead of prizes. When fairs decided to ban gambling, whimsical objects became the reward for winning a game. Although skill games and guessing games were sometimes called "gyp stands," game winners could be doubly proud because so few people ever seemed to win a prize.

Ball into the milk can, 1980

Ring toss, 1980

Football toss, 1979

Cat from a cat rack game

Guess your weight, 1960

Penny Arcade, 1937

Shooting gallery game, 1954

Arcade games had no prizes, just the satisfaction of playing the game better than most and for as long as possible.

It was an irresistible urge of human nature to want a souvenir, memento, or keepsake from the State Fair, so nearly everyone took something home. Animals, always a State Fair favorite, enticed potential adoptees with their plush fabrics or cheerful vinyl colors.

Souvenirs were tea-table quality at the first fairs, but beautiful wooden parlor games and ruby glassware soon gave way to kitschy chalkware and satin pillow covers.

▼ Lineup of chalkware

111

Villages

Entertainment also came with cultural connections. World's Fairs included villages from other societies such as Borneo, Alaska, or the Philippines. The Minnesota fair followed the popular trend with an easy history lesson at Native American, Swedish, and international villages.

Village, 1909

In 1896, the State Fair invited a band of Ojibway to live in an Indian Village on the fairgrounds. It started a successful association between Native Americans and the fair that continued well into the 1960s. Chippewa, Iroquois, Sioux, and Hopi joined in over the years. They dressed in the style of their ancestors; their historic dances and celebrated customs attracted appreciative crowds for many decades.

Indian Village, 1933

Mexican Village, 1970

Mexican Village market stalls opened in 1970 but a worldly focus was added in the 1980s when the area became the International Bazaar.

Mexican dancers, 1975

South American treasures, 1990s

Hawaii in Minnesota, 1990

Young America Center and Teen Fairs held programs tailored for youthful fairgoers. Exhibits, shows, and contests provided scholarly interest, while pop bands, folk singers, dancers, even the All-State Youth Orchestra, livened up diverse teen entertainment.

Heritage Square, 1990s

Entertainer outside State Fair Museum railroad car, 1980s

Old-fashioned was the focus at Heritage Square with historic buildings nestled between twentieth-century look-alikes; museums preserved artifacts from the past while exhibitors offered handmade pioneer-style crafts.

Claybourne Pots, 1970s

Credit River Stove Works, 1970s

The Midway spins round, or goes upside down
In a blur of tinsel and gold
With lights like tattoos, on a night sky once blue
In a permanent memory, of the Royal American Shows
To see for the devotee of the curious stare
With money to spend, to win prize dividends
At the Great Minnesota State Fair!

"THE GREAT MINNESOTA STATE FAIR" BY CHARLIE MAGUIRE

Fine Arts and Museum Exhibitions

arly art shows included traveling exhibitions from national museums as well as Minnesota Fine Art Competitions. The popular exhibits outgrew their original 1886 building and moved into the Main Building. By 1910, more space was needed and the Grandstand upper floor and balcony were redesigned into art exhibition rooms.

Finally, in 1914, museum exhibits and State Fair Fine Art exhibitions combined their shows and moved into space in the new Fine Art Galleries—where over 120,000 people viewed paintings that first year.

Painting and sculpture exhibit, 1880s

Fine Art Galleries, 1914

The Minneapolis School of Fine Arts, the forerunner to the Minneapolis College of Art and Design, advertised in the 1906 State Fair program. Opportunities for further education provided competition artists a better chance at a Blue Ribbon.

Interior of Fine Art Galleries, 1928

Fairgoers could study famous paintings loaned from museum shows—within arm's reach at State Fair galleries were Miro, Modigliani, Hopper, Braque, and Derain. In 1951, prints and drawings on exhibit were by Dali, Klee, Kandinsky, O'Keefe, Childe Hassam, Reginald Marsh, and Diego Rivera.

The Minnesota State Fair in 1922 presented Vice President and Mrs. Coolidge with Minnesota artist Cameron Booth's prize-winning oil painting.

When million-dollar exhibits from the nation's most heralded museums came to the fair, local artists helped organize shows and led tours for fascinated fairgoers.

Minnesota fine art superintendent Clement Haupers with a prize-winning sculpture by Evelyn Raymond, 1935.

WPA Federal Art Project painting demonstration, 1938

Finishing a painting for the fair, 1957

Pottery entry for the 1934 fair

Milkman sculpture attracts admirers, 1980s

Fine Arts Competition

In 1947, the "All American Show" boasted that America was the art center of the world; State Fair exhibitions included examples of the nation's outstanding art movements. Farsighted fairgoers could purchase oil paintings like a Milton Avery for $1,000, a Marsden Hartley for $2,200, a Robert Motherwell for $350, and a Max Weber for $2,800!

Grandstand art exhibit, 1948

Grandstand art exhibit, 1949

Minnesota artists were offered limited entry choices in fine art competitions in 1910: only oil paintings, watercolors, pastels, and black-and-white drawings could be entered. A decade later, competitions expanded dramatically with added categories for photography, sculpture, and prints, along with advertising design, costume design, stage design, and a section for applied art in jewelry, pottery, basketry, stenciling, weaving, metal and wood works. During those years it was called the State Fair Arts and Crafts Show. Years later, crafts were relocated to the handicrafts department and the art show became the permanent Fine Arts Show.

Advertising art show

▲ *Photography show*
▼ *Oil painting ready for exhibition, 1954*

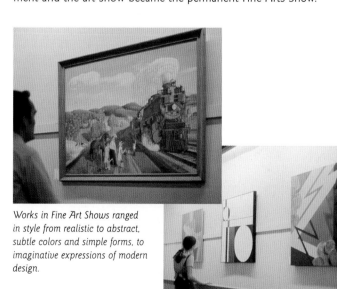

Works in Fine Art Shows ranged in style from realistic to abstract, subtle colors and simple forms, to imaginative expressions of modern design.

Contemplating a work of art, 1980s

Studying fine textile work, 1990s

Reflecting on an artistic style, 1980s

Many of Minnesota's best-known and most sought-after artists have been competitors at the State Fair—and their prices were very affordable. In 1955, St. Paul artist LeRoy Neiman's large oil painting was listed at $200. Other Minnesota artists were also modestly priced and collectors and local gallery owners made many opportune connections at the fair.

A closer look

After a move back to the Grandstand in 1954, and enduring decades on the move, the Fine Arts Show settled into the former Dairy Building in 1980.

Shopping for fine art at the fair, 2005

Crop Art ▱

The time-consuming art of gluing seeds to boards began as a rural, wintertime hobby. Finished pieces are exhibited at the fair alongside corn and grain competitions as a different view of the state's agricultural heritage. Judges critique work on neatness and creativity, but most important is the artist's use of Minnesota-grown seeds and foliage.

Art fans, young and old, liked the clever "seedy" arrangements, 1980s

David Steinlicht, First Place, 1996

Delores Doroff, Best of Show, 2000

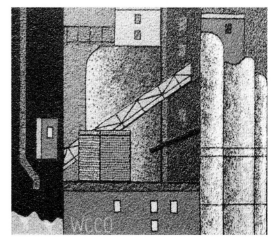

Linda Koutsky, Second Place, 1999

LILLIAN COLTON

State Fair Crop Art demonstration ▲
Barbra Streisand, 1974; Richard Nixon, 1969; Jesse Ventura, 1999; Eleanor Roosevelt, 2004 ▶

Lillian Colton began exhibiting her trademark portraits at the State Fair in 1966. Her realistic portrayals in poppy, wheat, wild rice, and cream of wheat won so many ribbons and best-of-shows that the fair decided to give Lillian her own exhibit space. Then, in 2004, her Crop Art was shown in a climate-controlled gallery at the Minneapolis Institute of Arts.

Creative Art on the Fairgrounds

Fairgoers are always within a few steps of whimsical outdoor sculptures that enliven plazas, streets, and walkways.

Sand castles made a fleeting appearance on the fairgrounds in the 1990s.

Minnesota's pioneer woman, 36 feet tall, made her debut in 1958 in celebration of 100 years of Minnesota statehood.

No one could miss the 24-foot gopher Fairchild who became the State Fair mascot in 1964. His nephew, "Fairborne," appeared in supporting roles.

Fairchild and friends peek from the fairground's oldest tree stump. Carved by Dennis Roghair in 1998.

Bust of Fairborne carved by Johnny Hunter in 1985.

Pioneer woman, painter, and farmer

Over a thousand shade trees were planted on the fairgrounds in 1892 and hundreds more followed in years to come. Tree sculptures gave new life to trees that had succumbed to old age or disease.

The Women's Buildings

Women finally received a building of their own at the turn of the nineteenth century. In 1897, the Minnesota Federation of Women's Clubs was given the former Racetrack Clubhouse to hold programs for women. The building was well furnished with chairs and rockers and places to attend musical performances, literary lectures, and afternoon readings. An attending nurse cared for tired children and offered mothers a cup of tea and a wafer. Programs were established for art day, library day, educational day, homemaking day, and school exhibitions. Attendance soared at the fair as a result of the first Women's Building.

Racetrack Clubhouse, 1900

The Clubhouse burned down in 1903 and women's programs moved temporarily into a vast open space at Institute Hall.

By 1907 the Women's Club State Fair Committee petitioned fair officials for a permanent building to house exhibits and demonstrations. The former Dairy Hall Building became the new Women's Building.

The old Manufacturer's Building was the last location dedicated exclusively for women's activities. Its stately architecture embraced home activities and creative competitions until the 1970s.

A handsome structure was erected to hold Minnesota State exhibits in 1904 at the St. Louis World's Fair, also called the Louisiana Purchase Exposition. When the exposition closed, the building was shipped in pieces to the Minnesota State Fairgrounds where it was reassembled on an attractive landscaped site. The building served as a hospital and a newspaper headquarters, but it was best known as the Rest Cottage for most of its years. KSTP was its final occupant in the 1960s.

The Minnesota State Exhibits Building in St. Louis was described as unusual; encircling the loggias were Byzantine columns described as a curious development from the Egyptian column. But the wide awnings and huge vases filled with flowering plants were inviting, and thousands visited the building during the St. Louis exposition.

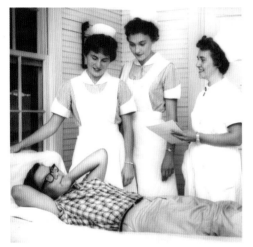

A model sick room in the 1907 Women's Building became taxed to the limit with two women in one bed and two sick policemen next door. The small space overflowed with ill fairgoers waiting for carriages to take them to the city. The St. Louis Building hospital briefly relieved the pressure with a physician and trained nurse in charge.

Decades later, a State Fair hospital was built. It was staffed by 2 physicians and 8 nurses and they treated 400 people in the first year.

Once settled comfortably on the fairgrounds, the Minnesota Building welcomed an eclectic variety of fair visitors for over fifty years. In 1913, the gracious verandas and bright interior rooms were furnished for increasing numbers of women and children attending the fair. The Rest Cottage interior became a cheerful assemblage of multicolored stained glass windows and embossed Egyptian columns surrounding Arts and Craft style rocking chairs.

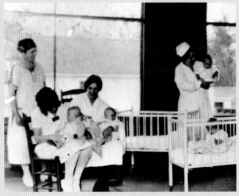

Fair nursery, 1925

The health of babies was a top-ranking subject for women at the fair. A baby contest planned for 150 babies opened with over 300 entries in 1913. Tots were examined and graded for nearly 100 attributes, then they were judged by well-known pediatric authorities. In 1915 the baby contest pitted city babies against country babies, and Minneapolis babies against St. Paul babies.

An exhibit of babies in newly invented glass-enclosed incubators operated at the fair from 1911 to 1923. They were extremely popular, but well protected from curious crowds. Nurses attended to the premature infants around the clock.

Multiple births attracted attention during the 1950s. The Seifert Quadruplets, born to Mr. and Mrs. Arthur Seifert of Sleepy Eye, were visited by many thousands of interested fairgoers. They were one-year-olds when they appeared at the fair in 1951.

Needlework

While agriculture was the prime focus for pioneering farmers, improving necessities at the farmhouse was just as important for a good life in Minnesota. Fairs in the 1850s promoted a small sampling of homemaking abilities in needlework, fancy articles, flowers, and butter making. But improving home skills brought resourceful and imaginative curiosity to both rural and urban families as fine cooking, precise needlework, skillful sewing, and other homemaking talents became lively competition at the State Fair.

Blue Ribbon winners for very fine needlework

Quilt and hooked rug inspections accompanied by a cup of tea in the Women's Building, 1935

Quilt display by senior citizens in 1970. Fair competitions included works of seniors, youngsters, and disabled artists.

Textile demonstration, 1938

Quilts were originally made for winter warmth, but quilters found the design possibilities irresistible. State Fair judges award needlework prizes based on workmanship, overall texture, thread type and size, beauty of design and color, neatness of seams, perfection of stitching, difficulty of project, and beauty of finished article. It isn't easy to take home a Blue Ribbon.

Yarn spinning demonstration

As people found more leisure time, articles once considered everyday necessities became hobbies. Rugs that covered splintered floors became fanciful designs that hung on walls because no one wanted to walk on them. Talented weavers and skillful sewers turn plain homespun fabrics into fine intricate linens, and demonstrations attract elbow-to-elbow audiences who view beautiful heirloom patterns re-interpreted by artists of the day.

Beaded purses, 1920s

Table linen cutwork winner, 1934

Hooked rug demonstration, 1926

Ribbon-winning dolls in native Japanese clothing, 1970s

Cutwork tablecloth

Changing styles reflected evolving fashions in competition categories. Official entry classes in 1920 included piano scarves, door stops, boudoir pillows, buffet scarves, bonbon cases, embroidered portieres, and between-meal cloths. Class 148 was entitled "Work of Old Ladies" and was open only to ladies 70 or older who entered patchwork quilts, mittens, slippers, socks, doilies, and tidies.

Hooked rug about to sail into the winner's circle, 1940s

Rosemaling, Carving, Collections ⚑

Collections and craftwork competitions comprise large categories that appeal to youngsters and adults alike. Educational, and often amazing, the beautiful work inspires rapt attention and speculation: "how long do you suppose it took to make that?"

Tables piled high with painted porcelain, rock collections, and fabric sewn into multitudes of shapes await a critical judge's eye.

Girls appreciating a pioneer family scene

There's something for everyone to admire in big competition displays

State Fair collections include minerals, buttons, stamps, coins, postcards, lapidary, and taxidermy. Collections reflect the interests of the times as entries such as woven hair pocket watch chains disappeared by the 1920s.

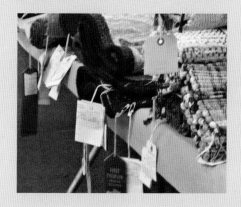

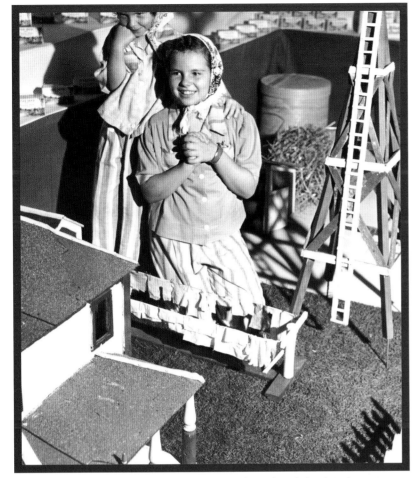

A dollhouse with Monday's wash on the line captured the fancy of two little girls in the 1940s

Handicraft categories came and went over the years reflecting changing interests and population growth. As categories like telescope construction and peasant painting disappeared, handcrafted items from other cultures entered to broaden and enhance competition displays.

One shipshape schooner, 1950s

▲ *Three Norwegians ready for the fair with complex rosemaling designs*
▼ *Covered wagon headed for the fair, 1950s*

Swedish painter completes a wood pail in the 1950s

Pretty as a pitcher, 1950s

Baked Goods

Baking took place all year long as bakers refined their recipes for State Fair competitions. Farm families retrieved fresh hen-house eggs and opened dusty flour sacks while city folk trekked to the corner grocery for products to make crusty breads, flaky pies, and high-rising cakes. Family and friends passed judgment and ate the losers—happy sacrifices on the way to a winning State Fair recipe!

Cake eaters testing for Mom, 1950s

One more ribbon—maybe, 1921

Checking the texture, 1950s

Donuts fresh from the kettle, 1950s

MINNESOTA STATE FAIR AND NORTHWEST DAIRY EXPOSITION

MIDWAY—BETWEEN THE TWIN CITIES

SEPTEMBER 1 to 8 NINETEEN TWENTY-THREE

Donuts by the baker's dozen

In the early 1900s, a daring man entered the women's world of baking competitions. He arrived at the fair with a large collection of cakes and registered a tutti-frutti cake along with other delicacies. The ladies didn't think it was a fair contest, but he went home with a couple of Second Place ribbons.

Flashlight test on the cake

When judgment day arrived, competitive bakers were on the road by dawn. Hundreds of hopefuls joined long lines, held carefully wrapped baked goods, and waited anxiously at crowded tables to register a freshly made culinary treasure.

Judge inspecting for a dome top, square corners, and an even crust

It's going to be a long day!

Baked goods must be entered on plain paper or plastic plates—no fancy china to keep track of at check-in

A bounty of yeast and sweet in 1951. Icing on the cake adds another dimension to the judging difficulty

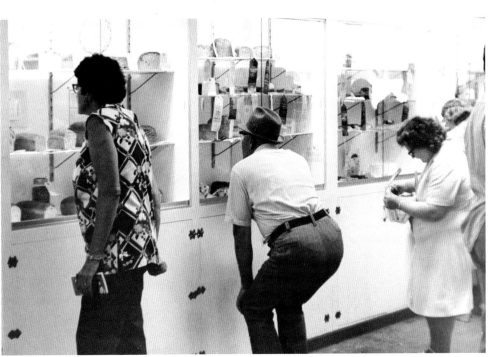

Breads and rolls are judged on size, shape, crust, flavor, lightness, color, and on the character of crumb!

Culinary Canning ▶

Cellars and pantries awaited freshly canned food in the days before electric freezers. Fall kitchens were crammed with bushels of produce, pots steamed with boiling water, glass jars waited in wire racks, rubber rings and lids sat nearby. Nothing comforted the soul like shiny rows of well-sealed fruit jars and the summer's harvest safely stored for winter.

Canned fruit and pickles earmarked for the fair in 1955

Checking to see who won, 1947

During World War I, competition rules stated that no canned products would be wasted; jars would be opened, tested, resealed, and returned to the competitor. World War II exhibits included Victory Garden produce from home gardens, rural gardens, and city gardens.

▲ *Cleaning the palate between tastings*
▶ *Judging fruit, 1955*

Checking on a fruitful harvest, 1950s

Premium book guidelines advised: "It is impossible to judge canned products fairly without opening the cans, as a beautifully appearing product may be absolutely unpalatable, the fruit or vegetables are not canned as ornaments but as food." It was a sage commentary on the beautiful rows of jars, gleaming in gemstone colors, laden with luscious fruits, lining the backlit display shelves.

Registering pickles and jams, 2006

Organizing the shelves took patience and perseverance, 2006

Appreciative would-be canners examine the canning division's selection of whole fruit, preserved fruit, preserves, jellies, conserves, jams, butters, pickles, relishes, and vegetables, 2006.

Education for Children at the Fair

There was more than Midway fun for thousands of kids at the fair. Programs and events showcased their talents, abilities, and passions—and spirited competitions proved their skill.

More than cookies: Girl Scouts demonstrated newfound talents from their booth

Scouts did duty at the fair with classes, exhibits, and activities—all uniformly well done. A troop from Granite Falls once hiked 196 miles to and from the fair. Five hundred Boy Scouts camped on the fairgrounds at the first statewide Boy Scout encampment.

Boy Scouts practiced a number of aptitudes during fair time—including how to peel potatoes

Garden produce ready for display at the 1934 fair

Boys from the gardening and canning contest, University of Minnesota Agriculture Department

Boys and Girls Clubs promoted discipline, education, practical experience, and equal opportunities from the garden to the kitchen.

State bread making contest, 1922

Winner of dramatic declamation award, 1935

Winner of humorous declamation award, 1935

Budding performers had ample audiences on which to practice their acting skills. The state spelling bee and a "Know your Minnesota" quiz contest tested a scholar's memory.

Style show in the auditorium, 1948

Fashion shows and sewing contests were among the most up-to-the-minute events at the fair. Clothing was judged on the suitability to occasion, individuality, beauty of design and color combinations, materials, trimmings, and perfection of stitch.

> Evelyn Olson,
> Eighth Grade, Age 14 years,
> Dist. 25 Isanti Co.
> There are a great many varieties of potatoes. The early Ohio is a leading oval punkish or flesh colored potato suitable for black, rich soil. It has light green stems and white flowers.

Winning potato essay by Evelyn Olson, Oxlip, Isanti County, 1919

The Potato Club for boys and girls taught about growing potatoes—all kinds. Potatoes were entered for competition, 32 paper-wrapped to a box and booklets were written about the characteristics of individual varieties. County fair winners went on to the Minnesota State Fair where an award became a treasured keepsake.

Educational Experiences

Youngsters from all over the state packed their duffel bags and wondered what life would be like living on the fairgrounds. Some lived in tents, others in dorms, many bunked in with their prize animals. Meals came from cafeterias, dining halls, or hotdog stands, and evenings were spent with newfound friends in fun-filled festivities. For most, it was the experience of a lifetime.

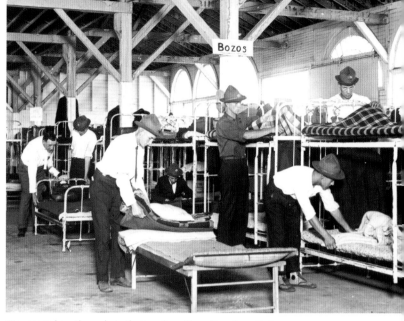

Boy soon to be wide-awake in the Farm Boys Camp Dormitory, 1937

The Farm Boys Camp started in the early 1900s. Two farm boys from each county competed for lodging and meals, along with free transportation to and from the fair. They studied exhibits of livestock, machinery, and agriculture, but they also had to work by ushering at the Grandstand and Livestock Pavilion.

Girls eventually joined the program and the Farm Boys Camp officially became the Minnesota State Fair Youth Camp in 1976.

Wooden dorms and recreation buildings were built in the 1920s to replace the early tents for the Farm Boys Camp

Shearing for a show

Blue Ribbon-winning Shropshire, 1920s

Grand Champion of 1948

FFA began their strong relationship with the fair in 1949 with a three-day livestock show and later a crop show. In 1956, with a focus on animals, the Children's Barnyard became a popular new FFA project at the fair.

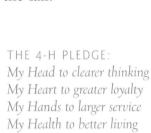

Opening in 1939, hundreds of 4-H participants moved into the state-of-the-art 4-H building, which included display space, a huge cafeteria, classroom space, and sleeping dorms. Livestock and agriculture were 4-H basics, but display spaces held abundant entries of youthful projects in other areas as well. Woodworking, weaving, cooking, welding, forestry, and health were but a few of the interests that kept 4-H'ers busy at the fair.

Handmade clothing rivaled store-bought frocks every time in 1951

4-H bunks for the boys with rules in plain sight, 1947

Staying overnight with friends in the dorms was half the fun of being in 4-H.

THE 4-H PLEDGE:
My Head to clearer thinking
My Heart to greater loyalty
My Hands to larger service
My Health to better living
For my club, my community,
My country, and my world.

The girl's dorm held closet-sized quantities of clothes— all in one bunk space

Upholstery and furniture making won awards in 1948

Serving the crowds, 1954

Mirror space was a little tight for a fancy hairdo

Canning and cakes, first premium lace,
Judging in red, white, and blue.
Needlework glory, that stitches a story
And invites you to be part of a family you never knew.
Ideas in paint or veneer, in seeds, on display it's all there.
You all are a part; all in life is an art
At the Great Minnesota State Fair!

"THE GREAT MINNESOTA STATE FAIR" BY CHARLIE MAGUIRE

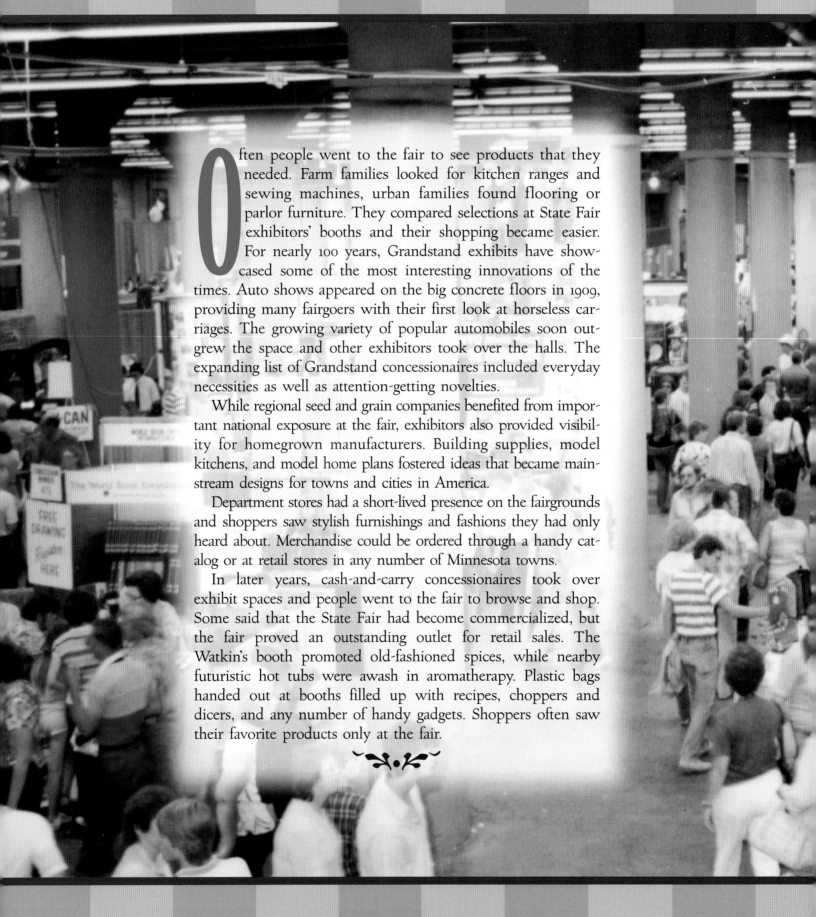

CHAPTER SEVEN
Exhibits & Concessions

Often people went to the fair to see products that they needed. Farm families looked for kitchen ranges and sewing machines, urban families found flooring or parlor furniture. They compared selections at State Fair exhibitors' booths and their shopping became easier. For nearly 100 years, Grandstand exhibits have showcased some of the most interesting innovations of the times. Auto shows appeared on the big concrete floors in 1909, providing many fairgoers with their first look at horseless carriages. The growing variety of popular automobiles soon outgrew the space and other exhibitors took over the halls. The expanding list of Grandstand concessionaires included everyday necessities as well as attention-getting novelties.

While regional seed and grain companies benefited from important national exposure at the fair, exhibitors also provided visibility for homegrown manufacturers. Building supplies, model kitchens, and model home plans fostered ideas that became mainstream designs for towns and cities in America.

Department stores had a short-lived presence on the fairgrounds and shoppers saw stylish furnishings and fashions they had only heard about. Merchandise could be ordered through a handy catalog or at retail stores in any number of Minnesota towns.

In later years, cash-and-carry concessionaires took over exhibit spaces and people went to the fair to browse and shop. Some said that the State Fair had become commercialized, but the fair proved an outstanding outlet for retail sales. The Watkin's booth promoted old-fashioned spices, while nearby futuristic hot tubs were awash in aromatherapy. Plastic bags handed out at booths filled up with recipes, choppers and dicers, and any number of handy gadgets. Shoppers often saw their favorite products only at the fair.

Premium List
MINNESOTA
STATE FAIR
and
NORTHWEST DAIRY
EXPOSITION
September 3d to 10th
1927

Grandstand exhibit hall, 1980s

Grains and Milling

Grains were Minnesota's pot of gold. The land was perfect for growing wheat and corn, rivers ran strong for turning grinding wheels, and savvy pioneers knew how to build the state into the milling capital of the world. And—all the best samples could be seen at the State Fair.

Postcard announcing State Fair exhibit

Victorian-style Minnesota Flour booth, 1893

An attention-getting Minnesota Flour booth was designed for the 1893 Chicago World's Fair, where it was a successful attraction for Minnesota's milling industry. The booth returned to Minnesota and was reassembled in the Main Building the following year.

Northrup King & Co.'s origins in Minnesota's agricultural landscape began in 1884. Colonel W. S. King, who ran the famous Bill King's Expositions in the 1880s, joined the company along with his son. Seed packet and hybrid pioneering brought international fame and success to the Minnesota company.

Cargill seed sample display, 1950s

Established in 1865, Cargill evolved into one of the country's largest privately-owned businesses. The Minnesota-based grain trader and agricultural commodities company exhibited in large and imaginative booths at the State Fair.

Well-known Minnesota products, and a few that were not so well-known, made unusual appearances in the exhibit halls. Competitions, like the Malting Barley Contest, enhanced the contents of bottles, barrels, and vats of beer from all around the state. Many became nationally famous brands.

Yes, it's still the Minnesota State Fair! The rolling fields of Stearns County once produced tobacco

Wool exhibit, 1940s

Wool, in the cool climate of the north, was a warm and comfortable necessity—and certain to be turned into something fashionable.

Minnesota Brewer's Association contest winners, 1940s

Enestvedt's hybrid seed corn, at the fair since the 1940s

Swift's Hatcheries for the best looking chicks, 1950s

Autos & Airplanes

Transportation exhibits became a fairgoer must-see. The 1909 Grandstand automobile show was the largest automotive show west of New York City. By the 1930s, high-style programs romanticized travel and nearly everyone wanted to buy a car. Auto exhibits eventually grew in size, dealers moved to huge suburban lots, and the Museum of Classic and Antique Cars opened near the Grandstand space.

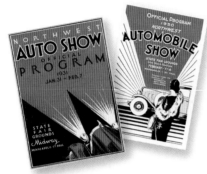

Auto show in the Livestock Pavilion, February 1929

Thanks to Henry Ford's ideas of mass production, the Northwest Auto Show became so large that it moved to the Livestock Amphitheater later in the year. Sponsored by the Minneapolis and St. Paul Auto Dealers Associations, it drew nearly 100,000 potential automobile buyers the first year.

First auto show, 1908

The Acme Roadster, Motor Buggy Manufacturing Company, Minneapolis, premium book ad, 1908

Two Minnesota firms made automobiles, the Pan company also built tractors.

Pan Motor Company, St. Cloud, 1922

Kaiser Frazer exhibit, 1950s

For many, the chance to see the newest in automobile models was at the fair.

Corvette display, 1950s

America's first sports car, the fast, two-seater made of fiberglass.

Oldsmobile exhibit, 1950s

Oldsmobile concept cars showcased futuristic design and advanced mechanical features.

Aircraft show with famous aviator Frank Hawks and his plane, 1927 ▲
Inside the Aircraft Show Building, 1927 ▶

It was the golden era of flight; Lindbergh flew across the Atlantic in 1927, and Frank Hawks set the first American transcontinental speed records. State Fair aircraft shows covered huge areas filled with crowds of aviation fans who were thrilled by personal appearances from famous aviators and arctic explorers. The expansive shows were thought to have been part of the largest airplane display ever presented at a state fair.

Heading for the huge aircraft show, 1927

Lively air shows included Curtiss-Wright's Pageant of Aviation Progress, exhibits of motors and wind tunnels, pushers and gliders, passenger aircraft, and Martin Bombers that were sent by the U.S. War Department. To attract local attention, a 1929 State Fair promotion "Carnival of the Skies" featured Miss Owatonna as Hera, Goddess of the Skies.

Big show tents held overflow aircraft exhibits, 1927

Airstream trailers, 1930s

Trailers made travel by car a new adventure, and sleek Airstream models were state-of-the-art for the time.

Harley-Davidson, 1931

For those interested in sport and speed, Harley-Davidson displayed enviable models for future test drives.

Farm and Home Building Products

Building material exhibits were important during the active building period of the 1800s. Fair exhibitors in 1887 earned premiums for the best specimens of Minnesota wood, granite, and marble, slate for roofing, flagstone for paving, and gold, silver, copper, zinc, and iron ores.

Permanent exhibit of Portland Cement Company, 1890s

Snap-on Tool display, 1947

Industrial Exhibit, 1904

An early experiment in electricity set in motion 841 machines connected by nearly a mile and a half of shafting. The $800,000 worth of machinery entertained crowds in 1888 with shaking and quaking, whines and rattles, all accomplished by machinery run entirely by new-fangled electricity.

Northwestern Bell Company, 1940s

Northern States Power, 1940s

Fairbanks, Morse & Co. State Fair reminder, 1909

An invitation penciled on the Fairbanks postcard read: "We invite you for another molasses pull Thursday night."

H ome improvement and remodeling products were big business at the fair. In the mid-1900s, eleven complete model houses were built in Grandstand exhibit areas to demonstrate the value of pine in construction of new homes.

Knotty Pine for attics and rec rooms, 1951

Zephyr ventilating awnings, 1948

Montgomery Ward Vinyl flooring, 1950s

Portland Cement Company model farm exhibit, 1940s

Models of farmhouses helped home builders and their customers visualize a new style of life in small-town America. Displays provided opportunities to make products known to the greatest number of people in one place, and many were manufactured in Minnesota.

U.S. Roofing & Siding, 1947

Model Farms and Kitchens

Anything that made life easier at home for both rural and urban families were among the most highly attended exhibits on the fairgrounds. Housing in the late 1800s was not efficient or very well-organized, especially kitchens. Before long, model houses, mock-up kitchens, and product exhibits at the State Fair became real-life versions of home design magazines. By the 1900s, ads for the newest wood-burning stoves and early water systems brought homemakers in record numbers to view life-changing displays in the exhibition halls.

The Minnesota Farm Women's Congress presented the fair with a complete Model Farm House in 1915. Innovative designs included a mudroom for farm boots, the latest in kitchen and bath fixtures, and innovative house planning ideas. It was visited by tens of thousands of farm women, but city dwellers also joined long lines at the door. The exhibit closed in 1918, but the building lived on for housing and meeting space.

Model farm kitchen display, 1920

Monarch and Paramount Range exhibit, Malleable Iron Range Company, 1922

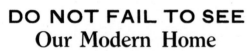

Crane Ordway Modern Home exhibit, premium book ad, 1921

Crane Ordway of Saint Paul placed advertising in premium books to promote their modern home. Fairgoers got a first-hand look at up-to-the-minute kitchen innovations.

Home water system, premium book ad, 1916

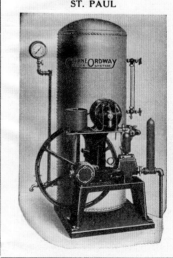
Sanitary water system, premium book ad, 1912

By the 1940s, nearly every homemaker became acutely aware of the need for better kitchen planning—and they knew that many of the latest designs could be seen at the fair. Educational institutions handed out step-saving kitchen brochures and fairgoers visited a host of exhibits that promoted vastly improved appliances. Cooking in the kitchen was going to get a lot easier!

Kitchen Floor Plan 2

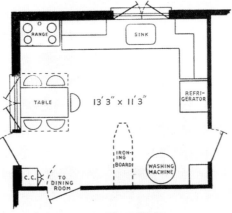

The L-Kitchen

University of Minnesota brochure, 1946

Better kitchen planning sometimes included space for ironing boards and washing machines!

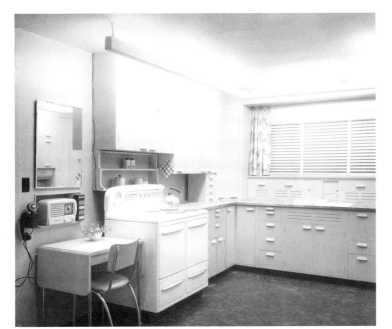

4-H State Fair model kitchen, 1948

Crosley kitchen with refrigerator, sink unit, stove, and cabinets, 1950

Loudon refrigerators and freezer, 1950s

Custom dining nooks, 1962

Washing, Ironing, and Sewing ⚐

Wash days benefited from new clothes washers shown at the State Fair each year, but the task remained daunting until the "automatic" washing machine came along in the 1940s. Garments still had to be wrung out and hung on clotheslines, but laundry day got a lot shorter.

"COSTS NOTHING,
I SAVE IN THE WEAR AND
TEAR OF THE CLOTHES"

The Washer that washes

State Fair program ad, 1908

Price Electric Company
Distributers

"Getzit
Electric
Washers"

"G
E
T
Z
I
T"

Price Electric Company ad, 1916

Price Electric Company

Do the Monday Washing with our
Clarinda "SAFETY" Electric Washer
Safe   Silent   Simple
No belts or exposed gears to injure the
clothes or children PRICE RIGHT.

Price Electric Company ad, 1923

Maytag display, 1947

A-B-C-Omatic washers, 1948

Clothes lines by E-Z-Way, 1947

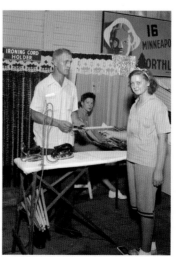

Ironing cord holders, 1947

Irons didn't fry the cord with the spring-mounted cord holder, but ironing was still a dreaded chore on hot days

Rudy Peterson Appliances, 1947

Ironing got a boost from the mangle—if one was a wizard at doing sleeves and collars without getting the fingers burned.

Sewing machines provided the first help for women making clothing—and the first actual machines in Minnesota were shown at the State Fair of 1858. Life changed dramatically as clothes were no longer tediously sewn by hand and warm quilts could be machine made more quickly. For decades, sewing machine exhibits for the modern seamstress held prominent spaces at the fair.

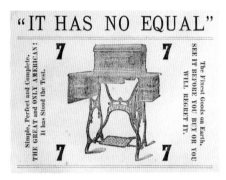

American Sewing Machine Company ad, 1887 premium list

Allied Sales sewing demonstration, 1962

Singer exhibit, 1963

Adler Automatic Zigzag machines, 1960s

Novel zigzag machines were fun but they didn't affect the art of hand quilting or embroidery. Now both hand-sewers and machine sewers won awards in creative competitions.

Department Stores

Department stores offered a sampling of their products in alluring displays. Fairgoing customers saw familiar brands and the latest merchandise they didn't know existed.

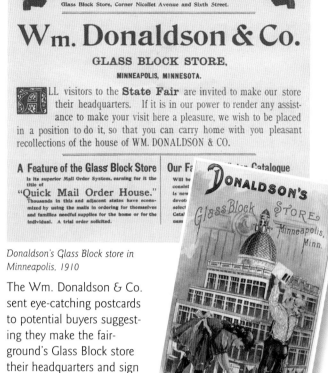

Donaldson's Glass Block store in Minneapolis, 1910

The Wm. Donaldson & Co. sent eye-catching postcards to potential buyers suggesting they make the fairground's Glass Block store their headquarters and sign up for a 300-page catalog.

Dayton's ramp store, 1940s

Dayton's built an actual store under the Grandstand Ramp. From socks to sofas, items on display represented the retailer's most popular departments. To buy products featured at the fair, shoppers went to Dayton's retail stores located throughout the state.

The Emporium, 1950s

Montgomery Ward style show, 1928

With few fashion magazines available, customers who wanted to see new wardrobe designs viewed them first at the Montgomery Ward style show. Long runways with lively models attracted huge crowds every year.

Sears merchandise tent, 1948

Merchandise orders took place in Sears tents along with a sign-up list for those wanting to be mailed a catalog. Small town family-run stores objected to out-of-state orders made at the fair, but free trade prevailed and Sears continued to arrange big exhibits into the 1950s.

Boutell's Furniture Store exhibit, 1947

Big spaces in Grandstand exhibit areas accommodated specialty home furnishing stores that set up model rooms with beautiful furniture arrangements. Intricate area rugs, moderne bars, high-tech television sets, and the ever-popular mattress testing display made fairgoers feel right at home.

Setchell-Carlson, 1951

Cardozo's King Koil mattresses, 1950s

Convertible Bars, 1966

Weyands carpets and rugs, 1947

Home Accessories, Clothing, and Jewelry

By the 1960s, big department stores, furniture, and appliance companies began to close their exhibits, as rural families frequented stores in neighboring cities and urban families found Southdale-style malls nearby. Small cash-and-carry kitchen gadgets, home accessories, hot fashions, and the latest fad took over every nook and cranny in big fair buildings. Booths dotted the avenues and browsing at fair time became an exhilarating, if exhausting experience.

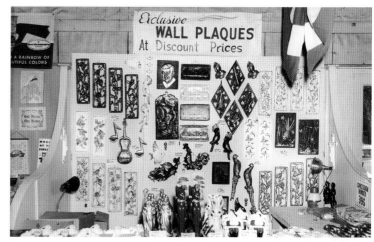

Exclusive wall plaques at discount prices, 1962

Northwestern Music Center, 1947

Decorative European products, 1960s

Faribo Blankets, 1970s

Minnesota's Faribault Woolen Mill Company began making blankets in 1865, and is the last woolen mill in America to make blankets in their entirety—from processing raw fiber to weaving it into blankets. In collaboration with Cargill, the two companies developed a revolutionary textile fiber from corn plants.

Oils, acrylics, and black velvet paintings, 1976

Jewelry in the Grandstand, 1970s

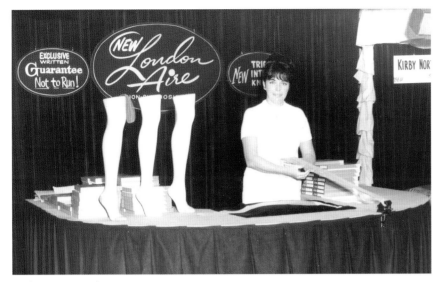

London Aire non-run hosiery, 1966

Red Wing Shoes, 1960s

Garibaldi's Boutique, 1976

Western hats, 1970s

Fashion statements got a head-to-toe start with a blitz of booths from local sellers as well as chic out-of-towners—and they all reported that they would be back the following year.

Crazy Louie's

Berman Buckskin, 1966

Swedish clogs, 1970s

I Didn't Know I Needed That ▷

Fairgoers took a deep breath, then embarked upon seemingly endless rows of crowded concession stands. Demonstrations pulled in gadget buffs and persuasive orators spoke eloquently. Colorful displays from baby buggies to geriatrics, smokers to exercisers, even education for a degree in psychology were nearly impossible to ignore.

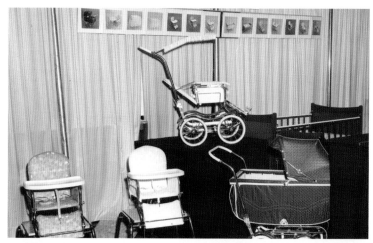

Rex baby products, 1966

Viking sewing machine hats, 1963

Sun and Rain Helmets, 1963

Hairpieces, 1966

Minneapolis Artificial Limb Company

Twister Exerciser, 1965

Geriatrics, for longer life past 40!, 1947

Mimeograph machine, 1954

Before the days of copy machines and cell phones, a mimeograph machine was the most common way to make copies, and a telephone receiver clip was only a neckache away from a hands-free phone.

Duncan telephone clip, 1963

University of Minnesota, 1970s

Breezy Point Resort, 1963

Bureau of Criminal Apprehension, 1955

All tuckered out, 1960s

Worn-out shoppers needed a vacation after visiting the concession stands. A fresh-air rest on a bench was worth a try, but it might have been time to follow the tantalizing aroma to the Pronto Pup stand.

Slicers and Dicers

Blender pitchman demonstrating his product, 1960s

Step right up, *see something you haven't seen on TV and you can't buy at the store....* Pitchmen had a sense of theater that went well beyond Toastmasters. Very good salespeople represented very good products, it was fun to listen—and maybe even buy one.

Egg recipe book for sale, 1980s

Seasoning demonstration, 1967

Peeler demonstration, 2005

Chopper, blender, mixer demonstration, 2005

Demonstrations made kitchen products look like they were easy to use, and most of the time it was true—but sometimes they just didn't work the same at home. As buyers became more interested in gourmet food and turned into culinary experts of their own, products at State Fair booths became more multifaceted.

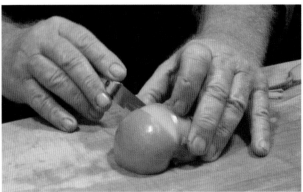

Melon cutting demonstration, 2005

It was hard to resist a Chef Harvey peeler gadget: they were sharp and worked well, and you could tell they were good by the down-to-earth demonstrations.

Fairgoers watched an apple turn into a beautiful dove sculpture with a mere flick of the wrist—and it drew crowds every time.

Welcoming doors, to fresh corridors,
Of apples and finely-shaped pears.
Agricultural churches, that worship ripe peaches
And the color of honey that bees get from fields,
Over there you see, not seen on T.V.,
A slicer-dicer without compare.
You can take it with you, buy one and get two,
At the Great Minnesota State Fair!

"THE GREAT MINNESOTA STATE FAIR" BY CHARLIE MAGUIRE

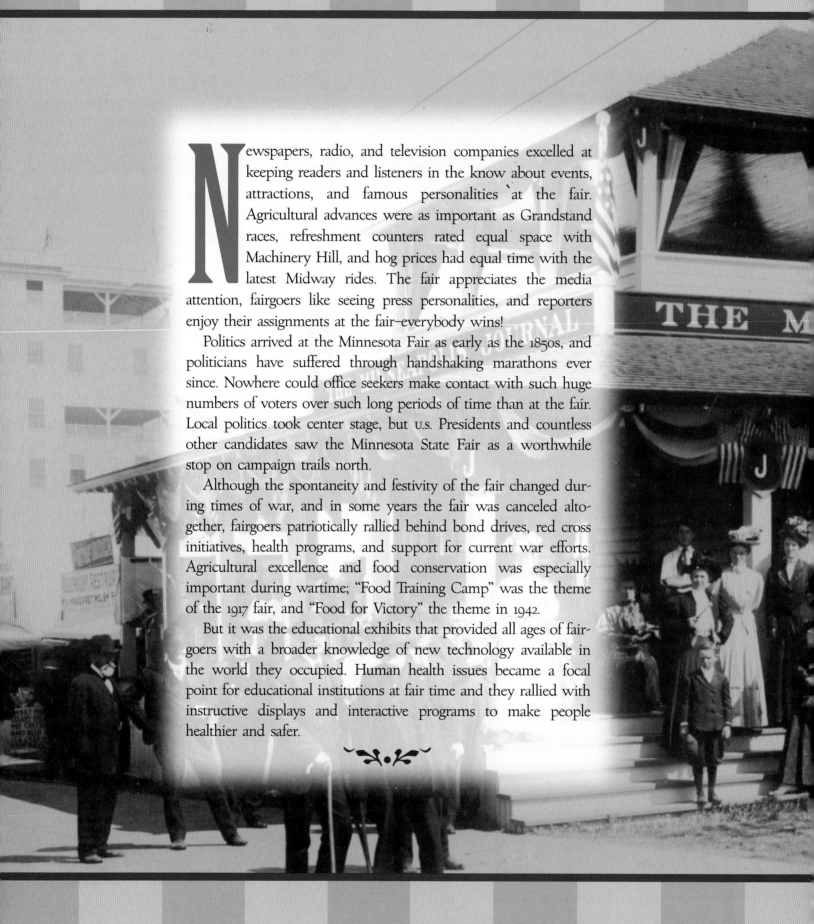

News, Politics, & Education

Newspapers, radio, and television companies excelled at keeping readers and listeners in the know about events, attractions, and famous personalities at the fair. Agricultural advances were as important as Grandstand races, refreshment counters rated equal space with Machinery Hill, and hog prices had equal time with the latest Midway rides. The fair appreciates the media attention, fairgoers like seeing press personalities, and reporters enjoy their assignments at the fair–everybody wins!

Politics arrived at the Minnesota Fair as early as the 1850s, and politicians have suffered through handshaking marathons ever since. Nowhere could office seekers make contact with such huge numbers of voters over such long periods of time than at the fair. Local politics took center stage, but u.s. Presidents and countless other candidates saw the Minnesota State Fair as a worthwhile stop on campaign trails north.

Although the spontaneity and festivity of the fair changed during times of war, and in some years the fair was canceled altogether, fairgoers patriotically rallied behind bond drives, red cross initiatives, health programs, and support for current war efforts. Agricultural excellence and food conservation was especially important during wartime; "Food Training Camp" was the theme of the 1917 fair, and "Food for Victory" the theme in 1942.

But it was the educational exhibits that provided all ages of fairgoers with a broader knowledge of new technology available in the world they occupied. Human health issues became a focal point for educational institutions at fair time and they rallied with instructive displays and interactive programs to make people healthier and safer.

The Minneapolis Journal booth by the Grandstand in the 1920s

Newspapers, T.V., and Radio ▶

Newspapers eagerly scour the fairgrounds in search of new products and events for their readers. They write about serious agricultural advances, interview eccentric personalities and sellers of newfangled merchandise, and describe the latest food fads and winning recipes. Readers can't wait to see it all for themselves.

St. Paul Pioneer Press, 1959

Star Tribune information center

Columnist Barbara Flanagan always had a nose for news. Happily, Lash LaRue did no damage with his bullwhip trick in front of fair onlookers, 1950s.

MPR

WLOL

The Cities 97

WCCO

WWTC

WAYL

Radio broadcasts attract audiences eager to put a face to a familiar voice. Many stations offer local musicians a chance to be heard on air as well as entertaining fairgoers. Radio personalities provide more than amusement: breaking news was often sent over fairground airwaves in the days before television.

Television news and variety shows play to fairgoers who come to see their favorite newscasters in person—or themselves on TV as they wave to friends at home.

KSTP's mobile television wasn't very mobile in 1947

WTCN TV, now KARE 11, 1963

KMSP TV

WCCO TV has some of the best giveaways— a big bag to carry all the other giveaways and a cooling fan for hot days.

Entertaining events always found media attention, but more serious programs like *The Market Report with Maynard Speece* and *George Grim Reports* were also daily features at the fair.

Dorothy Landis and Archie Philips married in the KSTP hot air balloon basket, 1928

Maynard Speece with a school contest winner

Bill Carlson interviewed hockey player and soon-to-be-governor Wendell Anderson

Politics and Legal Issues

Fairgrounds became soapboxes for all manner of political causes. Prohibition, gambling, and wages were among the hundreds of hot topics worthy of sign-up booths and active demonstrations. Bingo games created problems in 1944 when a protest group caused the arrest of 20 Midway game operators. The leader of the protesters was arrested for malicious libel, tried before a fairgrounds Justice of the Peace, and sentenced to 60 days in jail.

Socialist Labor Party booth, 1941

Prohibition booth volunteers

The Anti Saloon League signed up voters in 1941

▲ *United Packing House exhibit, 1947*
▼ *League of Women Voters booth, 1935*

Temperance movements successfully eliminated liquor sales during prohibition—but rumors hinted that spiked lemonade could be found behind the counters at a few soft drink stands.

National political parties vie for the most visible spaces on busy streets, roping in potential voters with a world-class list of enticements. Humorous buttons top the list, but unforgettable treats like a glass of root-beer milk were irresistible even to non-politicians.

Democratic-Farmer-Labor booth, 1960s

Minnesota Human Relations Agencies booth, 1947

Republican Party booth, 1962

Republican Party booth, 1962

UNITED STATES SUPREME COURT RULING

The State Fair was involved in an unusual United States Supreme Court landmark decision. The International Society for Krishna Consciousness did not want to have a booth at the fair, but were told they must solicit donations from a booth—and not throughout the public areas of the fair. A lawsuit resulted in 1977 and the Minnesota Supreme Court ruled that the State Fair could not limit the Krishnas to a booth under First Amendment free-speech rights, but the court also acknowledged the fair's rights in maintaining order in public areas. The Minnesota State Fair appealed to the U.S. Supreme Court and in 1981 the high court ruled in favor of the State Fair. The landmark decision prohibited open solicitation at the fairgrounds, but the ruling also applied to all public places throughout America, including shopping malls and airports.

Times of War

airgroundswere important forums for news and information during wartime. During the Civil War, news booths provided up-to-date reports on war activities. The Grand Army of the Republic participated in Grandstand "On to Victory" revues with sham battles that ended in thundering fireworks.

Volunteer soldiers in the 1898 Spanish-American War used fairground buildings for their quarters, holding marching drills in open fields and unoccupied spaces.

In 1918, near the end of World War I, The *Minneapolis Morning Tribune* reported: "From beginning to end, the fair promises to be a concentrated war training school for men, women and children. The grounds are said to contain more war exhibits than have been collected before in any place in the Northwest." The sale of war stamps was considered outstanding, and war-related exhibits occupied 85,000 square feet of space.

Red Cross booth, 1916.

Wartime exhibits provided important safety information for citizens.

Red Cross first aid exhibit during World War I, 1916

Large 8 x 10 glass negatives from the early 1900s that documented many important moments in Minnesota State Fair history are preserved at State Fair archives.

The war center, Arcade Building, 1940s

International Women's League booth for Peace and Freedom, 1940s

The floral flag with 21,000 red, white, and blue flowers was a feature of the 1942 fair. On Navy Day, a sailor stood at attention alongside each star.

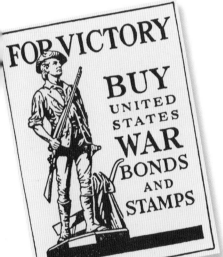

News and programs about World War II could be found everywhere on the fairgrounds. Troops marched in review, and anti-aircraft, machine guns, and tanks simulated actual battles.

Women war workers, with more than 7,000 members of the Red Cross, Liberty League, and the Y.W.C.A., joined eight marching bands for a colossal parade at the Grandstand. At the end of the event, a blitzkrieg parachute bombardment was staged on the infield with dogfights between a Japanese Zero and an American plane.

Auto racing was banned at the fair to conserve gas and rubber. Fairs were curtailed in 1942, 1943, 1944, and canceled entirely in 1945. In 1946 the polio epidemic became so severe that a much-anticipated World War II victory celebration was canceled.

German V-2 rocket on display after the war, 1947

WPA and Health Exhibits

People in the 1930s were living through serious times. Although prohibition was ending, drought was sweeping across the plains, and the Great Depression was overwhelming the country. The WPA stepped in with construction projects nationwide, but also with exhibits in collaboration with all manner of creative talents, fine arts, and ways to improve everyday life.

WPA Display Building, 1936

Mural painter, 1941

Federal Art project, 1936

Minnesota artist Knute Heldner held a painting by Elsa Jemne. She also painted the murals in the Minneapolis Armory and the Jemne Building in St. Paul was named after her. WPA Minnesota Art Projects at the fair were inspiration for many extraordinary mural projects, some of which survive through historic preservation efforts.

Home-sewn parade, 1938

Handmade twin snow suits in 1937

Music project choir performance, 1940

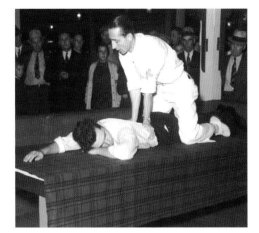

First aid demonstration, 1938

WPA booths also provided information for family health and safety.

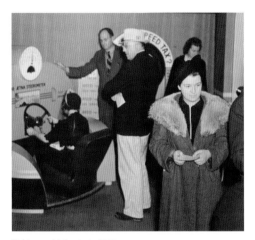

Taking a driving test, 1938

School lunch booth, 1938

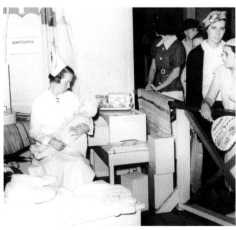

Nursery school booth, 1937

any early fairs had been seriously impacted by illness, such as typhoid fever that devastated the fairground encampment during the Spanish-American War. In later years, education and live demonstrations provided valuable health and fitness information for fairgoers.

University Health Booth, 1940s

The University of Minnesota Department of Health provided information on just about everything a fairgoer needed to know about nutrition and good health.

Sister Kenny spoke on poliomyelitis at the Territorial Pioneers building, 1945

The polio epidemic began in 1945 and became so serious by 1946 that the fair was canceled entirely.

Minnesota Resources

A big part of attending the fair each year was checking out the latest news about environmental education and recreation. The Conservation Building, later the Department of Natural Resources Building, provided fascinating exhibits of live fish, taxidermy, rock and mineral specimens, and information on the state's resources.

Conservation Building, 1963

As outdoor recreation and natural resources became more appreciated, Emergency Relief Administration workers, the forerunner of the WPA, began construction of the rustic log Conservation Building. Opened in 1934, the imposing structure houses exhibits inside, while the forested backyard supports native vegetation and a lively fishpond—wishful anglers gaze at perfect examples of the big ones that got away.

Fish and Game Building, 1917

The first Department of Fish and Game Building was home base for pioneering hunters and anglers.

Duck and otter on display, 1950s

Iron ore display, 1940s

Fish tank, 1950s

Game and fish exhibit, 1947

A cknowledgment of the region's spectacular natural environment and historic past were featured in State Fair exhibits and displays in the early 1900s.

Interior View of State Exhibits Building, 1926

Known as State Department Exhibits, as many as 36 divisions of the Minnesota state government filled entire buildings with displays. Successful administration projects even included marketable manufactured products.

State Exhibits Building, 1947

First Territorial Pioneer Cabin and Restaurant, 1900s

Membership in Territorial Pioneers is limited to persons who were citizens of Minnesota on statehood day, May 11, 1848, and their descendants. Their original Log Cabin held meeting space, artifacts, and an early dining hall, plus a large collection of pioneer portraits that hung next door in Institute Hall. Minnesota's Centennial was a gala event for the Pioneers: they moved into a new log cabin and pioneer portrait hall, and the thirty-six-foot Pioneer Woman statue out front watched over passers-by.

Interior of Territorial Pioneer Cabin, 1900

Twine house exhibit from Stillwater Prison, 1935

STATE FAIR MUSEUM

From little paper ticket stubs to an actual Royal American train car, the State Fair Museum in Heritage Square holds a vast collection of historic memorabilia. Photographs of celebrity entertainers, race car drivers, and Dan Patch line the walls, while badges from dedicated judges and loyal employees reside in cases next to souvenirs and costumes. Nearby, larger pieces of Minnesota history are also preserved: a St. Paul depot, linotype newspaper printers, and authentic log cabins.

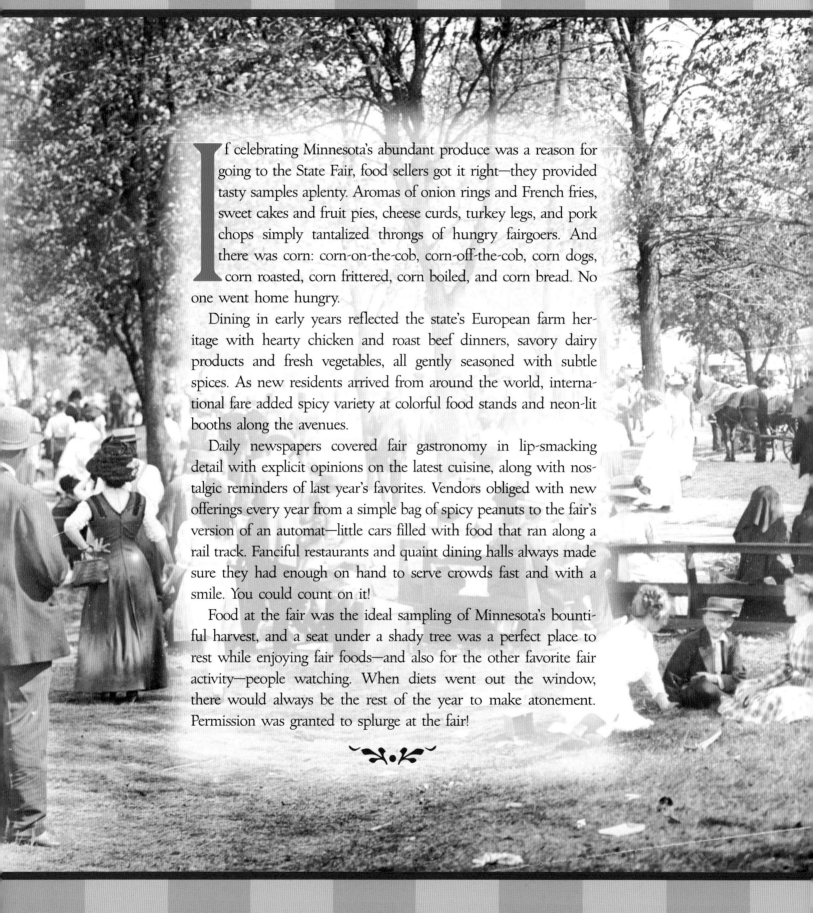

CHAPTER NINE

Food & Dining

I f celebrating Minnesota's abundant produce was a reason for going to the State Fair, food sellers got it right—they provided tasty samples aplenty. Aromas of onion rings and French fries, sweet cakes and fruit pies, cheese curds, turkey legs, and pork chops simply tantalized throngs of hungry fairgoers. And there was corn: corn-on-the-cob, corn-off-the-cob, corn dogs, corn roasted, corn frittered, corn boiled, and corn bread. No one went home hungry.

Dining in early years reflected the state's European farm heritage with hearty chicken and roast beef dinners, savory dairy products and fresh vegetables, all gently seasoned with subtle spices. As new residents arrived from around the world, international fare added spicy variety at colorful food stands and neon-lit booths along the avenues.

Daily newspapers covered fair gastronomy in lip-smacking detail with explicit opinions on the latest cuisine, along with nostalgic reminders of last year's favorites. Vendors obliged with new offerings every year from a simple bag of spicy peanuts to the fair's version of an automat—little cars filled with food that ran along a rail track. Fanciful restaurants and quaint dining halls always made sure they had enough on hand to serve crowds fast and with a smile. You could count on it!

Food at the fair was the ideal sampling of Minnesota's bountiful harvest, and a seat under a shady tree was a perfect place to rest while enjoying fair foods—and also for the other favorite fair activity—people watching. When diets went out the window, there would always be the rest of the year to make atonement. Permission was granted to splurge at the fair!

Outside the Dairy Building, 1900s

MINNESOTA
STATE FAIR
NORTHWEST
LIVESTOCK SHOW
Aug. 30 to Sept. 6
1930

Church Dining

Church meals are as old as the fair itself. Diners and dining halls were staffed by volunteers who put in long hours in hot kitchens along with church leaders who reeled in customers with ringing bells and persuasive chatter. Cooks fired up the grill and servers tied on aprons to dish up the next best thing to home cooking. Dining halls were important ways for church members to socialize with other members and to help churches financially. Fairgoers made these big dining rooms a family tradition.

Presbyterian Church diner, 1948

Hamline Methodist, 1912

Hamline Methodist opened in 1897 with volunteers who portioned out generous amounts of homemade ham loaf that brought diners back year after year.

Volunteer cook grilling hamburgers and onions, 1947

EPIPHANY DINER

Lines formed outside Epiphany Country Diner all day long for a chair at a red-checkered tablecloth in the 200-seat dining room. Delivering healthy sustenance to the masses required hundreds of church volunteers each year.

Diner coordinators serve meatloaf with a side of goodwill

WCCO weatherman Bud Kraeling enjoyed his annual dinner at the diner

Church dining stands didn't need elaborate kitchens. In the old days, a donated turkey could be cooked at home by Mom, carted to the fair by Dad, and served to customers by the rest of the family—all volunteer and all pure profit for church coffers.

Christ Lutheran Church Diner

Bethel Lutheran Church Diner

Bethel Lutheran Church Diner

St. John's of Little Canada, 1955

Benches, akin to backless church pews, were the preferred seating for many church dining stands. Hip-to-hip rows of backsides gave testimony to the good meals served at long wooden counters.

Bethlehem Lutheran Church, 1947

Mt. Olive Lutheran Church, 1948

Corpus Christi Diner, 1948

Cafés and Restaurants

The Banner Lunch Stand, 1912

Early cafés and restaurants operated under big tents that served customers at long open counters, but space inside was often tight and food selections were slim. Hot cook tents cooled off when gas service was installed on the fairgrounds in 1904, eliminating a ragged assortment of dangerous gasoline stoves. Over time, restaurants moved into permanent buildings that offered greater varieties of menu choices—food that became quintessential fair dining.

Rhines Café, early 1900s

Maple Leaf Café dishwashers behind the cook tent, 1900

Sizzling grills and steaming pots made for hot tents. Washing dishes in the back may have been a cooler job.

Train cars filled with food traveled on rails around Rail O'Matic's Smorgasbord buffet in the 1950s. Fairgoers took what they wanted, then found a table. Meals cost 50 cents and it took plenty of staff to keep the cars filled.

Robinson's dining specials were promoted in premium books, but fair foodies knew that the 800 seats at Jack Robinson's Cafeteria meant no waiting for lunch in 1951.

Busy fair "chefs" in 1947

By the 1940s, restaurant kitchens became the peak of controlled chaos as cooks prepared huge amounts of food each day for increasing numbers of hungry fairgoers.

Potatoes, peeled, boiled, and ready to serve, 1954

Fran's Breakfast, 1990s

Patiently waiting for waffles in the 1950s

Anticipating the next fair snack

The Arcade Building

The modern Arcade Building was completed in the 1940s and comes alive at fair time with appetite-grabbing food and high-spirited beer gardens. A mere stone's throw away from Midway glitter, it is the place to buck up courage after a defeat at ring toss or a giddy spin on the Tilt-A-Whirl.

The Arcade Building, 1950

The Arcade Building, 1980s

The souvenir menu from Buehler Biergarten advertised dancing to Whoopee John and his All-Star Dance Band and tempted fairgoers with a sampling of Minnesota's home-grown beers.

The Food Building

Grand Central Station for a snack is at the Food Building. Many stands remain in families for two or three generations and often cousins, aunts, uncles, and friends pitch in to help. Setting up and serving customers for long hours requires an unusually warmhearted group of people.

The Food Building, 1950

Danielson's and Daughters Onion rings, since 1956

Outside the Food Building, three generations of Danielson's and Daughters found generations of loyal fans for their world-class crunchy French-fried onion rings.

Mouse Hole cheese curd stand

We invented Batter Fried Cheese Curds in 1975

Cheese curds were at the top of the food chain at the fair. Lou and Audrey, Richard and Donna invented the batter-fried cheese curd business with one small deep fryer in 1975. The little business grew and grew and grew until it finally moved into a bustling building of its own.

Lynn's Lefse, 1980s

Lynn started serving lefse at the fair with a musical twist. Anyone who could sing the Lefse Song got one free, until the Sons of Norway Choir showed up: after they sang, the sign came down. Norwegians use white sugar and butter on their lefse, Swedes use brown sugar and butter.

Food Stands Along the Avenues

Food aromas wafted enticingly down streets at the earliest fairs, but the rambling array of cook shacks and food tents began to look a little tacky. As food stand guidelines were created, the drab old canvas tents were replaced, equipment was updated, and fairgoers found attractive counters with adequate seating and friendly service.

Hotdog stand, 1966

In the 1950s, little stands with small signs lined the streets, but catching a fairgoer's eye soon required larger structures with more attention-getting signage—and the race to attract customers began.

The line-up of food tents in 1900 ended with a booth serving buttermilk and ice cream

Henry's Bar-B-Q, 1970

Starched white dresses didn't stay clean for long at the turn of the century

Tom Thumb stand, 1980s

Tom Thumb mini-donuts were invented at the Minnesota State Fair by Jan Desmond in the late 1940s. She wanted a donut that could be carried around the grounds, and a dozen miniatures in a bag proved to be the runaway popular solution. Fresh mini-batches have traveled through fairs and celebrations in little bags ever since.

Understated food stands offered menus for all tastes, 1951

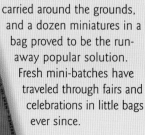

It's hard for a fairgoer to know where to look next, all the glitzy neon and flashing lights are attention-getters that simply can't be ignored. The lively buildings and animated signage turn fairground streets into electrifying festivals of their own.

Pronto-Pups, Corndogs, Hotdogs, and Hamburgers

On-a-stick or in a bun made it easier to eat on-the-run—the better to see more of the fair. There are hard choices to make in the hotdog department: pronto-pups, corndogs, wieners on a stick, foot-longs, chili dogs, brats, and plain old hotdogs that nestle in a soft bun surrounded by mustard, ketchup, onions, and relish. It makes a fairgoer hungry just to think about the possibilities!

Sky Dogs on display

Boxes and boxes of hotdogs on a stick, just waiting to be cooked in the 1940s

Pronto-pups were invented on the boarkwalk in Seattle in 1945 and first served at the Minnesota State Fair in 1947. Pronto-pup has it's own special batter and is a trademarked recipe.

Corndogs are made with corn meal batter

"Quality supreme, healthful and delicious" at Peters, 1947

If mustard isn't enough there's always chili, cheese, or onions

A busy lunch crowd, 1947 ▲
Coney Island Minnesota-style, 1962 ▶

While hotdogs outsold hamburgers every day at the fair, fairgoers who were happy to sit a spell could easily settle for second best, a classic hamburger with french fries and a chocolate malt.

Cheese on a Stick, 1980s

On-a-stick was pretty much reserved for hotdogs until the 1980s. But quirky minds invented other items that could be easily skewered, and competition was on to find the oddest snack that would stay put at the end of a stick.

▲ *Steichen's Store, 2006*
◀ *Ted Steichen and Amos Fink at the grocery scale in the 1940s*

Back behind the barns is a tiny market that stocks groceries and supplies. It's been there since 1933 and is only open during the fair. Canned foods, sodas, and a deli appeal to fairgoers, but clean-up and repair items make it a handy place for exhibitors as well.

Customers ordering Steichen's fresh ground hamburger also received the 1930 food market notebook that came with a bit of cheesecake on the cover.

Dairy and Princess Kay

Milk, cheese, and butter are the flavorful results of Minnesota's huge dairy production, and farmers in the state are among the nation's finest producers. As early as 1915, the State Fair butter contest had more entries than all other U.S. fairs put together.

Dairy Building and modern milk trucks, 1947

Over the years, dairy exhibits needed larger spaces. By the 1940s, the world's largest milk and dairy concession was a feature of the last big Dairy Building. Fine Art Exhibits took over the building in the 1950s.

Milk bar and dairy exhibit, 1940s

Dairy products exhibit, 1937

Lines at the milk stand, 1924

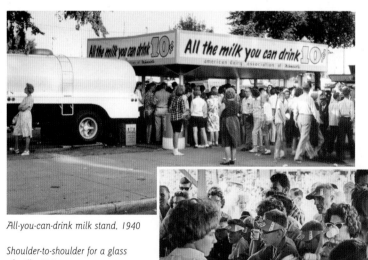

All-you-can-drink milk stand, 1940

Shoulder-to-shoulder for a glass of milk, 1962 ▶

182

Barberio Cheese House, 1966

Old Tyme cheese was an old tyme favorite at the Grandstand Cheese Shoppe. In earlier years, a complete cheese factory in full operation was featured at the 1892 Dairy Hall, and in 1911, fairgoers were amazed to see a 6,000-pound cheese manufactured at Pine Island.

Cheese and Butter

Butter sculptures were featured at the fair beginning in 1898. They were made in the shape of famous people or figures in interesting poses until Princess Kay came along and took over the butter sculpture art form.

Wrapping butter, 1955

Land O'Lakes Creameries installed a Dairy Building exhibit in 1939 to demonstrate the process of machine wrapping and boxing butter. Over the years, hundreds of thousands of butter buyers strolled by the popular booth.

Carved butter sculpture

Butter Statue of Liberty

Crowning Princess Kay

Princess Kay became the spokeswoman for the American Dairy Association of Minnesota beginning in 1953. She must come from a farm, and one that produces milk. The winning Princess Kay and her "court" sit on display in a 38-degree booth until their heads emerge as sculpture in ninety-pound blocks of Grade-A butter produced in New Ulm.

The first Princess Kay, Eleanor Thatcher, 1953

PRINCESS KAY OF THE MILKY WAY

Karen Bracken, Princess Kay of 1965, was the first to be sculpted in butter.

Following the fair, Princess Kays take their sculptures home to be used in worthy ways: a pancake breakfast fundraiser, Christmas cookies, a county-wide barbeque, topping for 2,000 ears of corn, or a butter head melt-down where people roll ears of corn on the melting head. But many Princess Kays froze their butter head sculptures intact.

Sweets and Treats

Between-meal-treats were found at all Minnesota fairs. Fresh-squeezed lemonade, Cracker Jacks, and ice cream cooled off early fairgoers, while hot roasted peanuts provided a needed boost of energy. Sweets waited until the twentieth century to make their appearance.

Coca-Cola came in bottles in 1948

Ives Ice Cream and Cracker Jack stand, 1909

Lee's Candies in a candy-box style booth

Mel's fudge was homemade—at the fair

Grandstand peanut stand, 1931

FROSTY LEMONADE

Gale Frost made lemonade for his family concession in the 1920s. He hand-squeezed the juice from several hundred lemons into a clean horse trough, added tens of pounds of sugar—to a young boy's taste—and 50-pound blocks of ice. All was stirred with a boat oar, ladled into big bottles, hoisted up on a seller's shoulder, and sold around the fair for 10 cents a cup. A long-time fair enthusiast, Gale Frost created a remarkable State Fair Museum in Heritage Square.

Gale Frost's old lemonade bottle on display at the State Fair Museum

184

Sweet Martha's Cookies started in the 1980s

Frosted malted, 1948

When days at the fair are hot, cool treats fly out of freezers fast.

Taffy stand with the animated taffy puller, 1980s

Honey Candy, 1980s

Honey candy and honey ice cream are true fair originals. Creamy ice cream is dished up next to the bee and honey exhibit, and sunflower seeds add crunch to the frosty delight.

Snow Cone, 1957

Cotton candy stuck to adults as well as kids, 2006

Ice cream cones between friends, 1947

Rainbow ice cream, 1963

Breakfast and all, in the church dining hall
Get there early, that's what to do
Kids in a wagon order a gallon of milk
Beer, and cheese curds, foot-longs and Pronto pups too
Sore feet, still more to eat, Mini-donuts without a care
Only twelve days a year, keep your calendar clear
For the Great Minnesota State Fair!

"THE GREAT MINNESOTA STATE FAIR" BY CHARLIE MAGUIRE

Frozen Delight, 1975

CHAPTER TEN
Recipes

As pioneer farmyards and barnyards once defined the Minnesota landscape, grain elevators and flour mills became the state's architectural icons. With bountiful fields of golden grains, fruit, vegetables, and meat and dairy products, Minnesota food companies became internationally famous. This vast harvest of good food was mirrored at the State Fair in first-rate exhibits and in culinary competitions. Recipes in handouts featured state products and were quickly gathered by fairgoers to be tried at home.

The recipes that follow were collected from delightfully diverse sources—an 1890s Washburn, Crosby Company cookbook, favorite 4-H recipes, ribbon-winning contestants, and State Fair superintendents. The late *Minneapolis Tribune* columnist Mary Hart published her favorites and Karen Humphrey edited *Great State Fair Recipes* published by the Minnesota State Agricultural Society and the American Dairy Association of Minnesota in 1976.

Minnesota's agricultural products flavored every recipe. Apples, blueberries, pears, plums, rhubarb, and honey rested in succulent combinations, and corn, beans, peas, potatoes, wild rice, and sunflower nuts celebrated the region's huge field crops. Turkey and pork braised in flavorful hot dishes, and State Fair baking competitions used wheat from the great flour mills. But it was no time to watch calories, as those delicious old recipes were rich in dairy cream, butter, and cheese.

To make unusual ingredients and directions more clear, friends tested recipes adjusting for missing ingredients or confusing directions. Testing parties and office tastings became festive get-togethers of old-fashioned Minnesota comfort food. Happily, a selection of great recipes from local products resulted. And not a single one on a stick—those treats can only be found at the fair!

Student bread makers, 1922

Butter, Cheese, Appetizers

Dairy products put Minnesota among the top states in the country for satisfying the nutritional appetite of a growing nation. Today, making old-fashioned cheese, butter, and potato bread in a modern kitchen is a fascinating journey back in time.

The following recipes may have been adapted for easy preparation, modern cooking methods, or ingredients that are readily available.

FARMER'S CHEESE

Farmer's cheese can be made easily in a home kitchen and it is even more fun to make with youngsters. Farmer's cheese replaces ricotta or cottage cheese in nearly any recipe. We used it in appetizers, cheesecake, and cookies—recipes to be found in coming pages.

- 1/2 gallon whole milk
- 1 cup heavy cream
- 1/3 cup white vinegar or lemon juice
- cheesecloth
- 1 teaspoon salt

Pour milk and cream into a large pot (not aluminum.) Bring to 190°F, or just to the boiling point. Remove from heat. Add vinegar and stir to mix; cool for 30 minutes or more; mixture will form into very small curds and whey. Pour the curds and whey into a colander lined with three layers of damp cheesecloth and drain off the whey for about 30 minutes. (The whey is nutritious; it can be saved and used for cooking and baking.) Pick up ends of cheesecloth and press out any remaining liquid. Put curds into a bowl, add salt, stir, and refrigerate. For a smooth cream-style cheese, add a little cream with the salt. For low-fat cheese, use 2% milk.

Sampling a round of American cheese

FARMER'S CHEESE CRACKER SPREAD

For a delicious cracker spread, top farmer's cheese or cream cheese with honey mint jelly or plum chutney from the jam and jelly recipe pages.

BUTTER

Our butter maker commented that "the experience of watching milk transform to butter is fun to watch, especially for the first time, it's one of those things you use often and take for granted." Butter can be made in a churn, or take turns shaking in a tightly covered jar for 20–30 minutes—or use a food processor.

- 2 cups heavy cream
- 1/2 teaspoon salt
- 1/2 cup ice water

Pour cream into food processor to 1/2 full. Blend. The cream will become sloshy, frothy, softly whipped, firmly whipped, coarse, then it will seize and collapse. The butter has separated from the milk; drain off the milk. Place butter in a cool bowl, add 1/2 cup ice water, and salt to taste. Knead mixture with two wooden spoons or by hand, pouring out water occasionally, when most of the water is removed the butter is ready. Makes about 1 cup.

Butter judge, Minnesota State Fair, 1947

FARMER CHEESE DIP

From Old Home Cottage Cheese: "In the heart of Minnesota's wonderful dairy country, we have located a modern sanitary 'Cheeserie.' A contribution to the good people of the great Northwest"

- 1-1/2 cups cottage or farmer's cheese
- 1/2 cup mayonnaise
- 1/2 cup cucumber, finely diced
- 1/4 cup green onion or chives, finely chopped
- 1/4 cup radish, finely diced
- 1 tablespoon dill weed
- Salt and pepper to taste

Beat cottage cheese until smooth. Add remaining ingredients. Refrigerate 3–4 hours or overnight. Serve with fresh vegetables or hearty crackers.

Old Home Cottage Cheese, 1930s

Boys and Girls Club breadmaking demonstration during World War I

STATE FAIR POTATO BREAD

The poster recipe for Minnesota State Fair Potato Yeast Bread was influenced by efforts to save on wheat and spend on potatoes. Our very creative baker started with the few ingredients listed on the poster and no directions. After several attempts, and the addition of butter and eggs, the bread has nice flavor, light texture, and great moisture content.

- 6–8 large potatoes
- 1 package dry yeast
- 6 tablespoons melted butter, divided
- 1/2 cup milk
- 1/2 cup sugar
- 2 teaspoons salt
- 8 cups bread flour
- 3 eggs, slightly beaten

Peel and cook potatoes in water until tender. Drain potatoes, reserving 3/4 cup of cooking water. Let water cool to 110–120°F; add yeast to dissolve. Mash potatoes with 2 tablespoons butter and milk. Measure out 4 cups. In a mixing bowl, combine sugar, salt, and 7 cups of flour. Thoroughly mix in potatoes, the dissolved yeast with the potato water, 4 tablespoons melted butter, and eggs. Turn out on a floured board and knead for 8–10 minutes, incorporating the last cup of flour and more if needed until dough is smooth and elastic. Place dough in a buttered bowl turning once to grease top. Cover, let rise in a warm place until doubled, about an hour. When dough has doubled, punch down and turn onto a lightly floured surface. Knead lightly and shape into two loaves. Put into buttered loaf pans. Cover, let rise until doubled, about an hour. Bake for 40–45 minutes (or until golden brown and hollow when tapped) in a 400°F preheated oven. Remove from pans to wire rack to cool.

SPAMPENADAS

From The National Best SPAM Recipe Competition and Leigh Walter of Burnsville, 1st Place, 2004 Minnesota State Fair.

- 1 12-ounce can SPAM Lite
- 4 green onions, sliced
- 3/4 teaspoon ground cumin
- 1/2 teaspoon garlic salt
- 1/2 teaspoon black pepper
- 1 jar of con queso dip
- 2 packages refrigerated pie crusts; or 4 9-inch pie crusts at room temp.
- 1 beaten egg
- Condiments: fat free sour cream, salsa, and extra con queso

Preheat oven to 425°F. Place SPAM Lite in a food processor and pulse until it begins to break apart. Add sliced green onion, cumin, garlic salt, and black pepper. Pulse until mixture is ground. Place mixture in a non-stick frying pan and cook over medium heat for 10 minutes. Stir in 1/2 cup con queso dip and let cool. Using a 3" or 4" circle cookie cutter, cut 6 circles out of each pie crust, for a total of 24 circles. Place 1 to 1-1/2 tablespoons of the SPAMpenada mixture into the center of each circle. Fold over and crimp edges into semi-circles. Brush top and sides with a beaten egg. Using a fork, make several holes in the top to allow steam to escape. Place on a nonstick cookie sheet. Bake on upper rack for 12–15 minutes or until golden brown. Makes 24.

GRANDSTAND SPAM

The creamy blend of blue cheese with a savory tomato-topping disappeared from our testing table in record time—everyone loved the spiced SPAM flavor.

- 8 white bread slices, crusts removed
- 1 cup mayonnaise
- 1 cup blue cheese, crumbled
- 2 tablespoons white wine vinegar

- 1 teaspoon dry mustard
- 1-1/2 cups tomatoes, finely chopped
- 1 cup SPAM, finely chopped
- 1/2 cup chopped fresh basil
- 2 tablespoons olive oil
- 1 garlic clove, finely chopped
- Salt and pepper to taste

Preheat oven to 450°F. Toast bread slices in oven 4 minutes until lightly browned. Mix mayonnaise, blue cheese, vinegar, and mustard together. In a separate bowl, mix tomatoes, SPAM, basil, olive oil, garlic, salt, and pepper. Spread cheese mixture on toasted bread and top with tomato mixture. Cut into fourths to serve. Makes 32 appetizers.

TANGY ZUCCHINI SQUARES

A great way to use extra zucchini in a recipe from the *Minnesota Farm Guide.*

- 4 eggs, slightly beaten
- 4 small zucchini, grated (about 3 cups)
- 1/2 cup onion, minced
- 1/2 cup parmesan cheese, grated
- 1/2 cup cooking oil
- 1 cup baking mix such as Bisquick
- 2 tablespoons fresh parsley, chopped
- 1/2 teaspoon salt
- 1/2 teaspoon paprika
- Salt and pepper to taste
- 1 clove garlic, minced

Preheat oven to 350°F. Grease a 9x13" oblong pan. Mix eggs, zucchini, onion, cheese, and oil. Stir in baking mix and seasonings. Spread into pan. Bake for 30 minutes, until golden brown. Cut into bite-size squares.

CHEESE CRISPS

- 1 cup cheddar cheese, coarsely grated
- 1/2 cup parmesan cheese, finely grated
- 4 tablespoons butter, very soft
- 1 cup flour

- 1/4 teaspoon dry mustard
- 1/4 teaspoon salt
- 1/8 teaspoon cayenne pepper
- 1/4 cup water, more if needed
- 1/4 cup finely chopped chives

Preheat oven to 350°F. Grease a 9x13" baking dish. Thoroughly mix cheeses and butter. Add flour, mustard, salt, and cayenne. Add water to make a spreadable consistency. Pat thinly into pan. Sprinkle with chives. Bake for 25–30 minutes. Cut into pieces.

National buttermaking champion Alfred Camp at the Minnesota State Fair, 1942

SPICED PECANS

An invigorating snack from the *Anoka County 4-H Cookbook*, 1984

- 1 cup sugar
- 1/8 teaspoon cinnamon
- 1/8 teaspoon nutmeg
- 1/3 cup water
- 1 tablespoon butter
- 1 teaspoon vanilla
- 2-1/2 cups pecan halves

Stir together sugar, cinnamon, nutmeg, and water in medium saucepan to soft-ball stage. Remove from heat; stir in butter and let stand 5 minutes. Stir in vanilla and pecans until mixture is thick. Turn out on cookie sheet, separating nuts. Cool and store in airtight container.

> GEDNEY PICKLES

GEDNEY DEVILED EGGS

Deviled eggs get a lively flavor boost thanks to an unusual magic ingredient: Gedney Dill Pickle Relish.

- 1 dozen eggs
- 2/3 cup mayonnaise
- 2/3 cup Gedney Dill Pickle Relish, drained
- 1 tablespoon dry mustard
- 1 teaspoon Worcestershire sauce
- 1/2 teaspoon salt
- 1/2 teaspoon pepper
- 4–6 drops hot pepper sauce
- Parsley or paprika for garnish

Cook eggs until hard, peel, cut in half lengthwise. Remove yolks and place in a medium bowl. Set whites aside. Mash yolks with a fork. Mix in remaining ingredients, except garnish. Spoon filling into hollowed-out whites. Sprinkle with parsley or paprika. Refrigerate until ready to serve.

In 1881, Gedney began packing pickles in Minnesota. In 1991, the company began making pickles from State Fair prize-winning recipes. Grocery store shelves held Kosher dills and bread & butter pickles, eventually the company added jams and preserves and more pickle recipes—all State Fair winners—nice going, Gedney Pickles!

Breads

Wheat was plentiful in Midwest kitchens thanks to Minnesota's world-renowned milling companies. Breads, rolls, and cakes were among the first food competitions held at the State Fair during early pioneer times.

The following recipes may have been adapted for easy preparation, modern cooking methods, or ingredients that are readily available.

STATE FAIR'S BEST BREAD

Minneapolis Tribune columnist Mary Hart featured her favorite State Fair winners every year. Described as the "champion bread baker of all time" the winning white bread recipe from Elaine Janas was included in Hart's book of favorite recipes published in 1979.

- 2 cups water
- 1/4 cup shortening, such as Crisco
- 6 cups bread flour
- 1/2 cup nonfat dry milk powder
- 1/4 cup granulated sugar
- 1 tablespoon salt
- 2 packages active dry yeast

Heat water and shortening to 120–130°F. Blend 2 cups of the flour, sugar, nonfat dry milk powder, salt, and dry yeast in large bowl of electric mixer. Add water-shortening mixture and beat until smooth, about 3 minutes. Gradually add remaining flour to form a firm dough. Knead until smooth—this will take 8 minutes if using a dough hook, 10 minutes if mixing dough by hand. When well-kneaded, place ball of dough in greased bowl. Let rise until double, 1 to 1-1/2 hours, depending on warmth of room. Punch dough down. Divide in half. Round up halves and let rest covered 15–20 minutes. Shape into loaves. Place in 2 greased 8-1/2x4-1/2" loaf pans. Cover with plastic wrap and let rise until light—you can feel the difference when you lift the pan. Bake at 350°F 45–50 minutes. Butter tops while warm for soft crust. Makes two loaves.

Russell-Miller Milling Company handout, 1932

PRIZE-WINNING GRAHAM BREAD

Mary Hart's favorite recipes featured the 1970 Purple Ribbon winner from Edna Soost. Hart wrote "whenever I have the time, I turn out a loaf or two."

- 1/2 cup milk
- 3/4 cup water
- 1 tablespoon sugar
- 1-1/4 teaspoons salt
- 1-1/2 cup graham flour
- 1-1/2 cup white flour
- 1 package active dry yeast
- 1 tablespoon shortening

Heat milk and water together to 160°F. Cool to 120°F. Pour in sugar and salt. Add a third of each flour and beat. Add yeast and beat again. Beat in more flour, add shortening. Add remaining flour and beat again. Put on lightly floured board and knead 10–15 minutes. Shape into a ball, place in greased bowl, cover, and put in warm place. When double, punch down. Let rise again. Shape into loaf. Put into greased pan and let rise until nicely above the pan. Bake at 375°F for 30 minutes, reduce temperature to 350°F and bake 20 minutes longer. Cool on rack, brush top with butter. Makes one loaf.

State Fair fruit and apple display

STATE FAIR ORANGE BREAD

Mrs. Myron Clark reluctantly shared her winning State Fair recipe stating that she had worked hard perfecting it. Her Blue Ribbon Fruit Bread recipe finally appeared in Mary Hart's *Minneapolis Tribune* column in the 1950s.

- 1 medium size orange
- 1/2 cup water
- 1 cup dates, cut up
- 1 egg
- 1 tablespoon butter, melted
- 2 cups flour
- 1 teaspoon soda
- 1/2 cup sugar
- 1/2 cup chopped nuts

Preheat oven to 350°F. Grate the orange rind. Squeeze the orange and place the juice in a measuring cup. Add water to make 3/4 cup liquid. Heat the juice and rind and add the dates. Remove from stove and let it stand. Beat egg and add melted butter, liquids, and dates to the egg. Add dry ingredients that have been sifted together. Mix in nuts. Beat all together. Place in bread pan that is greased and floured. Bake for about one hour. Makes one loaf.

MADE IN MINNEAPOLIS

This is the flour that made the loaf of bread which won the Grand Prize at the St. Louis World's Fair

The Pillsbury Cookbook, 1914

PILLSBURY QUICK NUT AND FRUIT BREAD

Bread recipes were an early Pillsbury specialty and they offered creative choices for bakers. Exhibits and displays created instant name recognition and recipe handouts were extremely popular.

- 2-1/2 cups sifted Pillsbury's Best Enriched Flour
- 3 teaspoons baking powder
- 2 teaspoons salt
- 1 cup sugar
- 1/4 cup shortening
- 1 cup finely cut dried peaches, apricots, or prunes
- 1/2 cup chopped nut meats
- 2 eggs, well beaten
- 1 cup milk

Preheat oven to 350°F. Sift together dry ingredients. Cut in shortening until mixture resembles coarse meal. Add fruit and nuts. Combine eggs and milk, add to dry ingredients; stir only until all flour is dampened. Turn into well-greased loaf pan. Push batter up into corners of the pan, leaving the center slightly hollowed. Bake for 1 hour. Makes 1 loaf.

CORN MUFFINS

While corn comes from all areas of the state, these muffins taste like the Green Giant might have supervised the cook himself. Fresh whole corn makes muffins extra flavorful and a perfect accompaniment to State Fair Chili.

- 1 cup yellow cornmeal
- 1 cup all-purpose flour
- 1/8 cup sugar
- 1 tablespoon baking powder
- 1/2 teaspoon salt
- 2 eggs
- 1 cup whole milk
- 1/4 cup butter, melted, cooled
- 1-1/2 cups frozen whole kernel corn, thawed

Heat oven to 425°F. Grease 16 muffin cups. In large bowl, mix cornmeal, flour, sugar, baking powder, and salt together. In separate bowl, whisk eggs, stir in milk, butter, and corn. Add to dry ingredients. Fill muffin cups 2/3 full. Bake 15 minutes or until brown on top.

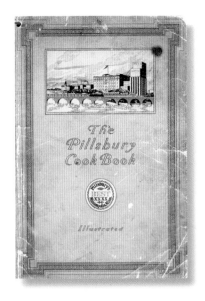

MARJORIE'S SOUR CREAM COFFEE CAKE

Marjorie Johnson is a Minnesota State Fair celebrity like no other. She pulls out her mixing bowls on numerous local television programs, and national audiences were entertained with her amusing cooking lessons on the Rosie O'Donnell and Jay Leno shows. Between appearances, Marjorie sent us her Blue Ribbon sour cream coffee cake recipe.

- 3/4 cup butter
- 1-1/2 cups granulated sugar
- 2 teaspoons vanilla
- 4 eggs
- 2-1/2 cups all purpose flour
- 1-1/2 teaspoons baking powder
- 1-1/2 teaspoons baking soda
- 1/4 teaspoon salt
- 1-1/2 cups dairy sour cream

STREUSEL
- 1/2 cup brown sugar, firmly packed
- 2 tablespoons butter, melted
- 1/2 cup chopped nuts
- 1/2 cup flaked coconut
- 1 tablespoon flour
- 1 tablespoon grated orange rind

POWDERED SUGAR GLAZE
- 1 cup powdered sugar
- 3–5 teaspoons milk
- 1/2 teaspoon almond or vanilla extract

Preheat oven to 350°F. In a large bowl place butter, sugar, and vanilla. Beat together until creamy and fluffy. Add eggs, one at a time, beat well after each. Sift together flour, baking powder, baking soda, and salt. Add to butter mixture alternating with the sour cream, starting and ending with flour mixture. Set aside.

Combine all streusel ingredients in a bowl until mixture is crumbly. Grease and flour two 9-inch round pans, put 1/4 of the batter in each pan. Spread out evenly. Sprinkle 1/4 of the streusel over each batter. Take the remaining batter and put it over streusel in each pan. Top each with remaining streusel. Bake for 30–35 minutes until done. Let rest in the pans on a wire rack for 10 minutes; remove from pans. Combine glaze ingredients in a bowl, stir until smooth. Dribble over tops of cooled coffee cakes. Makes two 9" coffee cakes.

TRAILWAY PUMPKIN BREAD

State Fair baking contests were popular with Boys and Girls Clubs and 4-H bakers. This recipe is from the *Anoka County 4-H Leaders Council Cook Book*, 1984.

- 3-1/3 cup flour
- 2 teaspoons baking soda
- 1-1/3 teaspoon salt
- 3 teaspoons cinnamon
- 3 teaspoons nutmeg
- 2 cups sugar
- 1 cup oil
- 4 eggs
- 2/3 cup water
- 2 cups canned pumpkin

Preheat oven to 350°F. Mix dry ingredients together in a mixing bowl. Make a well in dry ingredients and add all remaining ingredients. Mix together until smooth. Divide batter into three conventional bread pans that have been greased and floured. Bake for about 1 hour or until toothpick inserted in center comes out clean. Cool slightly in pans, then turn onto racks to finish cooling. Makes 3 loaves.

HIDDEN VALLEY POTATO CHEESE ROLLS

Blue Ribbon winner Stella Gilbertson was runner-up at the 2003 Minnesota State Fair for these Hidden Valley Family Friendly Food Contest rolls.

- 2 cups milk
- 1/4 cup sour cream
- 4–5 cups bread flour
- 1 tablespoon sugar
- 1-ounce Hidden Valley Ranch Original Ranch Salad Dressing & Seasoning Mix
- 1 cup mashed potato flakes
- 2 packages regular active dry yeast
- 2 eggs
- 1 cup shredded cheddar cheese (finely shredded works best)

In small saucepan, heat milk and sour cream until very warm (120–130°F). In large bowl, combine warm liquid, 2 cups flour, sugar, Hidden Valley Mix, mashed potato flakes, dry yeast, and eggs. Beat 4 minutes at medium speed. By hand, stir in shredded cheese and enough remaining flour to make a stiff dough. Turn out onto lightly floured board. Knead until no longer sticky, adding more flour sparingly as needed. Place in greased bowl, turning once to grease top. Cover; let rise in warm place until light and doubled in size, 45–60 minutes. Generously grease two 9-inch round cake pans. Divide dough into 24 pieces; shape into rolls (dough may be sticky, so use floured or oiled hands). Place 12 pieces in each prepared pan. Cover; let rise again in warm place until light and doubled in size, 30–45 minutes. Preheat oven to 375°F. Bake 15–20 minutes or until golden brown. Loosen sides with knife, if necessary, and immediately remove from pans to cool on wire racks. May lightly brush tops with softened butter, if desired. Makes two dozen rolls.

BLUEBERRY TEA CAKE

Washburn, Crosby Company was an important exhibitor at the Minnesota State Fair beginning in the late 1800s. The original Minnesota blueberry muffin was called a tea cake in *Washburn, Crosby's New Cook Book*.

- 1/2 cup butter
- 1 cup sugar
- 2 eggs
- 1/2 cup whole milk
- 2 cups flour
- 1 teaspoon salt
- 2 teaspoons baking powder
- 2 cups fresh blueberries
- 1 teaspoon vanilla

Preheat oven to 350°F. Grease 6 muffin pans. Cream together butter and sugar; add eggs and milk. Sift together flour, salt, and baking powder; add to batter. Dust blueberries with a little flour. Carefully stir blueberries and vanilla into batter. Fill muffin pans 2/3 full. Bake 25–30 minutes.

"How a Well Bred Maid Makes Well Made Bread"

CRUNCHY FIELD-CORN BREAD

Generations of Kelseys have grown State Fair prize-winning corn and this very rustic cornbread is the family favorite. It's also the perfect start for a crunchy cornbread dressing.

- 2 cups corn meal (freshly ground field corn)
- 2 teaspoons baking powder
- 1 teaspoon baking soda
- 1-1/2 teaspoons salt
- 2 cups sour milk or buttermilk
- 2 eggs, beaten
- 1/2 cup vegetable oil

Preheat oven to 425°F. Mix together corn meal, baking powder, baking soda, and salt. Add milk, eggs, and vegetable oil. Mix well. Turn into well-greased 13x9x1-inch pan and bake for 30 minutes. Pan must be shallow for good browning. Makes 12 servings.

The Kelsey family sorts corn for State Fair competition

Minnesota breakfasts benefit from farm fresh eggs and delicious dairy products. Add fresh apples and cheese to this sampling of morning basics and the day doesn't start any better than this.

The following recipes may have been adapted for easy preparation, modern cooking methods, or ingredients that are readily available.

HAM AND CHEESE PUFFS

In 1974, the official Minnesota Egg Lady handed out State Fair egg recipes with a lesson on the nutritional value of eggs. These ham and cheese puffs make a nearly perfect breakfast alongside a panful of Minnesota fried eggs.

- 1 cup water
- 1/2 cup butter or margarine
- 1 cup flour
- 1/2 teaspoon dry mustard
- 4 eggs
- 1 cup cooked ham, finely diced
- 1/2 cup shredded Cheddar cheese

Preheat oven to 350°F. Grease large cookie sheet. In 2-quart saucepan over medium heat, heat water and butter until melted and mixture boils. Remove saucepan from heat. With wooden spoon, stir in flour and mustard all at once until mixture forms a ball. Add eggs, one at a time, beating well after each egg until smooth. Beat in ham and cheese. Drop batter by spoonful onto prepared cookie sheet into 12 mounds, about 2 inches apart. Swirl top. Bake 35 minutes or until golden. Makes 12 puffs.

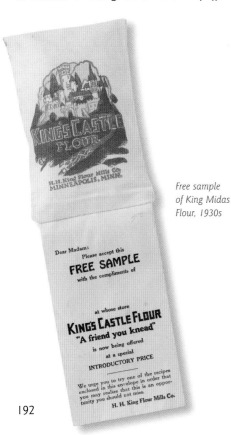

Free sample of King Midas Flour, 1930s

BREAKFAST BREAD PUDDING

This old-fashioned breakfast dish uses up that Blue Ribbon bread going stale and becomes a delicious start to the morning.

- Butter
- 6 slices white or potato bread
- 1-1/2 cups cheddar cheese, grated
- 6 slices bacon, diced and fried
- 3 large eggs
- 2 cups milk
- 1/2 teaspoon dry mustard
- 1/2 teaspoon salt
- 1/2 teaspoon pepper
- Pinch of cayenne

Preheat oven to 350°F. Generously butter an 8-inch square baking dish. In a large bowl tear bread into 2" pieces and mix with cheese and bacon. In a separate bowl beat eggs, add milk and seasonings. Add to bread-cheese-bacon mixture and mix well. Let stand 15 minutes. Pour mixture into baking dish. Bake until brown and puffy, 50–60 minutes. Makes 6 servings.

Queen Bee Flour Mills, 1920s

BAKED HAM AND EGGS

Eggs star in a tasty combination that would make any chicken proud.

- 3/4 cup green pepper, chopped
- 1/2 cup onion, chopped
- 1 tablespoon butter
- 1 cup cooked ham, chopped
- 2/3 cup grated cheddar cheese
- 6 eggs
- 1 cup milk
- 1 teaspoon dry mustard
- 1/4 cup chopped tomato

Preheat oven to 375°F. Butter a deep-dish pie plate. In small saucepan, cook peppers and onion in butter until tender. Stir in ham. Place in pie plate. Sprinkle with cheese. In medium bowl, whisk together eggs, milk, and mustard. Pour over vegetables and ham. Top with tomatoes. Bake 30–40 minutes, until center is cooked firm. Makes 6–8 servings.

PEAR AND ALMOND BREAD

Wooden cartons filled with pears covered tables at State Fair competitions, then they found their way into healthy breakfast breads.

- 1/2 cup butter, softened
- 1 cup sugar
- 2 eggs
- 1/4 cup sour cream
- 1 teaspoon vanilla
- 2 cups flour
- 1/2 teaspoon salt
- 1 teaspoon baking powder
- 1/2 teaspoon baking soda
- 1/8 teaspoon nutmeg
- 1 cup coarsely chopped pears
- 1/2 cup sliced almonds

Preheat oven to 350°F. Grease and flour a loaf pan. Cream butter, sugar, and eggs. Add sour cream and vanilla. Combine flour, salt, baking powder, soda, and nutmeg. Add to creamed mixture, beat well. Stir in pears and pecans. Pour batter into loaf pan, bake 60 minutes or until toothpick comes out clean.

CERESOTA SCOTCH SCONES

Ceresota cookbooks were loaded with interesting Minnesota flour recipes. Promotional literature included how to make everything from simple broth to Parisian cuisine, even in the early 1900s.

- 2 cups flour
- 2 teaspoons baking powder
- 1 tablespoon sugar
- 1/2 teaspoon salt
- 2 tablespoons butter
- 2 eggs
- 1/3 cup cream
- 1/2 cup currants

Preheat oven to 350°F. Combine flour, baking powder, sugar, and salt. Cut in butter. Stir in beaten eggs, then cream and fruit. Mix with a knife to a dough a little stiffer than for biscuit. Divide into two portions, roll each to a 1/2" thick round. Cut into 4 triangular segments, place on a greased baking sheet. Bake 15–20 minutes. Makes 8 scones. Serve with lots of butter and fruit jam.

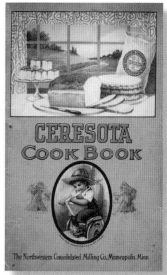

Ceresota Flour recipes from the early 1900s

LIZZIE'S CREAM MUFFINS

This 1886 recipe included the description "Popover-like flavor men love." The flavor is indeed popover-like; these dense muffins only rise a little during baking. A couple of muffins, topped by butter and jelly, would fortify a State Fair visitor for hours of walking around the fairgrounds.

- Butter for greasing muffin cups
- 3 eggs
- 1/2 cup heavy whipping cream
- 1-1/2 cups whole milk
- 2 cups flour
- 1 teaspoon salt
- 1 tablespoon butter, melted
- 1/4 teaspoon cream of tartar

Preheat oven to 400°F. Generously butter muffin cups. Separate egg yolks from whites. Beat egg yolks; add whipping cream, milk, flour, salt, and butter. Beat egg whites with cream of tartar until stiff, then fold them into the batter. Fill muffin cups to the top; bake 20 to 25 minutes. Muffins are done when they begin to color on top and a brown crust forms around the outside edge. Remove from oven, brush tops with melted butter. Makes 10–15 muffins depending on size of muffin cups.

The 1894 Farmer Magazine made recipe books available at their State Fair booth. "Every Recipe contributed by A Farmers Wife or Daughter"

OVEN APPLE PANCAKE

A hearty 4-H appetite was well satisfied with a flavorful dish from the *4-H Sampler Cookbook* of 1984.

- 2 apples, cored and sliced
- 2 tablespoons butter
- 1/2 cup milk
- 1/2 cup flour
- 3 eggs
- 1/2 teaspoon salt
- 3 tablespoons sugar
- Cinnamon to taste

Preheat oven to 400°F. Sauté apples in butter, pour into well-greased 2-quart baking dish. In a bowl mix remaining ingredients; pour mixture over apples. Cover. Bake 15 minutes. Remove cover and dot with a little additional butter, sugar, and cinnamon. Return to oven uncovered for 10–15 minutes. Serves 3–4.

APPLE OATMEAL CRUNCH

Healthy and hearty recipes come from Minnesota apple and grain growers. Great brunch crunch!

- 6 cups peeled, sliced apples
- 1 cup sifted flour
- 1 cup brown sugar, firmly packed
- 1/4 teaspoon cinnamon
- 1 cup butter
- 1 cup quick-cooking oats
- 1/4 cup chopped walnuts

Preheat oven to 350°F. Arrange apples in greased 8-inch square baking dish. Combine flour, brown sugar, and cinnamon. Cut in butter until crumbly. Add oats and walnuts; mix well. Sprinkle over apples. Bake 50–60 minutes or until apples are tender. Serve warm. Makes 9 servings.

CREAM OF WHEAT APPLE BAKE

For those who like hot cereal and a flavorful way to start out a cold day, this unusual breakfast dish is a true energy builder.

- 2 cups cooked Cream of Wheat
- 2 cups milk
- 3 eggs, beaten
- 1 cup sugar
- 3 apples, cored and sliced
- Sugar, nutmeg, butter for topping

Preheat oven to 350°F. Mix Cream of Wheat with milk, beaten eggs, and sugar. Pour one-third of mixture into a buttered baking dish, cover with apple rings, sprinkle with sugar and nutmeg, dot with butter; repeat twice, making three layers of pudding with apples on top. Bake for 30 minutes. Serve hot with milk or cream. Makes 6 servings.

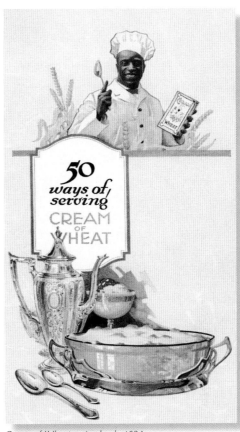

Cream of Wheat recipe book, 1924

McConnons Rainbow Road to Health and Happiness, 1900

EASY OLD-FASHIONED CINNAMON ROLLS

Aroma of cinnamon rolls baking in the oven come from a McConnons of Winona recipe. Baking products were sold "from wagon direct to consumer."

- 1/2 cup butter, softened
- 1 cup brown sugar
- 2 tablespoons cinnamon
- 2 cups flour
- 3 tablespoons sugar
- 3 teaspoons baking powder
- 1/2 teaspoon salt
- 1/2 cup butter
- 1 egg
- 2/3 cup milk

FOR ICING:
- 1/2 cup powdered sugar
- 1/4 cup milk

Preheat oven to 400°F. Grease a 9-inch square baking pan. Cream butter, brown sugar, and cinnamon together for filling. Set aside. Combine flour, sugar, baking powder, and salt in bowl. Cut in butter until crumbly. Whisk egg and milk together. Add all at once to the dry ingredients and mix to combine. Turn dough onto a floured surface or floured wax paper and pat into a 10-inch square. Spread filling on top and roll up like a jelly roll. Cut into 9 slices. Arrange slices in pan, cut side down. Bake for 20–25 minutes. Remove from pan and drizzle icing over: mix 1/2 cup powdered sugar with milk or cream to make a thin icing.

Fairgoers took a chance on Grocery Wheel Games in the 1930s. St Paul Home Brand products were the reward and lucky winners got a basket full—but they had to carry it home from the fair.

Vegetables

Although corn is a well-known crop throughout the state, two classes of bean, navy and pinto, encompass major commercial acreage in the state. In fact, Minnesota leads the country in green pea production. The state also holds the largest potato farming operations in America.

The following recipes may have been adapted for easy preparation, modern cooking methods, or ingredients that are readily available.

CORN PUDDING WITH CHIVES

One of Minnesota's largest crops is corn and this corn pudding wins the prize for flavor every time.

- I 16-ounce package frozen whole kernel corn, thawed
- 1/4 cup sugar
- I teaspoon salt
- 2 cups whole milk
- 4 eggs
- 4 tablespoons butter, melted and cooled
- 1/4 cup flour
- 1/4 teaspoon vanilla
- 1/4 cup finely chopped chives

Preheat oven to 350°F. Butter a 2-quart casserole. Finely chop half the corn or pulse in a food processor into coarse pieces with a tablespoon of water. Put into a large bowl, stir in remaining corn, sugar, and salt. Stir in milk, eggs, butter, flour, vanilla, and chives until well combined. Pour into buttered dish; bake in center of oven 60 minutes or more or until set. Let stand for 15 minutes to firm. Serves 8.

Norman Rockwell painted memorable ads for Green Giant corn. A print of "Gee whiz, there goes the last one" could be ordered in 1939 without advertising copy by sending ten cents to the Minnesota Valley Canning Company.

MAPLE WALNUT CARROTS

Towle's syrup recipes came inside little bucket-style handouts, two different recipes to a bucket.

- 4 cups sliced carrots
- 2 tablespoons butter, melted
- 1/4 cup finely chopped onion
- 1/3 cup Towle's maple syrup
- 1/2 cup chopped walnuts

Boil carrots in saucepan with enough water to cover until tender, 10–15 minutes. Meanwhile, combine butter and onion in saucepan; sauté until onion is tender; stir in syrup; add walnuts. Drain carrots; pour sauce over and gently mix to coat all carrot slices. Serves 6–8.

STICKS AND STONES

Peas and carrots are huge Minnesota crops and they combine into colorful vegetables for all ages.

- 4 carrots, scraped, halved, sliced lengthwise into 1/4" strips
- 1-1/2 cups frozen peas, thawed
- 3 tablespoons butter
- I teaspoon salt
- 1/4 teaspoon pepper
- 2 teaspoons sugar
- 2 teaspoons chopped parsley

Boil carrots in water until barely tender. Add peas, cook 3–5 minutes. Drain. Add butter to carrots and peas. Stir in seasonings, cook until hot. Makes 4–6 servings.

ZUCCHINI PANCAKES

This delicious combination of ingredients awaits baskets of zucchini overflowing from fall gardens.

- 5 small zucchini
- I medium red onion
- 1-1/2 teaspoons salt
- 2 eggs
- 2 tablespoons fresh chopped basil
- 4 tablespoons grated parmesan cheese
- 4 tablespoons flour
- 1/4 teaspoon salt
- 1/4 teaspoon pepper
- Oil for frying

Grate the zucchini and onion into a colander, sprinkle with salt. Let stand for 10 minutes, squeeze out excess water. In a large bowl beat eggs, stir in basil, cheese, flour, salt, and pepper. Add zucchini and onion. In a large skillet, heat 3 tablespoons oil until very hot. Drop zucchini batter in 1/3 cup measures into the hot oil. Completely brown one side, (about 2 minutes), turn and brown the other side. Remove to plate and keep hot. Repeat with balance of zucchini batter. Add more oil as needed. Makes 8–10 pancakes.

BUTTER PECAN ACORN SQUASH

Squash of all kinds would receive a tasty boost from this Towle's Syrup sauce.

- 2 large acorn squash
- Salt and pepper
- 1/3 cup butter
- 1/3 cup firmly packed brown sugar
- 1/4 cup Towle's maple syrup
- 1/2 cup chopped pecans

Preheat oven to 350° F. Cut squash into quarters, remove seeds, peel, and cut into 1" pieces. Place squash in a 9x9-inch casserole; lightly salt and pepper; bake covered for 20 minutes. Meanwhile, melt butter in small saucepan; stir in brown sugar, syrup, and pecans. Cook until sugar dissolves, stirring constantly. Pour over baked squash; bake an additional 10 minutes or until squash is tender, spooning mixture over squash occasionally. Serves 6–8.

ONION PIE

Northrup King provided educational booklets to onion growers with the advice: "A garden, no matter how small, is not considered complete until it is stocked with onions . . ."

- I cup Ritz cracker crumbs
- 1/4 cup butter, melted
- 2–3 cups thinly sliced sweet onions
- 2 tablespoons butter
- 2 eggs, beaten
- 3/4 cup half and half
- I teaspoon salt
- 1/4 teaspoon pepper
- 1/4 cup smoked cheese, shredded

Preheat oven to 350°F. Combine cracker crumbs in small bowl with melted butter; press into an 8-inch pie plate. In a skillet, saute onions in butter until soft. Pour into prepared crumb crust. In a medium bowl, combine eggs, half and half, salt, and pepper; pour over onions. Sprinkle with cheese. Bake for 30 minutes, or until knife inserted 1" from edge comes out clean. Serves 4–6.

Northrup King Onion Culture handout, 1908

ORANGE SWEET POTATOES

Brown sugar and a hint of orange become classic holiday fare for oven-baked sweet potatoes.

- 2–3 large sweet potatoes or yams
- 1/3 cup butter
- 1/3 cup brown sugar
- 2 tablespoons orange marmalade
- 1/2 cup pecan halves

Boil sweet potatoes in water until tender. Peel and slice in 1/2" slices. Place slices in buttered casserole. Melt butter in sauté pan, stir in sugar, add orange marmalade and pecan halves. When heated through, pour over sweet potatoes. Bake covered at 325°F for 20–30 minutes or until hot.

Holiday Hospitality *recipe book, Minneapolis Gas Company, 1967*

SWEET AND SOUR RED CABBAGE

The American Beekeeping Federation combined honey and wine vinegar for a perfect hot cabbage.

- 1 tablespoon butter
- 5 tablespoons wine vinegar
- 1 teaspoon salt
- 3 tablespoons honey
- 1 medium head red cabbage, shredded
- 2 apples, cored and diced

In a large skillet, melt butter. Add wine vinegar, salt, and honey. Stir in cabbage and apples. Cover and simmer 45–50 minutes. Serves 4–6.

Cabbage and apples in State Fair exhibits, 1900

Variety in Food
with Foley Kitchen Utensils, *1950*

POTATO CHEESE SCALLOP

Foley utensil demonstrations attracted large slicer-dicer audiences—and their recipes were just as good as their products.

- 2-1/2 pounds red potatoes
- 2 cups milk
- 1-1/2 cups cream
- 1 tablespoon crushed onion or garlic
- 1 teaspoon salt
- 1/4 teaspoon pepper
- 1/8 teaspoon grated nutmeg
- 3/4 cup grated cheese
- 1/2 cup whole wheat breadcrumbs

Preheat oven to 400°F. Butter a 2-1/2 to 3-quart baking dish. Peel and thinly slice potatoes into a 4-quart saucepan. Add milk, cream, garlic, salt, and pepper. Bring just to a boil. Transfer half the potato mixture into buttered dish. Sprinkle half the nutmeg, cheese, and breadcrumbs evenly over layer. Repeat. Bake 35–45 minutes until top is golden brown. Let stand 15 minutes before serving.

BRUSSELS SPROUTS

Sprouts, the little kids of the cabbage family, receive a playful dressing that real kids might like.

- 1-1/2 pounds Brussels sprouts, trimmed and halved
- 3 bacon slices, finely chopped
- 3 finely sliced green onions
- 1 teaspoon lemon juice
- 1/2 teaspoon salt
- 1/4 teaspoon black pepper

Cook Brussels sprouts in a 12-inch skillet with boiling salted water until crisp-tender, about 6 minutes, drain in a colander. Cook bacon in the same skillet over moderately high heat, stirring, until browned and crisp, about 3 minutes; add green onions and cook 1 minute. Reduce heat, stir in Brussels sprouts, lemon, salt, and pepper and cook for 3 minutes.

HOME BAKED BEANS

Senator Hubert Humphrey gave out food management and recipe bulletins in 1955. He knew his beans and that Minnesota was a leading producer.

- 1 pound dried navy beans
- 1/3 pound bacon or salt pork, diced
- 1 medium onion diced
- 8 cups water
- 1/4 cup molasses
- 1/3 cup brown sugar
- 4 tablespoons ketchup
- 2 teaspoons prepared brown mustard
- 1 teaspoon salt
- 1/2 teaspoon black pepper
- 1 tablespoon vinegar

Rinse and clean beans. Preheat oven to 300°F. Fry bacon or salt pork in a large Dutch oven. Add onion and fry until soft. Add remaining ingredients and bring to a boil. Cover the pot and place in oven. Bake about 4 hours, stirring every hour, Remove the lid and continue to bake until the liquid has thickened and beans are tender, 1 to 1-1/2 hours longer.

From U.S. Department of Agriculture, 1955

SPINACH AU GRATIN

The *Family Fare* booklet also held great recipe combinations that encouraged families to eat their vegetables.

- 10 ounces fresh spinach, chopped fine
- 1 tablespoon butter
- 2 tablespoons flour
- 2/3 cup milk
- 1/2 cup grated cheese, cheddar or swiss
- Salt and pepper
- Dash of fresh nutmeg
- 4 slices fried bacon, chopped
- 1/2 cup buttered breadcrumbs

Preheat oven to 350°F. Grease a medium oven casserole. Cook spinach a few minutes in a covered pan without adding water. Set aside. Melt butter in skillet, whisk in flour until bubbly, add milk and cook until thickened. Add cheese and stir until cheese is melted, add salt, pepper, and nutmeg. Mix in spinach and pour into casserole. Mix bacon with breadcrumbs and sprinkle over top. Bake about 20–30 minutes until crumbs are brown. Serves 4.

Fish, Poultry, Lamb, & Venison

In addition to great farm kitchen recipes for chicken, turkey, and lamb, many State Fair handouts offered a wealth of fish and game preparations.

The following recipes may have been adapted for easy preparation, modern cooking methods, or ingredients that are readily available.

TROUT SAUTÉED WITH BACON

The *Farmer Country Kitchen Cook Book* described this trout as having unequaled flavor—campers on the State Fairgrounds could fry their fish over a campfire in 1945.

- 8 slices bacon, diced
- 4 whole trout or 8 fillets
- Flour
- 1/4 cup slivered almonds
- Salt and pepper
- 4 sprigs parsley
- 4 lemon slices

Cook bacon in a large skillet and put to drain on paper towels. Add lightly floured trout to 1–2 tablespoons hot bacon fat in pan. Brown quickly, turn, add almonds, brown other side of fish, cook until flesh flakes, then add bacon. Garnish with parsley and lemon. Makes 4 servings.

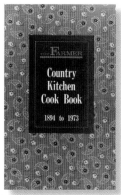

Farmer Country Kitchen Cook Book, 1894–1973

HONEY FRIED WALLEYE

From Minnesota Beekeeper honey recipes, this combination is certain to please fish lovers.

- 6 large walleye fillets
- 2/3 cup vegetable oil
- 1 egg lightly beaten
- 1 teaspoon honey
- 1-1/2 cups coarsely crushed soda crackers
- 1/2 cup flour
- 1/2 teaspoon salt
- 1/2 teaspoon pepper

Dry fillets on paper towels. Heat oil in a 10-inch skillet. Combine egg and honey. In a separate bowl, combine crackers, flour, salt, and pepper. Dip fillets in honey mixture, then coat with cracker mixture, pressing crumbs firmly into fillets. Fry about 3–4 minutes on each side.

CHICKEN CHOW MEIN

From the *4-H Cookbook of Anoka County*, 1984, this was reported to be a great tasting, good old-fashioned American Chicken Chow Mein.

- 1/2 cup chopped onion
- 2 cups diagonally sliced celery
- 2–3 cups roasted chicken or turkey
- 3 tablespoons oil
- 1 4-ounce can sliced mushrooms
- 1 1-pound can bean sprouts, drained
- 1 small jar chopped pimento
- 1-1/4 cups chicken broth
- 3–4 tablespoons soy sauce
- 3 tablespoons cornstarch
- Chow mein noodles or rice

In a large skillet cook onion and celery in oil until onion is tender. Stir in chicken, mushrooms (with liquid), bean sprouts, pimento, and chicken broth until hot. Blend soy sauce and cornstarch; stir into chow mein mixture. Cook stirring constantly until mixture thickens and boils. Cook stirring 1 minute more. Serve over noodles or rice. Serves 4–6.

CURRIED CHICKEN

The Northwestern Consolidated Milling company published it's *Cookery Book* of recipes using Ceresota flour. Curried chicken with coconut was a popular dish with Victorian cooks.

- 1 broiler-fryer chicken, cut up
- 3 tablespoons butter
- 1 onion, sliced
- 1–2 tablespoons curry powder
- 3 tablespoons shredded coconut
- 1 teaspon sugar
- 1 teaspoon salt
- 1 teaspoon flour
- 1 cup whole milk
- 1 cup water
- 1 tablespoon lemon juice

In a frying pan, fry chicken in butter to a light brown color. Remove chicken and set aside. Add onion to pan and fry until soft. Stir in curry powder, coconut, sugar, salt, flour, milk, and water. Add chicken and cook slowly for about one hour. Add lemon juice and serve with boiled rice. Makes 4–6 servings.

Ceresota Cook Book, *early 1900s*

OVEN BARBECUE CHICKEN

Minnesota Grown Broiler cooks made their barbecue chicken over smoking hot coals at the fair. This 1940s recipe does a great job in the oven.

- 4 pounds chicken pieces
- Oil
- 1/2 cup chopped onion
- 3 tablespoons butter
- 1 cup ketchup
- 1/4 cup vinegar
- 3 tablespoons brown sugar
- 2 teaspoons mustard
- 2 teaspoons Worcestershire sauce
- Salt and pepper

Preheat oven to 350°F. In a large skillet, fry chicken in hot oil until browned. Drain off fat and place chicken in a roasting pan. In skillet, sauté onion in butter until tender. Add remaining ingredients. Reduce heat and simmer for 10 minutes. Pour sauce over chicken and bake for 1 hour, or until chicken is tender and juices run clear. Baste occasionally. Serves 6.

Chicken Stand, 1940s

HONEY LEMON CHICKEN

From Minnesota Beekeepers Association best recipes, 1950s

- 1/3 cup flour
- 1 teaspoon paprika
- 1 teaspoon salt
- 2-1/2 – 3-pound chicken, cut up in pieces
- 1/3 cup butter
- 1/3 cup honey
- 1/4 cup lemon juice

Preheat oven to 375°F. Mix together flour, paprika, and salt. Roll chicken pieces in flour mixture. Melt butter in an oven casserole, roll chicken in butter. Bake chicken for 45 minutes. Mix honey and lemon together, brush on chicken pieces and bake an additional 15 minutes.

TURKEY WITH FRUIT SAUCE

Apples, oranges, and cranberries perfectly complement leftover turkey.

- 6–8 pieces leftover turkey or small turkey breast, roasted
- I tart apple, pared, cored, and diced
- 1/3 cup orange juice
- 3 tablespoons jellied cranberry sauce
- 4 tablespoons orange marmalade

In skillet, over medium heat, combine apple, orange juice, cranberry sauce, and marmalade. Cook until sauce is hot and apples are tender. Spoon sauce over hot turkey pieces or slices. Serves 6–8.

Turkey Stand, 1980s

HEARTY TURKEY PIE

Turkey came in many varieties at the fair, but from-scratch turkey pie at home was hard to beat.

- I can cream of potato soup
- 1/2 cup milk
- 3 tablespoons mayonnaise
- 2-1/2 cups cooked turkey, diced
- 1-1/2 cups frozen peas, carrots, and corn
- 1/2 cup onions, finely chopped
- Salt and pepper to taste
- Pastry for single crust pie

Preheat oven to 375°F. Heat soup, milk, and mayonnaise in heavy saucepan over low heat. Stir in turkey, vegetables, onions, salt, and pepper. Spoon into pie plate. Place pie crust over top, crimp edges to seal, and cut slits for steam to escape. Brush with melted butter. Bake for 20–30 minutes until golden brown. Let stand 10 minutes. Serves 4.

Turkey Stand by Poultry Building, 1965

SMOTHERED PHEASANT OR GROUSE

The Farmer Country Kitchen Cook Book suggested a garnish of tiny boiled carrots on this platter of succulent pheasant pieces.

- 2 pheasants or 4 grouse, skinned, quartered
- I tablespoon salt
- 1/2 cup flour
- 4 tablespoons butter, divided
- 1/4 cup chopped celery
- 1/4 cup chopped carrot
- 1/4 cup chopped onion
- 1/2 cup boiling water

Preheat oven to 350°F. Mix flour and salt in a brown paper bag. Shake pheasant pieces until well coated. Sauté celery, carrot, and onion in 2 tablespoons butter until tender. Place vegetables in shallow baking pan. Melt 2 tablespoons butter in skillet and brown pheasant pieces. Remove meat to baking pan, add water. Cover loosely with foil. Bake 1 to 1-1/2 hours, or until meat is tender. Makes 4–6 servings.

HONEY DUCKS

Duck hunters and their friends will appreciate this recipe made with Minnesota honey and sweet butter.

- 2 whole ducks, cleaned and rinsed
- I orange, quartered
- 2/3 cup honey
- 1/4 cup butter
- 3/4 cup orange preserves
- I tablespoon mustard
- I teaspoon garlic, minced
- I tablespoon orange-flavored liqueur

Preheat oven to 450°F. Place ducks in roaster pan and stuff each with orange quarters. Put in oven and immediately reduce heat to 350°F. Roast ducks uncovered for about an hour. In saucepan, simmer together remaining ingredients until syrupy. Just before done, coat the ducks with syrup, return to oven for 15 minutes to glaze. Serve remaining sauce over ducks. Allow 1/2 a duck per serving.

SOUR CREAM LAMB STEW

The Farmer Country Kitchen Cook Book, sold at the State Fair, was first published in 1894. This classic lamb stew remained through 50 years and 21 printings.

- 1-1/2 pounds cubed lamb shoulder
- 2 tablespoons butter
- 3 medium onions, sliced
- I medium green pepper, diced
- 1-1/2 teaspoons salt
- 2 teaspoons paprika
- 3/4 cup water
- I cup dairy sour cream

Brown lamb in butter. Add onions, green pepper, salt, and paprika. Cover and cook over low heat 15 minutes. Add water. Cover and cook 1 to 1-1/2 hours until lamb is tender. Mix in sour cream. Heat and serve with rice. Makes 4–6 servings.

LAMB PATTIES WITH CURRANT SAUCE

Quick and easy were the only requirements for tasty recipes from the lamb booklet.

- 2 pounds ground lamb
- 1/4 cup onion, finely chopped
- I cup bread crumbs
- I egg, beaten
- Salt and pepper
- 1/2 cup currant jelly
- I teaspoon mint, finely chopped
- 1/2 teaspoon orange peel, grated

Combine lamb, onions, bread crumbs, egg, salt, and pepper. Shape into patties 1" thick. Brown both sides in hot skillet. Reduce temperature and cook slowly until done. Mix together jelly, mint, orange peel. Spoon over lamb patties, cook until hot. Serves 6.

Lamb for Goodness Sake, 1940

VENISON COLLOPS

Turn-of-the-century recipes made liberal use of Minnesota fish and game populations. Washburn, Crosby's recipes were very sophisticated for the time.

- I thick venison steak
- Salt
- 2 tablespoons butter
- Dusting of cayenne
- 1/4 cup port wine
- 2 tablespoons currant jelly

Cut steak into 2" cubes. Season with salt. Melt butter in skillet, brown steak pieces quickly over a hot fire. Add cayenne, Port wine, and currant jelly. The 1910 cookbook advised: "Epicures would say 'Serve at once.' Most people prefer to let it simmer till pink."

Washburn, Crosby Company cookbook, 1910

Beef, Pork, & Ham

Hamburgers and hotdogs were just about everyone's favorite food at the fair. But fabulous recipes from exhibitors and State Fair associations turned home kitchens into aromatic little fairs of their own.

The following recipes may have been adapted for easy preparation, modern cooking methods, or ingredients that are readily available.

STATE FAIR MEATBALLS

Salem Evangelical Lutheran Church serves up big plates of meatballs and mashed potatoes, then tops the meal with fresh homemade blueberry pie à la mode and a cup of egg coffee. A long walk around the fairgrounds is nearly a dietary requirement.

- 3 pounds ground beef
- I egg
- I-2/3 cups breadcrumbs
- 1/4 teaspoon allspice
- I cup milk or water
- I tablespoon salt
- 1/4 teaspoon black pepper
- I cup chopped onions, sautéed in butter

Preheat oven to 325°F. Combine all ingredients and mix well. (additional allspice and nutmeg adds flavor) Form into 1-1/2" balls; place in shallow baking pan. Bake for 45–60 minutes. Makes about 36 meatballs.

For Swedish style, top meatballs with cream gravy after the meatballs come out of the oven:

- 3 tablespoons butter
- 3 tablespoons flour
- I can condensed beef broth
- I cup cream
- Salt and pepper

Melt butter in skillet; stir in flour. Cook until bubbly. Stir in beef broth, cream, salt, and pepper. Cook until sauce thickens. Pour over Swedish meatballs in serving dish.

MEATBALL SUNDAE
mashed potatoes
gravy & a meatball
$3.50

Salem Dining Hall sign, 2006

FAIR STAND CHILI CON CARNE

From *Great State Fair Recipes*, volunteers from Jehovah Lutheran Church served fairgoers hot chili at their sturdy dining hall tables.

- 2 pounds ground beef
- I medium onion, chopped
- 6 ribs celery, chopped
- 2 tablespoons butter
- 2–4 tablespoons chili powder (to taste)
- 2 cloves garlic, mashed
- 3 cups fresh, chopped tomatoes or one 15-ounce can diced tomatoes
- I 15-ounce can tomato sauce
- I cup strong beef broth
- Salt and pepper to taste
- 2 cans pinto or kidney beans, rinsed or I cup dried pinto or kidney beans, soaked overnight and cooked until tender

Brown ground beef, onions, and celery in butter. Mix in chili powder and garlic. Add tomatoes, beef broth, salt, and pepper. Simmer covered 1-1/2 hours, adding water if sauce becomes too thick. Add beans; simmer 30 minutes. Serve with corn bread or corn muffins. Serves 8.

SHORT RIBS IN DARK BEER

Famous Minnesota dark beer is the rustic base for this interesting combination of flavors.

- 6–8 pounds bone-in short ribs, trimmed of fat
- Salt and pepper
- Vegetable oil
- 1/2 pound bacon, cut into I" pieces
- 2 sweet onions sliced
- 3 carrots, diced
- I tablespoon flour
- I tablespoon brown sugar
- 2 bottles dark beer
- 1/2 cup red wine
- 3 tablespoons tomato paste
- 2 cups beef stock

Heat oven to 350°F. Salt and pepper ribs, dust with flour and sugar. In Dutch oven, heat oil and brown ribs on all sides. Remove ribs, drain fat, but don't clean pot. Add bacon, onions, and carrots, cook until browned. Stir in flour and sugar. Add beer, wine, tomato paste, and beef stock. Bring to a boil, add ribs. Cover pot and cook in oven for 2 hours. Take off lid and continue baking I hour to thicken sauce. Serve ribs with sauce.

HUNGARIAN GOULASH

Restaurants at the fair kept their kettles cooking all day long, and the goulash just got better and better.

- 3 slices bacon, chopped
- I large onion, minced
- Salt and pepper to taste
- 1/2 teaspoon caraway seed
- I pound each beef, pork, and lamb, cubed
- 1/4 cup flour
- 1/3 cup sweet Hungarian paprika
- I tablespoon whole allspice

Fry bacon with onion. Add salt, pepper, and caraway seed. When brown, add beef, cook for

15 minutes, add pork and lamb. Add flour, paprika, and allspice. Stir in I cup water or to cover meat. Stew gently until meat is tender, adding water if necessary. Serve over thick ribbon noodles. Makes 12 servings.

FARMHOUSE ROAST BEEF

Recipe and menu ideas were a popular combination for cooks. In 1931, old-fashioned, hearty red wine added a big flavor boost.

- 4–5 pounds beef chuck or arm roast
- Oil
- 2 tablespoons butter
- I large onion, coarsely chopped
- I tablespoon flour
- I can beef broth
- I tomato, finely diced
- I bay leaf
- I clove garlic, minced
- 1/2 cup red wine
- 12 carrots, halved, or 24 baby carrots
- 3 parsnips, peeled, cut in I" pieces
- 4–5 potatoes, peeled, quartered

Heat oven to 350°F. Dredge roast in flour, salt, pepper, and sugar. In a large skillet, brown meat in hot oil. Place meat in a Dutch oven or large casserole. Melt butter in skillet; add onions, sauté until soft. Add flour to onions and brown slightly. Stir in beef broth, tomatoes, bay leaf, and garlic, scraping up bits on the bottom of the pan. Add wine. Add liquid to the beef; cover and bake for 2 hours. Add carrots, parsnips, and potatoes; add additional beef broth if necessary; bake an additional 60 minutes or until vegetables are done. Serves 12–16.

Meat Recipes and Menus, *Minnesota State Fair and National Live Stock and Meat Board. 1931*

Meat in the Meal for Health Defense, *1950s*

BEEF BRISKET WITH ONION SAUCE

From *Meat Tops the Menu*, by the Minnesota State Fair and National Live Stock and Meat Board, this recipe was described as "One the Men Will Cheer."

- 4 pounds beef brisket
- I carrot, diced
- 1/2 cup celery, diced
- 2 teaspoons salt
- 6 peppercorns
- 6 whole cloves
- I egg
- I cup dry breadcrumbs

ONION SAUCE:

- 2 tablespoons sugar
- I tablespoon butter
- 2 onions, sliced
- 2 tablespoons flour
- 2 cups meat broth
- I teaspoon vinegar
- Salt and pepper

Put meat in large pot and cover with water. Add vegetables and seasonings. Simmer 3 hours, or until tender. Remove brisket, reserving broth, and slice. Place slices in shallow baking dish. Brush lightly with beaten egg. Sprinkle with crumbs and brown in 400°F oven. Make onion sauce. Brown sugar in butter, add onions and cook until tender. Add flour and brown. Add broth, vinegar, salt and pepper. Cook until smooth. Serve alongside brisket.

Meat Tops the Menu, 1936

OVEN PORK ROAST/FRESH HAM

Described as "Pork to Perfection," oven roasting aromas tempted impatient appetites.

- I 4–5 pound fresh bone-in pork leg roast or fresh ham
- Sage
- Garlic, mashed
- Salt and pepper
- 4 tablespoons flour

Preheat oven to 325°F. Score fat and rub roast with sage, garlic, salt, and pepper. Place in a roasting pan with rack. Roast to an internal temperature of 175°F, about 2–3 hours. Remove from oven and place roast on a warm platter to set. Skim fat from pan, leaving pan juices, whisk in 4 tablespoons flour, stirring until bubbly. Add water or broth to make about 2 cups, stir until thickened. Serve with carved roast. Potatoes and whole onions can be added during last 1-1/2 hour of roasting.

BAKED BONELESS HAM

Witt's Markets combined a savory Hormel ham in the oven with a sweet sauce simmering on the stovetop.

- I 3–5 pound cooked picnic ham
- I cup brown sugar
- 2 dozen cloves

Cover ham with brown sugar, stud with cloves. Bake in a 350°F oven until heated through. Serve slices with sauce.

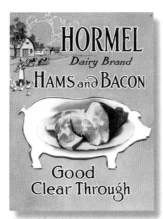

Hormel handout, 1950s

ORANGE SAUCE FROM WITT'S MARKET:

- 1/4 cup brown sugar
- 2 tablespoons orange juice
- I tablespoon grated orange rind
- I tablespoon sweet pickle juice
- 2 tablespoons honey

Combine in saucepan. Boil and stir 3 minutes.

HAM RAISIN SAUCE FROM KING MIDAS FLOUR AND PIGGLY WIGGLY STORES:

- 3/4 cup raisins
- I cup water
- 4 whole cloves
- 3/4 cup brown sugar
- I teaspoon cornstarch
- I tablespoon butter
- I tablespoon lemon juice
- Salt and pepper to taste

Simmer raisins, water, and cloves together for 10 minutes. Add remaining ingredients and cook, stirring constantly, until thick. Makes 2 cups.

STATE FAIR HAM LOAF

This St. Paul Hamline United Methodist Church recipe dates from 1930 and has been served at the church dining hall ever since.

- 1-1/2 pounds ground ham
- 1-1/2 pounds ground beef
- 3 cups dry breadcrumbs
- I small onion chopped
- 1/2 teaspoon salt
- 1/2 teaspoon pepper
- 1/2 teaspoon curry powder
- 1/2 teaspoon ground sage
- 1/2 teaspoon allspice
- 2 cups milk
- 3 eggs, slightly beaten

FOR THE SAUCE:

- 2 cups brown sugar, packed

- 2/3 cup vinegar
- 1/4 cup prepared mustard

Preheat oven to 325°F. Combine all ingredients except for sauce; pack mixture into large loaf pan. Combine sauce ingredients; spoon half of sauce over loaf. Bake for 1-1/2 hours. Spoon remaining sauce over loaf; continue baking 30–45 minutes.

CRANBERRY PORK CHOPS

Minneapolis and St. Paul daily newspapers gave out interesting recipe booklets "dedicated to the American Housewife."

- 4 thick pork chops
- Salt and pepper
- 1-1/2 cups fresh cranberries
- 1/4 cup water
- 1/2 cup brown sugar or honey
- 1/4 teaspoon cloves
- 1/4 teaspoon nutmeg

Preheat oven to 350°F. Brown pork chops, add salt and pepper. When brown, transfer to an oven casserole. Mix cranberries, water, sugar, cloves, and nutmeg, spread on top pork chops. Cover and bake 30 minutes, uncover and bake an additional 20–30 minutes until done. Serves 4.

SWEET AND SOUR PORK

It's all Minnesotan: Lake Pepin apple vinegar, soy sauce from soybeans, Red River Valley sugar, Minnesota pork, onion, and green pepper—and a little Hawaiian pineapple for a citrus splash.

- 2 pounds pork tenderloin, cubed
- I cup sliced onion
- I cup slivered green pepper
- I 8-ounce can pineapple tidbits
- 1/4 cup apple cider vinegar
- 1/4 cup brown sugar
- 2 teaspoons cornstarch
- 2 tablespoons soy sauce
- 1/2 teaspoon ginger
- 1/2 teaspoon salt

Brown pork in hot oil, add onion and green pepper and cook until lightly browned and pork is cooked. Drain pineapple liquid into a large measuring cup, add water to liquid to make 1-1/2 cups; add vinegar, brown sugar, cornstarch, soy sauce, ginger, and salt. Add to meat with pineapple tidbits; cook until sauce is clear and thickened. Serve over hot rice. Serves 4–6.

Hot Dishes, Soups, & Salads

Minnesota farmers are the largest pea producers in the nation and the fourth largest producer of dried beans. Minnesota is also unique in the production of wild rice having both cultivated paddy wild rice and traditional Native American hand-harvested wild rice. Beans and wild rice appear often in many fabulous Minnesota hot dishes.

The following recipes may have been adapted for easy preparation, modern cooking methods, or ingredients that are readily available.

TURKEY AND WILD RICE HOT DISH

This easy winner for turkey and wild rice is a fabulous combination from a very old, Old Dutch Potato Chip recipe.

- 1 cup wild rice
- 1 stick butter
- 1 small onion, chopped
- 1 cup sliced almonds
- 1 4-ounce can sliced mushrooms, drained
- 1 large jar pimento, diced
- 1/4 cup flour
- 1 tablespoon fresh chopped parsley
- 1-1/2 cup chicken broth
- 1-1/2 cup sour cream
- 3 cups cooked turkey or chicken diced
- Potato chips, finely crushed

Cook rice until tender. Heat oven to 350°F. In a large pan melt butter, sauté onion and almonds; add mushrooms and pimento. Stir in flour and parsley. Add chicken broth and sour cream, mix until smooth. Add cooked rice and turkey or chicken. Pour into a buttered casserole; top with potato chips. Cover and bake for 30 minutes, uncover and bake an additional 15 minutes or until hot. Serves 6–8.

Old Dutch State Fair handout, 1960s

Minneapolis Star and Tribune Newsettes Cookbook, 1961

CHINESE BEEF HOT DISH

High-tech for its time, the 1961 *Newsette* cookbook was printed in the Mimeograph Service Department of *The Star and Tribune* from stencils produced by the Electro-Rex, an electronic scanning device, on Rex Rotary stencil duplicators.

- 1-1/2 pounds ground beef
- 1 medium onion, chopped
- 3 stalks celery, chopped
- 1 can cream of mushroom soup
- 1 cup beef broth
- 1 8-ounce can diced tomatoes
- 2 tablespoons soy sauce
- 1 cup uncooked rice
- 2/3 cup sliced almonds
- 2 tablespoons butter

Preheat oven to 350°F. Brown beef, onion, and celery. Add soup, broth, tomatoes, soy sauce, and rice. Transfer to ovenproof casserole, bake for 30 minutes, stir. Coat almonds in melted butter, sprinkle on top and bake for an additional 30 minutes. Serves 6.

HAM AND SPAGHETTI CASSEROLE

Hormel ham, Creamette spaghetti, and good old mushroom soup combine perfectly in a flavorful taste-alike tetrazzini.

- 2 16-ounce packages spaghetti, broken into 2" pieces
- 2 cans condensed cream of mushroom soup
- 1-1/2 cups milk
- 1/2 cup dry white wine
- 1 cup chopped onion
- 1-1/2 cups fresh mushrooms, chopped
- 1 cup green olives with pimento, sliced
- 2 cups chopped baked ham
- 2 teaspoons Worcestershire sauce
- Salt and pepper
- 2 tablespoons parsley
- Parmesan cheese

Cook spaghetti in boiling salted water. Drain. Heat oven to 350°F. Combine soup and milk. Add remaining ingredients. Toss thoroughly with spaghetti. Put in a greased 2-1/2 or 3 quart casserole. Top with cheese. Bake uncovered 40 minutes or until heated in center and bubbly around the edges. Serves 8–10.

CHICKEN CHUN KING

The water chestnuts are Chun King, but the rest is pure old-fashioned comfort food, Midwest style. Tasters gave this dish their hearty approval.

- 1 16-ounce package frozen broccoli cuts, thawed
- 4 chicken breast halves, cut into 8 pieces
- 1 cup shredded cheddar cheese
- 1 can cream of mushroom soup
- 1/2 cup real mayonnaise
- 1 8-ounce can sliced Chun King water chestnuts, drained
- 1 can French fried onion rings
- 1/2 cup salted cashew pieces

Preheat oven to 350°F. Place broccoli in greased 9x13-inch pan; place chicken pieces over broccoli. Sprinkle cheese on top. Mix soup with mayonnaise and water chestnuts; spread over cheese. Bake for 40 minutes. Top with onion rings and cashews; bake 20 minutes longer. Serves 6–8.

Chun King food booth, 1965
Recipes from Chun King, 1960s

SPLIT PEA SOUP

Many Minnesota peas end up in the hands of the Green Giant, but others find their way into soup.

- 1 pound dried split peas
- 1 pound ham, diced
- 3 cups chopped onion
- 3 carrots, shredded
- 3 celery stalks, including leaves, finely chopped
- 2 garlic cloves, chopped
- 1/2 teaspoon dried thyme
- 1/2 teaspoon dried marjoram
- 1/2 teaspoon pepper
- Salt to taste
- 4 cups chicken broth
- 3–4 cups water

Combine all ingredients in large pot and bring to boil. Reduce heat to low, cover and simmer 3 hours. Stir occasionally and add more water if necessary. Makes 10–12 servings.

NAVY BEAN SOUP

Navy beans top the list for Minnesota bean growers and it's no wonder when navy bean soup tastes as good as this. Ham hocks can be used instead of bacon.

* 1 pound dry navy beans
* 1/2 pound bacon
* 1 medium onion, chopped
* 1 16-ounce can diced tomatoes
* 1 cup carrot, shredded
* 2 1/2 cups beef broth
* 2 tablespoons brown sugar
* 1 clove garlic, minced
* 2 tablespoons parsley
* 1 tablespoon basil
* Salt & pepper to taste

Rinse beans. Place in large soup kettle, cover with cold water and soak overnight or boil gently for 2 minutes and let stand for 1 hour. Drain beans. Fry bacon until semi-crisp, drain, add to beans. Sauté onion in bacon drippings, add to beans with all remaining ingredients. Bring to a low boil. Reduce heat; cover and simmer 2–3 hours or until beans are tender. Serves 6–8.

Watkins Almanac and Home Book
with tested recipes, 1942

CLASSIC WILD RICE SOUP

This delicious soup recipe was offered to fairgoers from the Minnesota Cultivated Wild Rice Council.

* 1/2 cup onion, chopped fine
* 6 tablespoons butter
* 1/2 cup flour
* 4 cups chicken broth
* 2 cups cooked wild rice
* 1/2 cup grated carrots
* 1 cup cooked chicken, cubed
* 3 tablespoons slivered almonds
* 1/2 teaspoon salt
* 1 cup half and half
* 2 tablespoons dry sherry

In a large saucepan, sauté onion in butter. Add flour, stirring until bubbly; gradually stir in broth. Stir in wild rice, carrots, chicken, almonds, and salt; simmer 5 minutes. Stir in half and half and sherry; heat through. Makes 6 servings.

CHUNKY TOMATO SOUP

The University of Minnesota brochure recommended twenty-five tomato plants for every person in the family! This chunky tomato soup is the answer for a bumper crop. It's from Ceresota Flour Mills in the early 1900s.

* 2 tablespoons butter
* 2 carrots, grated
* 1 small turnip, grated
* 2 small onions, finely chopped
* 2 tablespoons flour
* 4 cups vegetable broth
* 8 tomatoes, finely chopped
* 1/2 teaspoon mace (nutmeg)
* 1 teaspoon salt
* 1/2 teaspoon pepper
* 1 cup whole milk

TOMATOES
Minnesota's Health Food

UNIVERSITY OF MINNESOTA
Agricultural Extension Service
U.S. DEPARTMENT OF AGRICULTURE

Tomatoes, Minnesota's
Health food, 1941

Melt butter in a large soup pot. Add carrots, turnip, and onion, cook until soft. Stir in flour. Add broth, tomatoes, mace, salt, and pepper. Simmer for 1 hour. Purée in a sieve or food processor, or leave chunky. Add milk. Heat and serve. Serves 6–8.

TURKEY CHUTNEY SALAD

This hearty salad made with turkey and sweet cream provides energy-boosting staying-power for a sunny day of hearty activities.

* 1/4 cup mayonnaise
* 2–3 tablespoons chutney
* 1 teaspoon curry powder (optional)
* 3–4 tablespoons cream
* 1/4 cup celery, chopped
* 1/3 cup chopped dried cranberries
* 1/4 cup chopped green onion
* 1/4 cup chopped pecans
* 2–3 cups diced turkey
* Salad greens

In a small bowl, combine mayonnaise, chutney, and curry powder. Stir in cream to moisten. In a larger bowl, combine celery, dried cranberries, green onion, pecans, and turkey. Toss with dressing. Serve on salad greens. Serves 4–6.

FRUIT SALAD WITH TANGY DRESSING

This dressed-up fruit salad features honey, plums, pears, apples, and grapes that all appeared at State Fair Agricultural Competitions.

* 1 cup honey
* 1/4 cup sugar
* 3/4 cup cider vinegar
* 1/8 teaspoon salt
* 1 teaspoon paprika
* 1 cup salad oil
* 1/4 teaspoon celery seed
* 1 cup plum quarters
* 1 cup apple, diced
* 1 cup pear, diced
* 1 cup seedless grapes
* 1 head lettuce

Mix together honey, sugar, vinegar, salt, and paprika in saucepan. Bring to a boil for one minute. Cool. Add oil and celery seed. Assemble fruit in medium-sized bowl. Toss with dressing. Serve on chopped lettuce. Makes 4–6 servings.

CREAMETTE SHRIMP SALAD

Creamette handouts for this "tasty, tempting, and delicious" salad state that it is made to "just fit the fork."

* 1 package Creamettes elbow macaroni
* 1 green pepper, finely chopped
* 2 tomatoes, chopped
* 4 radishes, chopped
* 2 cups small cooked shrimp
* 1–2 cups mayonnaise
* Lettuce leaves
* 3 eggs, hard-boiled, sliced

Boil Creamettes in 2 quarts of rapidly boiling water with 2 teaspoons of salt, 8 minutes or until tender. Drain and chill in cold water. Combine pepper, tomatoes, radish, and shrimp with mayonnaise. Toss with Creamettes. Place servings on lettuce leaves and garnish with eggs. Serves 6.

Delicious Recipes made
with Creamettes, *1950s*

Cookies & Desserts

Local companies like Watkins and Nordic Ware distributed their popular cookbooks at State Fair booths and always attracted large crowds. *Great State Fair Recipes*, published by the Minnesota State Agricultural Society and American Dairy Association of Minnesota, appear throughout these recipe pages.

The following recipes may have been adapted for easy preparation, modern cooking methods, or ingredients that are readily available.

CHOCOLATE CHIP COOKIES

From *Great State Fair Recipes*, tasters thought that these were simply the best tasting chocolate chip cookies.

- 8 tablespoons softened butter
- 6 tablespoons granulated sugar
- 6 tablespoons dark brown sugar
- 1/2 teaspoon salt
- 1/2 teaspoon vanilla
- 1/4 teaspoon cold water
- 1 egg
- 1/2 teaspoon baking soda
- 1 cup all-purpose flour
- 1 cup semi-sweet chocolate chips
- 3/4 cup coarsely chopped pecans (optional)

Preheat oven to 375°F. In a large mixing bowl combine butter, white, and brown sugar, salt, vanilla, and water. Beat with a large spoon until the mixture is light and fluffy. Beat in the egg and baking soda, add the flour, beating it in 1/4 cup at a time. Gently fold in the chocolate chips and nuts. Coat a cookie sheet evenly with butter. Drop the batter by tablespoons, leaving about 1-1/2" between cookies. Pat down the tops of each cookie. Bake for about 12 minutes, or until the cookies are firm to the touch and lightly brown. Makes about 30 cookies.

Great State fair Recipes, A Collection of Minnesota State Fair sweepstakes-winning recipes from 1906 to 1975.

BUTTERSCOTCH ICE BOX COOKIES

Ice box and refrigerator makers handed out booklets at the fair with recipes and advice: "true progress is the liberation of a people from drudgery . . . Ice Box cookery is a further contribution to this progress . . ."

- 1/2 cup butter
- 1 cup brown sugar
- 1 egg
- 1/2 teaspoon vanilla
- 2 cups flour
- 1/2 teaspoon soda
- 1/2 teaspoon cream of tartar
- 1/2 teaspoon salt
- 1/2 cup walnuts, finely chopped

Cream together butter and sugar. Beat in egg and vanilla. Mix flour, soda, salt, and cream of tartar together; add to creamed mixture. Add nuts and mix until well blended. Shape into a 2" roll in waxed paper. Chill in ice box until firm. Cut thin slices as wanted and bake on cookie sheet in 375°F oven about 6–8 minutes or until lightly browned.

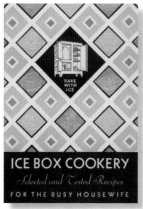

Ice Box Cookery for the Busy Housewife, *1920s*

CHOCOLATE BROWNIES

Also from *Great State Fair Recipes*, these scrumptious prize-winning chocolate brownies were judged as excellent.

- 2 squares unsweetened chocolate
- 1/2 cup butter
- 1 cup sugar
- 2 eggs
- 1/2 cup all-purpose flour
- 1/2 teaspoon baking powder
- 1/2 teaspoon salt
- 1 teaspoon vanilla
- 1 cup coarsely chopped walnuts or chocolate chips

Preheat oven to 350°F. Melt the chocolate in a small heavy saucepan over low heat, stirring constantly. Set aside to cool. In a mixing bowl, cream the butter and sugar together until light and fluffy. Beat in the eggs, one at a time, then the cooled chocolate. Sift the flour, baking powder, and salt together into the mixture. Beat for 10–15 seconds, or until the ingredients are well combined. Stir in vanilla and walnuts. Lightly butter an 8-inch square baking pan, pour in the batter. Bake brownies in the center of the oven for 30–35 minutes. Cool and cut into 2" squares. Makes 16 brownies.

FARMER'S CHEESE COOKIES

Making the cheese, then making the cookies could easily become a family tradition. (To make your own cheese, see page 188.)

- 1 cup butter at room temperature
- 2 cups sugar
- 1-1/2 cups farmer's or ricotta cheese
- 2 eggs
- 2 teaspoons vanilla
- 4 cups flour
- 1 teaspoon salt
- 1 teaspoon baking soda
- 1 teaspoon baking powder

ICING:
- 1/2 cup milk
- 1/2 teaspoon butter
- 1/2 teaspoon shortening
- 3–4 cups powdered sugar
- 1 tablespoon grated lemon rind

Preheat oven to 350°F. Beat butter and sugar until light and fluffy. Beat in cheese, eggs, and vanilla. Add flour, salt, baking soda, and baking powder. Drop by tablespoon amounts on greased baking sheet. Bake for 10–12 minutes. Cool on wire racks. In small saucepan, heat milk, butter, and shortening. Remove from heat, gradually add sugar and lemon rind. Spread icing on cookies. Makes about 3 dozen cookies.

LEMON COOKIE TART

This 1953 State Fair sweepstakes winner appeared in Mary Hart's column in the *Minneapolis Morning Tribune*. It used an unusual ingredient—potatoes—to enhance its texture and taste.

- 1 cup sifted flour
- 2 tablespoons sugar
- 1/3 cup butter
- 2 tablespoons milk
- 3/4 cup sugar
- 1 tablespoon butter, melted
- 1 egg
- 1 medium potato cooked and grated
- Grated rind of one lemon
- 1 tablespoon lemon juice

Preheat oven to 300°F. Sift flour and sugar together. Cut in butter as for pastry, stir in milk. Pat a small amount in bottom and up the sides of small muffin tins. Refrigerate while making filling. Mix sugar, butter, egg, potato, lemon rind, and juice together. Fill the tarts. Bake for 8 minutes at 300°F. Increase temperature to 375°F and bake until slightly brown, approximately 10 minutes. Makes about 20 1-1/2" tarts.

Admiring all the winning ribbons in 1957

SUNFLOWER COOKIES

A Red River Valley sunflower contest produced a winning cookie that is simply delectable.

- 2 cups sugar
- 3 cups flour
- 1 teaspoon soda
- 1 teaspoon baking powder
- 1 cup butter
- 1 cup shortening
- 1 teaspoon vanilla
- 1 cup toasted, salted sunflower meats
- 1 cup flake coconut

Mix dry ingredients, cut in butter and shortening. Add vanilla, sunflower meats, and coconut. Shape into four 2-inch diameter rolls and refrigerate 2 hours. Preheat oven to 350°F. Slice cold dough into cookies. Bake about 10 minutes. Makes about 9 dozen cookies.

APPLE CRUMBLE

4-H Club members published cookbooks with their favorite recipes and many of them were served at state fairs nationwide.

- 4–5 cups sliced baking apples
- 1/2 cup water
- 1 teaspoon cinnamon
- 1/3 cup granulated sugar
- 1/3 cup brown sugar
- 6 tablespoons butter, soft
- 1 cup flour
- 1/8 teaspoon salt
- 2 teaspoons vanilla
- 1/2 cup chopped almonds

Preheat oven to 350°F. Grease an 8x8-inch baking dish. Place apples in prepared dish. Pour 1/2 cup water over all. Sprinkle with cinnamon. In a bowl, cream together sugars and butter. Blend in flour, salt, vanilla, and almonds. Sprinkle mixture evenly over apples. Bake 40–50 minutes, until apples are tender and crust is golden.

Doing dishes at the 4-H Dining Hall, 1954

Nordic Ware, Unusual Old World and American Recipes, *1950s.*

PEACHES A LA CRÈME

Molds have been used to fashion dessert sculptures for hundreds of years and Nordic Ware makes beautiful shapes for cakes as well as exotic crèmes.

- 2 envelopes unflavored gelatin
- 1/3 cup water
- 1 cup half and half
- 16 ounces cream cheese, softened
- 2 cups cream
- 1 cup sugar
- 1 10-ounce package frozen peaches, thawed, finely diced
- 1 10-ounce package frozen peaches, thawed, sliced

Soften gelatin in 1/3 cup water. Scald half and half, add gelatin, stir until dissolved. Cool. Beat cream cheese until light. Slowly beat in cream. Add sugar. Add diced peaches. Combine with half and half mixture. Pour into lightly oiled ring mold or custard cups. Refrigerate several hours until set. Unmold; add peach slices.

DESSERT PEARS

Pears appeared in fruit competition at the Minnesota State Fair as early as 1880. This recipe will brighten up the end of any meal.

- 4 tablespoons butter
- 1-1/4 cups brown sugar
- 5 pears, quartered and cored
- 3/4 cup sour cream
- 1/2 cup chopped walnuts or pecans

Preheat oven to 400°F. Melt butter in the oven in an 8x8-inch square or round pan. Remove from oven. Sprinkle sugar over melted butter, add pears and turn to coat with butter and sugar sauce. Bake 20–30 minutes until slightly soft, basting with sauce two or three times during the baking. Transfer pears to dessert plates. Spoon sour cream, extra sauce, and nuts on top. Makes 5 servings.

Watkins Home Doctor and Cookbook, *1913.*

ALMOND PISTACHIO BISQUE ICE CREAM

Watkins booths have been popular State Fair attractions for decades. Their books provide hundreds of creative recipes using everyday spices and nuts. Pistachios were a favorite nut in the early 1900s.

- 2-1/2 cups milk
- 3 eggs
- 1 cup sugar
- 1/2 cup almonds, finely chopped
- 3/4 cup pistachios, shelled, peeled, finely chopped
- 1 teaspoon almond extract
- 1 tablespoon vanilla extract
- 1 cup heavy whipping cream

Whisk together milk, eggs, sugar, and nuts until smooth. Pour into a heavy saucepan. Cook over low heat until mixture thickens, about 20 minutes. Do not boil or it will curdle. Cool. Stir in vanilla and almond extracts. Whip cream and fold into mixture. Pour into bowl that fits in freezer compartment. Every 30 minutes, pull the bowl out and mix ingredients until frozen. To serve, place in refrigerator for 1 hour, stir well before spooning into bowls.

Cookin' with Honey, All-Honey Recipes, *1974*

MINNESOTA HONEY SUNDAE

From the Minnesota Beekeepers Association comes a State Fair favorite.

- Vanilla ice cream
- Honey
- Salted sunflower nut-meats

Drizzle honey over scoops of ice cream, top with salted sunflower meats.

ADD CHOCOLATE SAUCE FOR A TRULY DECADENT TREAT:

- 1 cup chocolate chips
- 1/2 cup honey
- 3/4 cup evaporated milk

Melt chocolate. Add milk and honey and blend. Makes 1-3/4 cups.

Cakes

State Fair ribbon winners, renowned milling companies, newspaper columnists, exhibitors, 4-H'ers, and Betty Crocker provided fairgoers with wondrous assortments of cake and frosting recipe combinations. Many are time-honored classics from the early 1900s.

The following recipes may have been adapted for easy preparation, modern cooking methods, or ingredients that are readily available.

CHEESECAKE WITH FARMER'S CHEESE

Cheesecake-making skills are considered high art at the fair. Tasters said this cheesecake was just right—not too dense, not too fluffy, not too cheesy.

- 6 tablespoons butter
- 1/2 cup sugar
- 1 teaspoon vanilla
- 2 cups graham cracker crumbs, divided
- 2 8-ounce packages cream cheese
- 1 cup farmer's or ricotta cheese
- 1-1/2 cups sugar
- 4 eggs, slightly beaten
- 3 tablespoons flour
- 1-1/2 teaspoons vanilla
- 2 cups sour cream
- 1/2 cup butter, melted

Preheat oven to 375°F. Cream butter, sugar, and vanilla together. Blend in 1-3/4 cups graham cracker crumbs. Press into a 10-inch spring-form pan or baking dish. Bake for 8 minutes, cool.

Cream together cream cheese and farmer's or ricotta cheese. Beat in sugar and eggs until smooth. Add flour and vanilla. Stir in sour cream and butter; mix thoroughly. Pour into prepared pan. Sprinkle remaining graham cracker crumbs on top. Bake at 325°F for about 1 hour 15 minutes. Cool and refrigerate. Serve with raspberry sauce.

Cheese on display for State Fair competition.

ZUCCHINI FUDGE CAKE

This popular 4-H recipe combination won praises from the baker and her fellow tasters.

- 1/2 cup butter, softened
- 1/2 cup vegetable oil
- 1-3/4 cups sugar
- 2 eggs
- 1 teaspoon vanilla
- 1/2 cup buttermilk
- 2-1/2 cups flour
- 1/3 cup cocoa
- 1 teaspoon soda
- 1 teaspoon baking powder
- 1/2 teaspoon salt
- 1/2 teaspoon cinnamon
- 1/3 cup chopped nuts
- 2 cups finely diced zucchini
- 1/4 cup chocolate chips
- 1/4 cup brown sugar
- 1/4 cup chopped nuts

Preheat oven to 325°F. Grease and flour a 9x13-inch pan. Cream butter with oil and sugar. Slowly beat in eggs, vanilla, and buttermilk. In a separate bowl, combine dry ingredients. Slowly beat this into the creamed mixture. Stir in zucchini. Pour batter into pan. Sprinkle with chocolate chips, brown sugar, and chopped nuts. Bake 40–45 minutes.

APPLE CAKE WITH CARAMEL SAUCE

The best of Minnesota apple recipes from State Fair exhibitors Alice and Gary McDougall.

- 1/2 cup oil
- 1-1/2 cups sugar
- 2 eggs
- 1 teaspoon vanilla
- 2 cups flour
- 1 teaspoon soda
- 1/2 teaspoon salt
- 1 teaspoon cinnamon
- 1 teaspoon nutmeg
- 4 cups diced apples
- 1/2 cup chopped walnuts
- 1/2 cup raisins (optional)

Preheat oven to 350°F. Grease and flour a bundt or deep cake pan. Blend together oil, sugar, eggs, and vanilla. Add flour, soda, salt, cinnamon, and nutmeg. Fold in apples, walnuts, and raisins. Bake for 55–60 minutes.

SERVE WITH CARAMEL SAUCE:

- 1/2 cup white sugar
- 1/2 cup brown sugar
- 1/2 cup cream
- 1/2 cup butter

Combine, stir over medium heat until thick.

RHUBARB COCONUT CAKE

A winning combination for all that rhubarb in the garden is from the *4-H Sampler Cook Book.*

- 1-1/2 cups brown sugar
- 1/2 cup butter or margarine
- 1 egg
- 1 cup sour or buttermilk
- 2 cups flour
- 1/2 teaspoon salt
- 1 teaspoon soda
- 1 teaspoon vanilla
- 1-1/2 cups rhubarb, chopped
- 1/2 cup walnuts, chopped

Preheat oven to 350°F. Mix all cake ingredients together. Put in a 9x13-inch cake pan.

MIX TOPPING:

- 1/2 cup sugar
- 1 teaspoon cinnamon
- 1/2 cup coconut

Sprinkle on top of cake. Bake 30–45 minutes.

CARROT CAKE WITH CREAM CHEESE ICING

A classic from the 1940s and described as a family standby from Virginia Roberts at Occident Flour.

- 1 cup all-purpose flour
- 1 teaspoon baking soda
- 1 teaspoon baking powder
- 1 teaspoon cinnamon
- 1/2 teaspoon salt
- 2/3 cup vegetable oil
- 1 cup sugar
- 2 beaten eggs
- 1/3 cup chopped walnuts
- 1-1/2 cups grated carrots

Preheat oven to 325°F. Grease and flour one 8-inch square pan. Sift together flour, soda, baking powder, cinnamon, and salt. In a separate bowl, beat together oil, sugar, and eggs. Add to dry ingredients. Blend in nuts and carrots. Pour into pan. Bake for 45–60 minutes until toothpick inserted in center comes out clean.

FROST WITH CREAM CHEESE FROSTING:

- 1/4 cup butter, softened
- 8 ounces cream cheese, softened
- 1-2 cups powdered sugar, sifted
- 1 teaspoon vanilla
- Grated lemon rind

In medium bowl, thoroughly beat cream cheese and butter. Gradually add powdered sugar and beat until smooth. Beat in vanilla extract, and lemon rind.

Occident Home Baking Institute, 1944

CHOCOLATE CAKE WITH CHOCOLATE FROSTING

A 1950s Mary Hart column favorite from 14-year-old prize-winner Nancy Bolduc.

- 1-1/2 cups sugar
- 1/2 cup butter
- 1 teaspoon vanilla
- 3 eggs separated
- 2 cups cake flour
- 1 teaspoon baking powder
- 1 teaspoon soda
- 1 cup milk
- 2 squares chocolate

Preheat oven to 350°F. Grease 2 round layer cake pans. Cream sugar and butter, add vanilla and egg yolks. Sift together flour, baking powder, and soda. Melt chocolate. Add dry ingredients and milk alternately to the creamed mixture. Add chocolate. Fold in stiffly beaten egg whites. Pour batter into cake pans. Bake 30 minutes.

FROST WITH CHOCOLATE FROSTING:

- 2 tablespoons shortening
- 1 tablespoon butter
- 2 squares semi-sweet chocolate
- 5 tablespoons cream
- 2 cups sifted powdered sugar
- 1/2 teaspoon vanilla

Melt shortening and butter together. Melt chocolate separately, add to shortening. Add powdered sugar. Add heated cream a little at a time, mix in vanilla.

LEMON CHIFFON CAKE

Great State Fair Recipes by ribbon-winner Margaret P. Boyd

- 2-1/4 cups sifted cake flour
- 1-1/2 cups sugar
- 3 teaspoons baking powder
- 1 teaspoon salt
- 1/2 cup oil
- 6 egg yolks, unbeaten
- 3/4 cup cold water
- 1 tablespoon grated lemon rind
- 6 egg whites
- 1/2 teaspoon cream of tartar

Set out a 10-inch angel food tube pan. Preheat oven to 325°F. In mixing bowl, sift together flour, sugar, baking powder, and salt. Make a well in center and add oil, egg yolks, water, and rind. Beat until smooth. In another bowl beat egg whites and cream of tartar until they form very stiff peaks. Pour egg yolk mixture gradually over beaten egg whites, gently fold with rubber scraper until blended. Pour into ungreased pan. Bake for 65 minutes. Invert and let hang until cold. Serve slices with fresh strawberries and whipped cream.

PINEAPPLE UPSIDE DOWN CAKE

Betty Crocker's pineapple upside down cake was the pick for the best recipe of 1924.

- 1 cup soft butter, divided
- 1 cup sugar
- 3 eggs
- 2 cups flour
- 2 teaspoons baking powder
- 1/2 teaspoon salt
- 2/3 cup whole milk
- 1 teaspoon vanilla
- 1 cup brown sugar
- 1-1/2 cups pineapple pieces, very well drained
- 6 maraschino cherries, halved
- 1/2 cup chopped walnuts

Preheat oven to 350°F. In a large bowl cream 1/2 cup butter and sugar. Add well-beaten eggs. Sift flour with baking powder and salt. Add to mixture alternately with milk and vanilla. Melt remaining 1/2 cup butter in a round 10-inch baking dish or ovenproof skillet. Whisk in brown sugar until smooth. Arrange pineapple, cherries, and walnuts on brown sugar. Spoon cake batter over mixture in pan. Bake for 40–50 minutes. When cake is done, remove from oven, put large plate on top of baking dish, carefully turn upside down. Allow syrup to run on cake a few minutes before removing baking dish. Serves 8.

CRUMB CAKE

During wartime in 1943, General Mills kitchens developed recipes using limited food products—and they were good.

- 2 cups sifted Gold Medal flour
- 1 cup sugar
- 1 teaspoon each cloves, nutmeg, and cinnamon
- 1/2 teaspoon salt
- 1/2 cup shortening
- 1 teaspoon soda
- 1 cup buttermilk
- 1 egg, beaten
- 1 teaspoon vanilla
- 2 tablespoons molasses

Preheat oven to 350°F. Grease and flour an 8-inch square pan. In large bowl, sift together flour, sugar, spices, and salt. Cut in shortening until very fine. Remove half of mixture for topping. Dissolve soda in buttermilk. To mixture in bowl, mix in egg, vanilla, and molasses. Add buttermilk and soda. Pour into pan, sprinkle reserved crumb mixture over top. Bake 30–40 minutes. Makes 9 servings.

Beginning in the 1920s, Betty Crocker State Fair Cooking Schools were packed with eager learners.

Betty Crocker's Minnesota Kitchen, 1970s

Betty Crocker's 15 prize recipes from 1921 to 1936; Your Share, how to prepare appetizing, healthful meals with foods available today, 1943

Coupon for a Gold Medal cookbook, 1910

Pies & Puddings

Pies were the preferred dessert in dining halls at the State Fair until sweets on a stick came along. But milling companies and fruit exhibitors made sure everyone had a souvenir or recipe booklet to make their favorite Midwest desserts at home.

The following recipes may have been adapted for easy preparation, modern cooking methods, or ingredients that are readily available.

APPLE PIE

Ann Pillsbury's 1945 recipe book provided "basic recipes with fascinating variations to help make your baking fun." Modern bakers may want to use refrigerated pie crust, and add extra sugar and cinnamon, plus a pinch of nutmeg.

- Pastry for 2-crust pie
- 6 cups tart cooking apples, pared and sliced
- 2 tablespoons flour
- 1/2 cup sugar
- 1/4 cup brown sugar, firmly packed
- 1/2 teaspoon cinnamon
- 1/8 teaspoon salt
- 1 tablespoon lemon juice
- 1/4 cup butter

Preheat oven to 400°F. Fit one pastry loosely in 9-inch pie pan. Trim and brush lightly with butter. Put apples in pan. Combine dry ingredients and sprinkle over apples. Dot with lemon juice and butter. Moisten edges of pastry, place second pastry over top and seal edges with fork or fingers. Cut a few gashes in center for steam. Sprinkle sugar on top. Bake for 15 minutes, then reduce heat to 350°F and bake for 45–55 minutes, or until apples are tender.

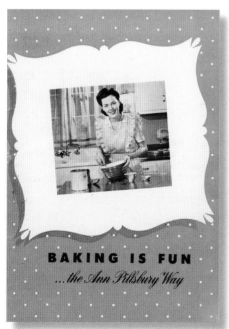

BAKING IS FUN
...the Ann Pillsbury Way

Baking is Fun . . . the Ann Pillsbury Way, 1945

State Fair fruit display, 1911

GRANNY'S STRAWBERRY PIE

This simple pie from the 4-H "Whistling Workers" in the 1984 cookbook was described as simply exquisite.

- 1 baked cooled pie shell
- 1/4 cup cold water
- 1/2 cup sugar
- 3 tablespoons cornstarch
- 4 cups sliced strawberries
- 1 teaspoon lemon juice
- 4 cups whole strawberries

Heat water, sugar, and cornstarch. Mix in sliced strawberries. Cook about 10 minutes until mixture is clear and thick. Add lemon juice. In cooled pie shell, place 2 cups whole strawberries. Pour cooked mixture over all. Add remaining strawberries on top. Cool in refrigerator. Serve topped with ice cream or whipped cream.

BLUEBERRY-GRAHAM-CRACKER PIE

This popular 1950s recipe is easy and delicious when cold-weather cravings for blueberry pie become irresistible.

- 1/2 cup butter, melted
- 16 graham crackers, rolled fine
- 1/4 cup brown sugar
- 1 8-ounce package cream cheese, softened
- 1/2 cup sugar
- 2 eggs
- 1 teaspoon vanilla
- Cinnamon
- 1 lemon juice
- 1 can blueberry pie filling

Preheat oven to 375°F. Mix butter, crackers, and brown sugar; press into bottom and sides of a 9-inch pie pan. Beat cream cheese, sugar, eggs, and vanilla, and pour over cracker crust. Bake for 15 minutes. Remove from oven and sprinkle with cinnamon. When cooled, mix lemon juice and pie filling and pour over custard. Refrigerate pie for several hours.

SOUR CREAM RHUBARB PIE

When the rhubarb plant is poking up pretty pink stalks, this is the pie to make.

- 1 deep dish pie crust
- 2 eggs
- 3/4 cup dairy sour cream
- 1-1/4 cups sugar
- 2 tablespoons flour
- 1-1/2 teaspoons vanilla
- 1/2 teaspoon salt
- 3 cups chopped fresh rhubarb
- 1/4 cup packed brown sugar
- 1/4 cup flour
- 1/8 teaspoon cinnamon
- 3 tablespoons butter

Preheat oven to 450°F. Bake pie shell per directions. In a large mixing bowl, stir together eggs and sour cream. Stir in sugar, flour, vanilla, and salt. Stir in chopped rhubarb. Pour the filling into the baked pastry crust. Cover pie loosely with foil. Bake in a 450°F oven for 15 minutes. In a small mixing bowl, stir together brown sugar, flour, and cinnamon. Cut in butter until mixture resembles course crumbs. Take pie from oven, remove foil, and sprinkle with topping mix. Bake uncovered for an additional 30–40 minutes until filling is set. Serves 8.

THE OCCIDENT PANTRY PALS INVITE YOU TO TRY
OCCIDENT FLOUR *Tested Recipes*

Occident Flour Tested Recipes with Pantry Pals Speedie, Tastie, and Easie, 1950s

Occident Mills packaging flour, 1900

LEMON MERINGUE PIE

Great State Fair Recipes from Emmaus Lutheran Church included a satin-smooth filling and an easy mix-and-press crust for those who hate to roll pie crust.

- 1-1/2 cups flour
- 1 tablespoon sugar
- 1/2 teaspoon salt
- 1/2 cup oil
- 3 tablespoons milk

Preheat oven to 375°F. With a fork, thoroughly mix all ingredients together in a 9" pie pan. Press mixture evenly and firmly over the sides and bottom of pan with floured fingers. Prick with fork and bake 15 minutes or until browned.

PIE FILLING:

- 1-1/2 cups sugar
- 1/3 cup cornstarch
- 2 tablespoons flour
- 1-1/2 cups hot water
- 3 slightly beaten egg yolks
- 3 tablespoons butter
- 1/2 teaspoon grated lemon peel
- 1/2 cup lemon juice

In a saucepan mix sugar, cornstarch, and flour. Gradually stir in hot water. Bring to a boil, stirring constantly. Reduce heat, cook and stir 5 minutes. Stir small amount of hot mixture into egg yolks, then return to hot mix. Bring to boil and cook 4 minutes, stirring constantly. Add butter and lemon peel. Slowly add lemon juice. Pour into shell.

MERINGUE:

- 3 egg whites
- 1/4 teaspoon cream of tartar
- 6 tablespoons sugar

Preheat oven to 400°F. Beat egg whites and cream of tartar until foaming. Gradually add sugar, beating to dissolve sugar and form stiff peaks. Immediately spread over hot filling, sealing edges well. Bake for 10–12 minutes until delicately brown. Cool.

Sleepy Eye Flour Mills hot weather fan for the fair

CLASSIC PUMPKIN PIE

The 1886 issue of the *Farmer* magazine suggested that pumpkin pie is appreciated at harvest time by the farm hands, but carrots are a great substitute—and anyone who could tell the difference would be smarter than most. To take the test, simply substitute mashed carrots for the pumpkin.

- Pastry in 9-inch pie
- 1-3/4 cups cooked mashed pumpkin or canned pumpkin (15-ounce can)
- 1/2 cup brown sugar
- 1/2 cup white sugar
- 1/2 teaspoon salt
- 1 teaspoon cinnamon
- 1/4 teaspoon ginger
- 1/4 teaspoon nutmeg
- 1 cup milk or evaporated milk
- 3 eggs, beaten

Heat oven to 450°F. Combine pumpkin, sugars, and seasonings. Heat milk. Combine with pumpkin. Add beaten eggs and stir thoroughly. Pour into pie shell and bake for 10 minutes. Reduce heat to 350°F and continue baking for about 40–45 minutes or until knife inserted in center comes out clean. Cool and serve with cinnamon whipped cream.

State Fair display of pumpkins and gourds, 1911

BLUEBERRY PUDDING BOWL

This very old-fashioned pudding sat on the back of a wood-burning stove and stayed warm until dinner was finished.

- 1/2 cup butter
- 1-1/4 cups sugar
- 1 teaspoon cinnamon
- 5 cups slightly-dry bread cubes
- 4 cups blueberries
- 1/2 cup water
- Cream or milk

Preheat oven to 325°F. Butter a medium baking dish. Cream butter and sugar. Add cinnamon, bread cubes, blueberries, and water; mix thoroughly. The mixture will be rather dry. Put into baking dish. Bake for about 45 minutes. Serve warm drenched with cream or milk. Makes 6 servings.

Gardeners Association, 1911

BREAD PUDDING

Leftover bread goes straight into a flavorful pudding, along with a decadent whiskey sauce.

- 10 slices white bread
- 6 tablespoons butter, softened
- 1-1/2 cups half-and-half
- 1 cup whole milk
- 4 large eggs
- 1/2 cup sugar
- 1 teaspoon Watkins vanilla
- 1/4 teaspoon Watkins almond extract
- Dash cinnamon
- 1/4 teaspoon salt

Preheat oven to 350°F. Butter a 2-1/2 or 3-quart baking dish. Butter bread and cut into cubes. Arrange evenly in baking dish. Whisk together half-and-half, eggs, sugar, vanilla, almond, cinnamon, and salt, making sure sugar is dissolved. Pour pudding mix over bread, pushing bread down to absorb liquid. Let set 15 minutes. Bake for 50–60 minutes, until custard is still soft in the middle. It will continue cooking when removed from oven.

SERVE WARM WITH WHISKEY SAUCE:

- 1/2 cup butter, melted
- 1/2 cup sugar
- 1 egg
- 1/4 to 1/2 cup bourbon whiskey

Melt butter in saucepan, add sugar and egg, whisking to blend well. Cook over low heat, stirring constantly, until mixture thickens. Whisk in bourbon to taste.

J. R. Watkins Company, Winona, 1940s

Preserves & Candies

Once a requirement for storing fruit and vegetables over long winters, jams, jellies, conserves, and pickles became State Fair competition fundamentals. Canners arrived with colorful jars and high hopes of winning a ribbon. Great State Fair Recipes provided savory combinations, and for those who don't can, freezing preserves colors and flavors.

For food safety when canning and preserving, follow guidelines for handling of jars and processing available from your county extension office.

The following recipes may have been adapted for easy preparation, modern cooking methods, or ingredients that are readily available.

OVERNIGHT RASPBERRY JAM

From *Great State Fair Recipes* and Mrs. Roy A. Johnson.
- 4 cups sugar
- 4 cups raspberries
- 2 tablespoons water
- 1 tablespoon lemon juice

Boil sugar, berries, and water together for 8 minutes. Add lemon juice and stir well. Let stand for 24 hours in an open crock. Stirring occasionally. Put jam in sterilized jars; seal. Store in refrigerator or freezer.

Tupperware State Fair Booth, 1950s

APPLE BLUEBERRY JAM

This no-nonsense ribbon winner appeared in the *Minneapolis Tribune* Mary Hart column, from Mrs. Augusta Carlson in 1950.
- 2 cups blueberries
- 2 cups apples, cored and diced
- 3-1/2 cups sugar

Boil until thick or until jam sets when dropped onto chilled saucer. Put into hot sterilized jars and seal.

CRANBERRY RELISH

From *Great State Fair Recipes* and Annemarie Plunkett.
- 4 cups fresh cranberries, washed
- 10 ounces orange marmalade
- 1 lemon
- 1 orange
- 1/8 teaspoon salt

Put cranberries in a food processor, cover and process until evenly chopped. Some berries will remain whole. Blend the chopped berries with orange marmalade. Add the juice of a lemon and orange. Add salt. Bring just to a boil. Ladle into sterilized jars, cover with 1/8-inch hot paraffin, tilting jars in a circular motion to achieve a tight seal.

Kerr, a "Jarring Experience," 1935

WATERMELON PICKLES

Great State Fair Recipes, Mrs. Ralph Buzick
- Rind from 1 watermelon (2 pounds)
- 4 tablespoons Kosher noniodized pickling salt
- 4 cups sugar
- 2 cups white vinegar
- 1 tablespoon broken cinnamon sticks
- 1-1/2 teaspoon whole cloves

Trim off all green and pink part of rind. Cut rind into 1" cubes. Soak overnight in salt water (4 tablespoons salt to 1 quart water.) Drain and cover with fresh water and cook until almost tender. Drain watermelon. Make a syrup of sugar, vinegar, and spices. Heat to boiling. Allow to set for 15 minutes. Strain out spices. Add the drained rind and cook until clear and transparent. Pack in pint jars and seal. Process in a boiling water bath canner 5 minutes.

Canning was important during the early 1900s. Boys and Girls Clubs demonstrated the latest techniques from the University of Minnesota.

TOMATO PEACH CHUTNEY

2005 Blue Ribbon Honey Recipes, Sonia Jacobsen
- 2-1/2 cups tomatoes, peeled, chopped, and seeded
- 2 cups peaches, peeled, chopped
- 1 cup green pepper, chopped
- 1-1/3 cups honey
- 3/4 cup white vinegar
- 1/2 cup golden raisins
- 1/2 cup onion, chopped
- 1 teaspoon curry powder
- 1/2 teaspoon ground ginger

In a large saucepan, combine all ingredients. Cook over medium heat for 1 hour or until thickened. Stirring frequently. Ladle hot chutney into sterilized jars and seal. Makes 1-1/2 pints.

PLUM CHUTNEY

As an appetizer, serve this old-fashioned chutney on top of farmer's cheese or cream cheese with crackers.
- 5 cups ripe plums, cut in chunks
- 1-1/2 cups golden raisins
- 1 cup candied ginger, coarsely chopped
- 3 cups sugar
- 2-1/2 cups apple cider vinegar
- 1/2 teaspoon salt
- 1/2 teaspoon ground cloves
- 1/2 teaspoon ground allspice
- 2 sticks cinnamon

Combine all ingredients in large saucepan. Heat to the boiling point, stirring frequently. Reduce heat and simmer uncovered 1-1/2 to 2 hours stirring often until mixture is thickened. Remove cinnamon sticks. Cool. Freezes well for future use.

Honey comes in colors: Dark honey is from bees that worked a field of buckwheat, medium, from fall wildflowers, light golden from clover and sunflowers, and white honey is from alfalfa fields or basswood trees.

HONEY MINT JELLY

Spoon this mint jelly over soft cheese such as farmer's or brie and serve with crackers. It is also the perfect accompaniment for lamb chops. *Great State Fair Recipes*, Mrs C. Arlt.
- 1 cup water
- 1/2 cup vinegar
- 1-3/4 cups sugar
- 1-3/4 cups honey
- 1/2 bottle liquid pectin
- Green food coloring
- 1/2–1 teaspoon spearmint extract

Mix together water, vinegar, sugar, and honey in a medium saucepan. Bring to a boil. Add pectin and boil 1/2 minute. Remove from heat. Add spearmint. Cool and serve. To can, pour into sterilized glasses; pour paraffin to cover.

MUSTARD PICKLES

From *Great State Fair Recipes*, Mrs. Ernest Bach
- 3 quarts cucumbers, sliced
- 1/2 pint onion slices
- 1 cup salt
- 1/2 cup flour
- 2 tablespoons mustard
- 2 tablespoons turmeric
- Vinegar
- 2 cups sugar

Put cucumbers and onion in salt brine overnight (1 gallon water and 1 cup salt.) Mix flour, mustard, turmeric, and a little vinegar to mix. Put mixture in a one-quart container and fill to capacity with vinegar. Transfer to saucepan, add sugar, cucumbers, and onions and bring to a boil. Boil until they turn color, stirring continually. Put in jars and seal.

Sliced pickles ready for the judges, 2006

HONEY CARAMEL CORN

There is popcorn and then there is Honey Caramel Corn. This recipe from the Minnesota State Fair bee and honey superintendent would be the best.
- 4 quarts popped corn
- 2 cups nuts
- 3/4 cup honey
- 1/4 cup light corn syrup
- 1 cup brown sugar
- 1 teaspoon salt
- 1/2 cup butter
- 1 teaspoon vanilla
- 1 teaspoon baking soda

Preheat oven to 225°F. Place popped corn and nuts in an uncovered roasting pan. In a separate saucepan, boil honey, corn syrup, brown sugar, salt, and butter for five minutes, stirring constantly. Stir in vanilla and baking soda. Pour mixture over popcorn and nuts and stir to coat. Bake 1 hour, stirring at 15-minute intervals. Pour out to cool. Store in closed container.

Corn originally grew only in dark colors; golden corn has evolved over hundreds of years.

OLD FASHIONED PEANUT BRITTLE

4-H'ers gobbled up peanut brittle for extra energy on fairground treks in 1984.
- 2 cups sugar
- 1 cup light corn syrup
- 1/2 cup water
- 1 cup butter
- 2 cups raw peanuts
- 1 teaspoon baking soda

In 3-quart saucepan, heat together sugar, corn syrup and water, stirring until sugar dissolves. When syrup boils, blend in butter. Stir frequently. Add peanuts when temperature reaches 280° F on a candy thermometer. Stir constantly to 305°F; remove from heat. Quickly stir in baking soda, mixing well. Pour onto two buttered cookie sheets. Loosen from pans when candy hardens. Break into pieces. Makes 2-1/2 pounds.

COCOA FUDGE

Making good use of their products, Watkins produced great recipe booklets for 1935 homemakers to pick up at the fair.
- 2 cups sugar
- 2/3 cup milk
- 1/3 cup Watkins cocoa
- 2 tablespoons butter
- 1 tablespoon vinegar
- 1 teaspoon Watkins vanilla
- 1 cup chopped walnuts

Cook sugar, milk, and cocoa together until boiling. Add butter and vinegar. Boil, stirring until soft ball stage. Remove from fire, allow to cool to lukewarm without stirring, then beat until it loses its shiny appearance. Add nuts and vanilla. Pour into buttered 8x8-inch pan. When firm, cut in squares.

Watkins Almanac, 1935

TEN-MINUTE PICKLES

These amazingly delicious pickles may be a home-kitchen Blue Ribbon. Slightly sweet and slightly tangy, they keep for a long time refrigerated, but are usually gone within the week. Adding onion, garlic, dry mustard, or dill brings out different flavors.
- 1-3/4 cups sugar
- 2 teaspoons pickling salt
- 1 cup white vinegar
- 1 teaspoon celery seed
- 5 cucumbers, sliced across or lengthwise

Place cucumber pieces in 3–4 sterilized jars with lids. Heat sugar, salt, vinegar, and celery seed until sugar melts. Cool slightly. While still warm, pour over cucumbers in jars. Cover and refrigerate.

TOFFEE BARS

King Midas flour selected Baking Queen winning recipes each year. Mrs. Walfred Johnson won in the 1950s for these toffee bars.
- 2 cups sifted flour
- 1 cup brown sugar, packed
- 1 cup butter
- 1 egg yolk
- 1 6-ounce package semi-sweet chocolate pieces
- 1/2 cup chopped nuts

Preheat oven to 350°F. Combine flour and brown sugar in mixing bowl. Cut in butter and egg yolk until thoroughly blended. Pat into ungreased 15x10-inch jelly roll pan. Bake 10–22 minutes, until golden brown. Sprinkle immediately with chocolate pieces. Let stand a few minutes to melt, then spread evenly over surface. Sprinkle with nuts. Cut into bars while warm.

Baking Queens favorite recipes, 1950s

RAZZY TRUFFLES

From the Ghirardelli Chocolate Championship Blue Ribbon recipe contest, Loretta Ratajczyk won first place at the 2004 Minnesota State Fair for her razzy truffles.
- 3/4 cup butter, softened
- 1/4 cup raspberry preserves
- 1-1/2 teaspoons almond flavoring or extract
- 1/2 cup Ghirardelli Unsweetened Cocoa
- 1/2 teaspooon cinnamon
- 5 cups powdered sugar
- 1 tablespoon whipping cream
- 1 12-ounce package Ghiradelli Semi-Sweet Chocolate Chips

Cream butter on medium- to high speed with electric mixer. Add raspberry preserves and almond flavoring. In separate bowl, mix cocoa, cinnamon, and powdered sugar, and add to the above with the whipping cream. Mix until well blended. Chill until firm; at least one hour. Shape into approx. 1" balls. Melt the chocolate chips (double boiler recommended). Dip balls into the melted chocolate and place on a cookie sheet or other pan lined with parchment or wax paper. Refrigerate for a quick set up of the chocolate.

Recipe Index

APPETIZERS

Cheese Crisps, 189
Farmer's Cheese Cracker Spread, 188
Farmer's Cheese Dip, 188
Gedney Deviled Eggs, 189
Grandstand SPAM, 189
SPAMpendas, 188
Spiced Pecans, 189
Tangy Zucchini Squares, 189

BREAD

Cornbread, 191
Pillsbury Quick Nut and Fruit Bread, 190
Prize Winning Graham Bread, 190
State Fair Orange Bread, 190
State Fair Potato Bread, 188
State Fair's Best Bread, 190
Trailway Pumpkin Bread, 191

BREAKFAST ROLLS AND MUFFINS

Blueberry Tea Cake, 191
Ceresota Scotch Scones, 192
Corn Muffins, 190
Ham and Cheese Puffs, 192
Hidden Valley Potato Cheese Rolls, 191
Italian Crème Coffee Cake, 192
Lizzie's Cream Muffins, 193
Marjorie's Sour Cream Coffecake, 191
Old-Fashioned Cinnamon Rolls, 193

BREAKFAST EGGS AND PUDDINGS

Apple Oatmeal Crunch, 193
Baked Ham and Eggs, 192
Breakfast Bread Pudding, 192
Cream of Wheat Apple Bake, 193
Oven Apple Pancake, 193

BUTTER AND CHEESE

Making Butter, 188
Making Farmer's Cheese, 188

CAKES

Apple Cake with Caramel Sauce, 204
Carrot Cake and Cheese Icing, 204
Cheese Cake with Farmer's Cheese, 204
Chocolate Cake and Frosting, 205
Crumb Cake, 205
Lemon Chiffon Cake, 205
Pineapple Upside Down Cake, 205
Rhubarb Coconut Cake, 204
Zucchini Fudge Cake, 204

CANDY

Cocoa Fudge, 209
Honey Caramel Corn, 209
Old Fashioned Peanut Brittle, 209
Razzy Truffles, 209
Toffee Bars, 209

COOKIES

Butterscotch Ice Box, 202
Chocolate Chip, 202
Farmer's Cheese Cookies, 202
Lemon Cookie Tart, 202
Sunflower Cookies, 203

DESSERTS

Almond Pistachio Ice Cream, 203
Apple Crumble, 203
Chocolate Brownies, 202
Dessert Pears, 203
Minnesota Honey Sundae, 203
Peaches a la Crème, 203

FISH

Honey Fried Walleye, 196
Trout Sautéed with Bacon, 196

MAIN DISHES

Chicken Chow Mein, 196
Chicken Chun King, 200
Chinese Beef Hot Dish, 200
Fair Stand Chili Con Carne, 198
Turkey and Wild Rice Hot Dish, 200
Ham and Spaghetti Casserole, 200

MEATS

Baked Boneless Ham, 199
Beef Brisket with Onion Sauce, 199
Cranberry Pork Chops, 199
Farmhouse Roast Beef, 198
Hungarian Goulash, 198
Lamb Patties with Currant Sauce, 197
Oven Pork Roast, 199
Short Ribs in Dark Beer, 198
Sour Cream Lamb Stew, 197
State Fair Ham Loaf, 199
State Fair Meat Balls, 198
Sweet and Sour Pork, 199
Venison Collops, 197

POULTRY

Curried Chicken, 196
Hearty Turkey Pie, 197
Honey Ducks, 197
Honey Lemon Chicken, 196
Oven Barbecue Chicken, 196
Turkey with Fruit Sauce, 197
Smothered Pheasant or Grouse, 197

PRESERVES AND PICKLES

Apple Blueberry Jam, 208
Cranberry Relish, 208
Honey Mint Jelly, 208
Mustard Pickles, 209
Plum Chutney, 208
Raspberry Jam, 208
Ten-Minute Pickles, 109
Tomato Peach chutney, 208
Watermelon Pickles, 208

PUDDINGS AND PIES

Apple Pie, 206
Blueberry-Graham Cracker Pie, 206
Blueberry Pudding Bowl, 207
Bread Pudding, 207
Classic Pumpkin Pie, 207
Granny's Strawberry Pie, 206
Lemon Meringue Pie, 207
Sour Cream Rhubarb Pie, 206

SALADS

Creamette Shrimp Salad, 201
Fruit Salad with Tangy Dressing, 201
Turkey Chutney Salad, 201

SAUCES

Ham Raisin Sauce, 199
Orange Sauce from Witt's Market, 199

SOUP

Classic Wild Rice, 201
Navy Bean, 201
Split Pea, 200
Tomato, 201

VEGETABLES

Baked Beans, 195
Brussels Sprouts, 195
Butter Pecan Acorn Squash, 194
Corn Pudding with Chives, 194
Maple Walnut Carrots, 194
Onion Pie, 194
Orange Sweet Potatoes, 195
Potato Cheese Scallop, 195
Spinach au Gratin, 195
Sticks and Stones-peas and carrots, 194
Sweet and Sour Red Cabbage, 195
Zucchini Pancakes, 194

Food is the number one reason people go to the State Fair. We're thrilled to offer flavors of the fair in this book. Family friend Madeline Betsch took charge of an unusual variety of recipe sources. Her organizational knack and never-ending enthusiasm made short work of a towering stack of recipe publications—then she arranged for tastings "in the field" by friends and family.

Boundless gratitude goes to Ann Burckhardt, master cook of Minnesota food, who reviewed recipe collections from the State Fair Museum, antique booklets purchased at the fair, and handouts picked up from fair exhibitors. Ann cooked up solutions to recipe discrepancies and kneaded them into shape for modern kitchens.

Compliments to the Blue Ribbon Group, who arrange food company competitions for State Fairs in Minnesota and nationwide. They contributed winning recipes for SPAMpendas, Hidden Valley Potato Cheese Rolls, and Razzy Truffles.

Thanks go to recipe testing and tastings in the kitchens of: Pat Barker, Judith Benton, Margaret Johnson, Winnie Johnson, Marjorie Johnson, Christine Judge, Allan Klein, Lydia Kohls, Harriet Lansing, Anna LeSueur, Doug Oakley, Eleanor Oakley, Sandy Rensink, Lois Schlampp, Katie Searl, Jennifer Totoritis Searl, Lisa Sten, Janet Strand, Mary Jo Sutherland, and Tom Thomas.

Index

Principal entries for each topic are provided here. Entries noted in **boldface** refer to photographs.

Administration Building, **29**
Aerial acts, **84–85**
Agricultural products, 38, **44–55**
  corn and grain, **48–49**
  fruit, **52**
  honey, **53**
  produce, **55**
Air
  aeronauts, 70
  airplanes, **83**, **141**
  balloons, **19**, 70, **82**
  dirigibles, 70, **82**
  flying machines, 70
  thrill shows, **82–84**
  wing-walkers, 70, **83**
Amusements
  aerial acts, **84–85**
  areas, 96
  auto polo, **78**
  Bug House, **106**
  Dancing Waters, **107**
  daredevil auto, **78–80**
  demolition derby, **78–79**
  early, **21**
  fireworks, 70, **86–87**
  fortune-tellers, **96**, **97**
  fun house, **106**
  games, 21, **110**
  Glass House, **106**
  London Fog, **106**
  Lux Memory Doll House, **107**
  Midway, **94–113**
  motorcycles, **81**
  Motordrome, **107**
  races, **80–81**
  revues, **88**
  rides (*see* Rides)
  sham battles, **86**
  sideshows, **96–99**
  thrill shows, 70, **78–85**
    high-wire, **84**
    Swenson Thrillcade, **79**
  train crashes, **79**
Anderson, Governor Wendell, **159**
Animals
  buffalo, **68**
  cattle, 60, **61**
  dogs, **69**
  goats, **65**
  horses, **68**, **74–75**
  poultry, **67**
  sheep, **65**
  swine, **64**
Architects
  Brodi, James, 14
Architecture
  Beaux Arts, **32–33**
  exposition style, **30–31**
  farm style, **28–29**
  modern, **36–37**
  W.P.A. style, **34–35**
Art
  creative, **121**, **126–127**
  crop, **120**
  fine, **116–119**
  needlework, **124–125**

tree sculptures, **121**
Automobiles
  Acme Mfg. Co., **140**
  auto daredevils, **78–80**
  auto polo, **78**
  Chitwood, Joie, **78**
  demolition derby, **78–79**
  drivers, **76–77**
  exhibits, **140–141**
  Museum of Classic and Antique
    Cars, **140**
  Northwest Auto Show, **140**
  Pan Motor Co., **140**
  racing, **73**, **76–77**
  Swenson Thrillcade, **79**
Baked goods, **128–129**
Balloons, **82**
  ascension, **19**, 70
  race, **82**
Bands, **90–93**
  concert, 90
  marching, **93**
Bandstands, **90–92**
Barns (*see* Buildings)
Beekeeping, 53
Berg, Dr. Elmer, **62**
Bicycle daredevils, **80**
Bonnie & Clyde, **99**
Boyer, Lillian, **83**
Boys & Girls Club, **20**
Boy Scouts, **132**
Brodi, James, 14
Buildings
  History of, viii
  Administration, **29**, **37**
  Agricultural Hall, 9, 14
  Agriculture, 17, **45**
  Agriculture Horticulture, 17, **32**,
    35, **44**, **45**
  Aircraft Building, **141**
  Animal barns, **28**
  Arcade, **35**, **176**
  Baldwin Park Bandshell, **92**
  Bandshell, **92**
  Bee and Honey Exhibit, **53**
  CHS Miracle of Birth, **69**
  Cattle Barn, **28**, **33**, **60**
  Children's Barnyard, **69**
  Conservation, **168**
  Coliseum, **36**
  Creative Activities, **37**
  Dairy Animal Products, **36**
  Dairy/Fine Arts, **119**
  Dairy Hall, **30**, **33**
  Drivers Club, **30**
  Education, **36**
  Electric City, **37**
  Empire Commons, **36**
  Entrance, 13, **30**
  Exposition, 14
  Fair Administration Building, **37**
  Farm Boy's Camp, **23**
  Fine Arts, 33, **116**
  First Agriculture, **44**
  Food, **37**, **177**
  4-H, **34**, 67
  Fish and Game, **31**, **168**
  Food, **37**, **177**
  Grandstand, 12, **18–19**, **32**, **35**,
    70–73, 90
  Greenhouse, **22**
  Hippodrome/Coliseum, 58, **59**, 107
  Honey, **53**
  Horse, **34**

Institute Hall, **30**
Judging Arena, **60**
Judging stands, **73**
J. V. Bailey House, **22**
Livestock Amphitheater, 16,
  56–58, **140**
Machinery Hall, **31**, **40**
Main, 14, 15
Manufacturers/Women's, **32**, **122**
Merchandise Mart, **37**
Minnesota Building (St. Louis
  World's Fair), **123**
Minnesota Driving Club, **30**
Modern Living, **37**
Music Gazebo, **73**
Officer's Cottage, **22**
Plaza Park Bandstand, **91**
Poultry, **28**, **33**, 66
Progress Center, 33
Racetrack Club House, **122**
Rest Cottage (St. Louis World's
  Fair), **123**
Sheep and Poultry Barn, **34**
Sheep Barn, **28**
State Exhibits/Progress, **33**, **169**
State Fair Police Headquarters, **29**
State Fair Museum, **113**, **169**
State Fair Souvenir Shop, **37**
Streetcar entrance, 11
Swine Barn, **64**
Tent city, **23**
Territorial Pioneers Cabin, **169**
Warner Coliseum, Lee and Ann, **36**
Women's Building, **20**, **32**,
  114–115, **122–123**
"Bumper Crop Fair," 47
Canning, **130–131**
Carlson, Bill, **159**
Carnival companies
  Gaskill Carnival Company, **96**
  Philadelphia Toboggan Company,
    105
  Royal American Shows, **100–101**
Cash, Johnny, **89**
Cattle, **60–61**
  Campbell Aberdeen Angus, **61**
  Mayowood Farm Holstein, **61**
Celebrities, **89**
  Cash, Johnny, **89**
  Denver, John, **89**
  Hope, Bob, **89**
  Keillor, Garrison, **89**
  Linkletter, Art, **89**
  Nelson, Willie, **89**
Chickens (*see* Poultry)
Children
  Boys and Girls Clubs, **132**
  Boy Scouts, **132**
  Children's Barnyard, 134
  Education for, **132–133**
  4-H, **135**
  Farm Boys Camp, **134**
  FFA, 134
  Potato Club, **133**
  Style show, **133**
Clay, Cassius. M., 5
Cochran, Jay, **85**
Collections and crafts, **126–127**
Collins, Emory, **77**
Colton, Lillian, **120**
Commercial exhibits (*see* Exhibitors,
  commercial, and Concessionaires)
Commissioners, State Fair [cross-
  indexed by name]
Competitions

baking, **128–129**
canning, **130–131**
creative, **126–127**
crop art, **120**
fine arts, **116–119**
needlework, **124–125**
sand castle, **121**
Concessionaires
  auto and airplane, **140–141**
  department store, **148–149**
  farm, **142–143**
  grain and milling, **138–139**
  home appliance, **146–147**
  miscellaneous, **150–153**
  model farm and kitchen, **144–145**
  slicers and dicers, **154–155**
Contests
  Rooster Crowing, **66**
  talent, **93**
Cookbooks (*see* Recipes index)
Coolidge, Calvin, 29, **116**, **162**
Corn and grain, 48–49
County exhibits, **46–47**
  Isanti, **47**
  Meeker, **47**
  Olmsted, **46**
  Otter Tail, **47**
  Stearns County, **139**
  Washington, **47**
  Wilkin, **47**
Creative Arts
  baked goods, **128–129**
  canning, **130–131**
  collections and crafts, **126–127**
  needlework, **124–125**
Crops, **48–53**
Dairy
  barns (*see* Buildings)
  butter, **183**
  concessionaires, **182–183**
  Princess Kay, **182–183**
Dan Patch, **75**
Denver, John 89
Department of Natural Resources,
  168
Dining (*see* Food)
Dogs, 69
Ducks (*see* Poultry)
Eisenhower, Gen. Dwight D., 29
Employees, 1
Endicott, Wild Bill, **77**
Esterly reaper, 4
Exhibitors, commercial
  Adler Sewing Machine, **147**
  Airstream, **141**
  Berman Buckskin, **151**
  Boutell's, **149**
  Cargill, **138**
  Ceresota, 49
  Chef Harvey, **155**
  Claybourne, Pots, **113**
  Crane Ordway, **144**
  Credit River Stove Works, **113**
  Dayton's, **148**
  Donaldson's, **148**
  The Emporium, **148**
  Fairbanks, Morse & Co., **142**
  Faribault Woolen Mills, **150**
  Foot, Schulze & Co., **15**
  General Mills, 49
  Harley-Davidson, **141**
  C. J. Hoigaard Co., **23**
  Jewell Nursery, **17**, **55**
  Josten, **15**

Kemps ice cream, 53
King Koil, **149**
Lee Overalls, **42**
Maytag, **146**
Minnesota Tent and Awning, **23**
Montgomery Ward, **143, 148**
Nathan Ford, **15**
Neal, H. G., **23**
Northern States Power, **142**
Northrup King, **55, 138**
Northwestern Bell, **142**
Pillsbury, 15, 49, **91**
Pioneer Hybrid Corn, **48**
Portland Cement Co., **142, 143**
Red Wing Shoes, **151**
Robin Hood, 49
Sears Roebuck & Co., 29, **148**
Singer Sewing Machine, **147**
Swedish Clogs, **151**
Washburn Crosby, 49
Fairborne, State Fair mascot's nephew,
    121
Fairchild, State Fair mascot, **1, 121**
Fairgrounds
    Hamlin, **11–12**
    Kittonsdale, 8
Fairs
    agricultural, viii
    "Balloon," 4
    Bridge Square, 4
    Hamline, 11–12
    Minnesota Territorial Fair, 1, 2
    Owatonna State Fair, 7
    Red Wing state and county, 6, 93
    Rochester State Fair, 6
Farm Boys Camp, **23, 134**
Farmers' Institute, **30**
Farm machines, **20,** 142
    Allis-Chalmers, **41**
    Case Engine, **43**
    Fairbanks Morse & Co., **41**
    Farmall, **41**
    Ferguson Tractors, **41**
    Great Minneapolis Line, **40**
    Independent Silo Company, **40**
    International Harvester, **41**
    John Deere, **41**
    Minneapolis-Moline, **41**
    Oliver, **41**
    Twin City Gas Tractors, **40**
    Wege Concrete Machinery, **40**
Ferris, Carl, **83**
Fine Arts, **116–119**
Fireworks, 70, **86–87**
Flanagan, Barbara, **158**
Flowers, **54**
Food, **170–185**
    Arcade Building, **176**
    cafés and cafeterias, **174–175**
    church dining, **172–173**
    corndogs, pronto-pups, hotdogs,
        hamburgers, **180–181**
    Food Building, **177**
    stands, **178–179**
    sweets and treats, **184–185**
Fort Snelling, **5**
4-H, **135, 145**
FFA (Future Farmers of America),
    69, **134**
Frakes, Frank, **83**
Frost, Gale, **184**
Fruit, 52
    apples, **50,** 52
    strawberries, **52**

Games, 21, **110** (see Amusements)
Gardens
    flower, **22**
    Gates Ajar, **22**
    greenhouse, **22**
    Liberty Bell, **22**
Goats, **65**
Governors
    Johnson, John A., 72
    Ramsey, Alexander, 38, 63
Grandstand, 12, **18–19, 32, 35,**
    70–73, 90
Great Northern Railroad, **24**
Grimm, George, 106, 159
Hamline (Minn.), 1, 11
Hammond, V. O., **27**
Harding, Pres. Warren G., 29
Hart-Kaiser, **ix**
Haugdahl, Sig, **77**
Hayes, Pres. Rutherford B., 8, **162**
Heritage Square, 113
Hill, James J., 56, 58
Honey, **53**
Hope, Bob, **89**
Horses, 62–63
    Budweiser, **68**
    Clydesdales, **68**
    Dan Patch, **75**
    draft, 59, **62, 68**
    milk wagon competitions, 62
    racing, **74–75**
    riding, **63**
    rodeo, **68**
    Swift and Co., **68**
Jewell Nursery, **17, 55**
Johnson, Gov. John A., 72
Keillor, Garrison, **89**
Kiddieland, **105**
King, Col. William S., 9
Kinney, Sister, **167**
Le Duc, William G., 1
Linkletter, Art, **89**
Livestock shows, 56, **60**
Machinery Hill, **20, 40–43**
Maguire, Charlie (lyrics of), 27, 69,
    93, 113, 135, 155 185
Middleton, Kitty, **83**
Midway, 94–113
    amusements (see Amusements)
    carnival companies, **96, 100,** 105
    games, **110**
    revues, **88**
    rides, 21, **97-109**
    sideshows, **98–103**
    villages, **112**
Milling companies, 49
    Ceresota, 49
    General Mills, 49
    Pillsbury, 49
    Robin Hood, 49
    Washburn Crosby, 49
Minneapolis Woolen Mills, 9
Minnesota Fair Commissioners, 1
Minnesota State Agricultural Society,
    viii, 2, 5, 6, 9
Minnesota Territorial Fair, 1, 2, 4
Mondavi, Robert, **52**
Motorcycles, **81**
Natural Resources, Department of
    Conservation Building. **168**
Needlework, **124–125**
Nelson, Willie, **89**
News media, **156–159**
Oldfield, Barney, **77**

Owatonna, **6**
Parades
    cattle, **19, 59**
    draft horse, **59**
Parking lots, **25**
Pigs (see Swine)
Police, State Fair, 29
Political organizations, **160–161**
Politicians
    Clay, Cassius M., 5
    Coolidge, Pres. Calvin, 29, **162**
    Eisenhower, Gen. Dwight D., 29,
        163
    Hayes, Pres. Rutherford, 8, **162**
    Johnson, Gov. John A., 72
    Ramsey, Gov. Alexander, 38, 63
    Roosevelt, Pres. Theodore, 29, **162**
    Vilas, Col. William F., 6
Postcards, souvenir, **26,** 27
Postmark, State Fair, **26**
Poultry, **66**
Prize ribbons, ix
Programs, **16**
Races
    auto, **73, 76–77**
    balloon, **82**
    horse, **19, 74–75**
    motorcycle, **81**
    stock car, **77**
    tractor, **43**
Radio, **158**
Railroads
    Lake Superior & Mississippi, 8
    Minneapolis & St. Louis, **24**
    Northern Pacific, 8, **24**
    St. Paul & Pacific, 8
Ramsey County Poor Farm, 11, 29
Ramsey, Gov. Alexander, 38, 63
Recipes (see Recipes before general
    index)
Red Cross, **164**
Red Wing, **6**
Revues, **88, 107**
Rickenbacker, Eddie, **76**
Rides
    Astro-Liner, **108**
    Cannon Ball Coaster, **97**
    carousel, **105**
    Coney Island Switchback Railway,
        97
    Double Space Wheel, **100, 104,**
        109
    Ferris wheel, 101, **104**
    four-wheel Ferris wheel, **101, 104**
    Giant slide, **105**
    lagoon boat ride, **97**
    Mad Mouse, **109**
    Man in Space, **108**
    Matterhorn, **109**
    roller coaster, **21**
    Sky Ride, **108**
    Space Tower, **108**
    Super-Loop, **109**
    Thunder Bolt, **109**
    Tilt-A-Whirl, **105**
    train, 21, **105**
    Ye Old Mill, **104**
Ripley's, **98**
Rochester, **6**
Roosevelt, Pres. Theodore, 29, **162**
Roy, Gladys, **83**
Saint Paul Growers Association, **50**
Savage, Marion, 75
Schrader, Gus, **77**

Sedlmayr, Carl Jr. 85
Sellner, Herbert, 105
Sewing machines, **147, 152**
Sham battles, **86**
Sheep, **65**
Shows
    auto, **73, 78–79,** 136
    cattle, **60**
    fireworks, **85–86**
    horse, **59**
    Northwest Livestock, **60**
    revues, **88**
    sham battle, **86**
    thrill, 70, **79**
Sideshow girls, **102–103**
    Club Lido, **103**
    Covette, Ricki, **103**
    Gypsy Rose Lee, 102
    Rand, Sally, **102**
Sideshows, **96–103**
Sousa, John Philip, **90**
Souvenirs, 111
    chalkware, **111**
    postcard, **26–27**
Speece, Maynard, **159**
State Fair mascot, **1, 121, 214**
Steele Family Singers, **93**
Steichen's Store, **181**
Stevens, Col. John H., 56
Streetcars, **24**
Street names, i
Swine, **64**
Tent city, **23**
Territorial Capitol, **4**
Thrill shows (see Amusements)
Tractors, **42–43**
Train crashes, **79**
Turnblad, Swan, **76**
University of Minnesota, **45, 52, 145,**
    153, 167
U.S. Presidents
    Coolidge, Calvin, 29, **162**
    Harding, Warren G., 29
    Hayes, Rutherford B., 8, **162**
    Roosevelt, Theodore, 29, **162**
U.S. Supreme Court, 161
Vegetables
    corn, **48, 55**
    onions, **55**
    potatoes, 50, **51**
Veterinarians
    Berg, Dr. Elmer, **62**
Vilas, Col. William F., 6
Villages
    International, 112
    Mexican, 112
    Native American, 112
    Swedish, 112
Wallenda Family, **84**
Wars
    Spanish-American, **164,** 167
    World War I, **164**
    World War II, **165**
Wine, **52**
W.P.A. [Works Progress
    Administration], **34, 166–167**
Wright Company, **83**
Young America Center and Teen Fairs,
    113
Zacchini Act, **85**

Image Credits

MINNESOTA STATE FAIR

Photos not listed below are from Minnesota State Fair archives and museum.

HENNEPIN HISTORY MUSEUM

Newspaper, 11; crowd, 13; windmill, 28; fish and game, 31; horse in tent, 75; 1907 balloon race, 82; military band, 91; 1908 Auto show, 140

MINNESOTA HISTORICAL SOCIETY

Reaper, Whitney's Gallery, 4; Capitol, 4; store, 7; piano, 15; oval, 18; train, 21; train, 24; main gate, 25; main entrance, 25; police, 29; Institute Hall, 30; WPA artist, 34; stone cutters, 35; Machinery Hill, 40; prize-winning wheat, Paul W. Hamilton, 49; woman with flour, Kenneth M. Wright, 49; produce man, Paul W. Hamilton, 50; exhibit building, 53; 1930 tower, 73; 1925 race, 74; horse in blanket, 75; Kiser, 76; Schraeder, 77; elephant, Charles P. Gibson, 79; start of race, George E. Luxton, 82; flame diver, W. Allen Mortenson, 85; Pillsbury band, Charles P. Gibson, 91; sideshow, 1917, 96; fat people, 98; midway, Steve Plattner, 99; fan dancer, Kenneth M. Wright, 102; slide, Steve Plattner, 105; village, Potter-Hibbard, 112; Indian village, Monroe P. Killy, 112; Fine art galleries, Works Progress Administration, 116; Clement Haupers, WPA painter, potter, 117; Lillian Colton, 120; nursery, 123; hooked rug demonstration, 125; cutwork, Kenneth M. Wright, 125; who won, 130; 1932 boys, 132; state breadmaking contest, 132; declamation winners, 133; Pan Motor Co., H. M. Schawang, 140; Harley-Davidson, 141; model kitchen, 144; League of Women Voters, 160; women at republican party, 161; Dewey booth, George Miles Ryan, 163; Red cross, 164; peace headquarters, 165; display building, Works Progress Administration, 166; Federal Art Project, Kenneth M. Wright, 166; all other WPA photos, 166; WPA, Sister Kenny, 167; cabin interior, 169; volunteer cook, 172; 1924 milk stand, *Minneapolis Journal*, 182; two girls, frozen delight, Steve Plattner, 185

OLMSTED HISTORICAL SOCIETY, AL CALVANO

Scale, 7; menu, 7; Olmsted display, 46

INDIVIDUALS

A Prairie Home Companion, vii, 89

Bruce Adomeit: *Minneapolis Journal* photo, 157

Carol Brekken: judge badge, 44; badge, 49; vase, pillow, 111

Chuck and Margaret Donley: Cotton Candy, 185

Enestvedt's Seed Co: 139

Epiphany Church: 172

Barbara Flanagan: 158

Bob Johnson: Turnblad, 76

Ron Kelsey: 191

Marcia McEachron: Tumbelina, 178

Midwest Dairy Association: Thatcher and Bracken, 185

Richard Mueller: cheese curds, 177

Keith Olson: Portland Cement, 142

Chuck and Genee Parrish: Fairchild; 1911 bandstand, 91; cigar, 111; Minnesota Building, 123, farm boys camp, 134; Donaldson's Glass Block, 148

Addie Pittelkow: milk pail, 182

H. Rosenhaus: Chef Harvey items, 155

Carolyn "Lynn" Staff: Lefse photo, 177

Jimmy Steichen: 1940 photo, 181

Janet Strand: piggy bank, 111

KATHRYN KOUTSKY AND LINDA KOUTSKY

Real estate office, old view, 4; balloon, 9; expo, 9; overview, 11; shoe-makers, 15; exterior, 16; postcard, 16; prize herd, 16; interior, 17; 1905, 18; ticket, 19; exhibit, 20; necklace, 21; entrance, 22; tent city, 23; badge, 24; streetcar, 24; postcards, 26, 27; administration, 29; Grandstand, Manufacturer's, Agriculture Building, 31; Poultry, Dairy Buildings, 33; Case, 43; dome, 44; memo book, 49; Jewell postcard, 55; Swift, 68; Dan Patch illustration, music, 75; race programs 1924, 1952, 76; postcard, 77; postcard, 83; Lindquist, 90; second bandstand, 91; double space wheel, 104; cat, panda, 110; shopping, 119; state exhibits, 123; dress, 124; sidebar photos, 126; cakes and breads, 129; product shots, 131; Olson images, 133; Northrup King, 138; postcard, 142; Portland Cement, 143; U of M brochure, 134; Harper's, Franklin Mint, 162; buttons, 163; ad, 175; menu, 176; Ive's, 184.

KENT FLEMMER AND ANITA SADLER

Photography of artifacts, badges, sculptures, museum posters, and photographs

Suggested Reading

- Marling, Karal Ann, *Blue Ribbon: A Social and Pictorial History of the Minnesota State Fair.* Minnesota Historical Society Press, 1990. Karal Ann Marling observed that writing about the State Fair taught her everything she knows about Minnesota. The fair never ceases to change and never ceases to be great. It tugs at our heartstrings, our pocketbooks, our waistlines, and our consciousness.

- Humphrey, Karen, *Great State Fair Recipes.* Minnesota State Agricultural Society and the American Dairy Association of Minnesota, 1976. Karen commented on the multigenerational cooking and baking connections she observed as she collected State Fair ribbon-winning family recipes for this book (out of print).

- Nelson, Derek, *The American State Fair.* St Paul, Motorbooks International, 1999.

Funders

Coffee House Press is an independent nonprofit literary publisher. Our books are made possible through the generous support of grants and gifts from many foundations, corporate giving programs, individuals, and through state and federal support.

This book was made possible with special project support from the Elmer and Eleanor Andersen Foundation, Jennifer Haugh, Stephen and Isabel Keating, Mary Kinney, Allan and Cinda Kornblum, Ethan James Litman, and Laura Thorpe. A special media partnership with the *St. Paul Pioneer Press* enabled us to introduce readers to this book, and to their heritage.

Coffee House Press receives general operating support from the Minnesota State Arts Board, through an appropriation by the Minnesota State Legislature and from the National Endowment for the Arts, a federal agency. We receive major general operating support from the McKnight Foundation, and from the Target Foundation. Coffee House also receives assistance from: the Buuck Family Foundation; the Patrick and Aimee Butler Family Foundation; Allan and Cinda Kornblum; the Lenfesty Family Foundation; Rebecca Rand; Charles Steffey and Suzannah Martin; the law firm of Schwegman, Lundberg, Woessner & Kluth, P.A.; the James R. Thorpe Foundation; the Woessner Freeman Foundation; the Wood-Rill Foundation; and many other generous individual donors.

This activity is made possible in part by a grant from the Minnesota State Arts Board, through an appropriation by the Minnesota State Legislature and a grant from the National Endowment for the Arts. MINNESOTA STATE ARTS BOARD

TARGET.

PIONEER PRESS
TwinCities.com

Part of the proceeds of this book help support the Minnesota State Fair Foundation which preserves and improves the fairgrounds and supports State Fair agricultural, scientific, and educational programs.

We've had the good fortune to experience more than one hundred and fifty years of the Minnesota State Fair through fabulous historic photographs and colorful illustrations. Gratefully, the fair will go on into the future, bigger and better, furthering progressive agriculture, animal excellence, cultural encouragement, lively amusements, first-rate entertainment, educational opportunities, and attention-grabbing exhibits—along with a bounty of wonderful food!

Theodore Roosevelt said it first: "speak softly, and carry a big stick," and some fairgoers thought "why not food on a stick?" After the introduction of the Pronto-pup, the race began to find out how many food products would actually stick to a stick. Concessionaires joined in lively contests to create the most unusual concoctions; fairgoers tried as many quirky foods as they could down in one day, and food on a stick became a uniquely popular, if occasionally dubious, culinary curiosity at the fair. To add to the variety, all manner of healthful and delectable cuisine quickly arrived at the fairgrounds and most fairgoers declared that food is the number one reason they go to the Minnesota State Fair.

Thanks for joining us on our pictorial fun-filled days at the fair.

Now let's go to the real fair!

Mammoth
4-H Club
FUTURE FARMERS OF AMERICA
Stock Show
Million Dollar
ART
EXHIBIT
Mammoth
FARM CROPS
and
GARDEN
EXHIBITS
AGRICULTURE
Gigantic
HORSE SHOW